Springer Texts in Education

Springer Texts in Education delivers high-quality instructional content for graduates and advanced graduates in all areas of Education and Educational Research. The textbook series is comprised of self-contained books with a broad and comprehensive coverage that are suitable for class as well as for individual self-study. All texts are authored by established experts in their fields and offer a solid methodological background, accompanied by pedagogical materials to serve students such as practical examples, exercises, case studies etc. Textbooks published in the Springer Texts in Education series are addressed to graduate and advanced graduate students, but also to researchers as important resources for their education, knowledge and teaching. Please contact Natalie Rieborn at textbooks. education@springer.com or your regular editorial contact person for queries or to submit your book proposal.

More information about this series at http://www.springer.com/series/13812

Robert S. Fleming • Michelle Kowalsky

Survival Skills for Thesis and Dissertation Candidates

 Springer

Robert S. Fleming
Rohrer College of Business
Rowan University
Glassboro, NJ, USA

Michelle Kowalsky
Campbell Library
Rowan University
Glassboro, NJ, USA

ISSN 2366-7672   ISSN 2366-7680   (electronic)
Springer Texts in Education
ISBN 978-3-030-80938-6   ISBN 978-3-030-80939-3   (eBook)
https://doi.org/10.1007/978-3-030-80939-3

This Springer imprint is published by the registered company Springer Nature Switzerland AG
The registered company address is: Gewerbestrasse 11, 6330 Cham, Switzerland

Preface

Throughout your life, you have embarked on many journeys, and you have met and interacted with many interesting people and ideas along the way. This book was written to serve as a travel guide for your academic journey of a lifetime, for individuals preparing to embark on a graduate degree. Travel through the thesis or dissertation stage of your journey will be one of the most interesting, challenging, and (ideally) meaningful experiences that you will undertake in your personal life and professional career.

Your success in this important pursuit in your academic and professional career will be built upon developing and implementing a realistic travel plan. You have likely successfully completed a number of smaller voyages along the way in your graduate studies, such as completing a course project or working on a team. If you are honest with yourself, you know that you may not always have taken as much time as you could have (or should have) to prepare in a manner that led to optimal completion of that project. It is now time to embrace fully the reality that your planning will likely need to be some of the most detailed and comprehensive that you will ever create, both personally and professionally.

Throughout this book, we describe many steps in navigating the successful development and defense of a thesis or dissertation. While initially you may find the tasks unfamiliar and difficult, we are confident that by the time you successfully complete the process, you too will be proud of the unique journey you have experienced. By sharing the story of your voyage with others, you will be able to connect with those who are on a similar quest, with those who have already completed the journey, or with those who are using their new experiences and skills to create their ideal lives.

Our mission in writing this book is to provide students who are about to enter this important phase of their graduate studies with a useful guide and roadmap for negotiating the research and writing processes successfully. We refer to the process of completing a dissertation manuscript as a unique new trip which requires mastery of survival skills along the way. Naturally, this sage travel advice is also relevant to those completing a thesis project as part of a master's degree, or for those creating a professional-level academic research project for the first time. Independent researchers may also find these experiences helpful for organizing journal article projects, sustaining collaborative writing efforts, or finding new research interests.

As all who have traveled before would agree, a plan with a roadmap is the most essential of travel tools, and one which most of us wished we pursued earlier, and in more detail!

As with most significant things that you choose to undertake in life, having a realistic preview of what you are getting into, as well as a viable plan for working toward your goals, will lead you most reliably toward success. In reading the various chapters of this book, you will gain an informed, "street-smart" understanding of the dissertation process. You will find a sound plan to guide you toward your desired destinations: the successful research, writing and defense of your thesis or dissertation; the completion of your graduate program; the awarding of your academic degree; and maybe even your dream job. This guide will help you to focus in order to finish.

Your success in this endeavor will require you to develop and properly implement a *proactive* plan for your travel, and to learn how to survive the most common aspects of the process that others have found challenging. In years past, most individuals preparing to take a long road trip or vacation would usually take the time in advance to meticulously plan their route, including when they would depart, the roads they would travel, where they would make rest stops or procure overnight accommodations, and how soon they would expect to arrive at their destination. Yet today, many travelers do not take the time to engage in proactive travel planning; rather, they jump in their car and request travel assistance as they go, perhaps through an app on their smartphone, relying on a quick web search of reviews about possible destinations, or simply following spontaneous decisions they made along the way.

While this convenient *reactive* approach to planning may get you to your desired travel destination, it is detrimental as a dissertation strategy since it is both inefficient and unfocused. This research endeavor will certainly be a journey unlike any other you have attempted! Therefore, we instead recommend a *proactive* approach. A planned, detailed, and well-thought-out analysis of where you need to go, and how you might get there will help you reach your goals with a minimum number of problems and setbacks. Similarly, your attention to the skills required for survival of the journey, especially as you become aware of them in advance, will help clear your path. This book provides both the incentive and the reflection tools you will need to plan in advance, in as much detail as possible, your most ambitious scholarly journey to date.

The various chapters of this book follow a logical sequence that will assist you as you prepare for, embark upon, and navigate through the steps of the thesis or dissertation process. Of course, you may enter the guide and return later at a different point in your travels, as you need! You will come to understand that encountering a number of challenges or detours in your travels is to be expected, even with the best of travel arrangements. However, by developing and following a realistic and proactive plan, you will avoid the significant challenges or roadblocks that some candidates have unfortunately encountered. Throughout the book, we recount the experiences and suggestions frequently mentioned by students themselves or by their research advisors. Naturally, we have removed specific details of subject matters, genders, and situations, in order to protect everyone's true identities. Our goal is to give you enough actionable information from those who came before and who really want you to succeed by knowing how to handle a variety of issues which may arise during the process. Our frank discussion of the necessary survival skills for thesis and dissertation candidates will help you efficiently complete your project, and as a result, receive your advanced degree.

Many thesis or dissertation travelers have been in denial about the depth and detail required to successfully complete this type of work. They often got frustrated and spent way too much additional time trying to finish the process (if they finished at all), or they exhausted precious mental and physical energy by ending up in stressful situations. Some worried about a process they could have organized in a much better way, and others stalled in a series of unnecessary steps or unproductive revisions due to lack of written plans, focus or follow-through. In the worst-case outcomes, many students have spent extensive time and money on this process, but failed for whatever reason to produce a final manuscript or to receive an officially awarded degree.

The guidance in this book is intended to enable you, as a thesis or dissertation candidate, to navigate this challenging process successfully. It will focus on several key aspects of a successful journey, including the various steps of the research process and the people and resources you will work with along the way. Of course, specific tools and strategies will be specified by your own programs and those will be very important to your success. Yet common issues are shared among candidates in many types of programs, so it will be worthwhile to know what to expect and potentially what to avoid. In addition to discussing your responsibilities throughout the dissertation process, we will consider the roles of your research advisor or supervisors, of committee members, and of fellow candidates as well. The working relationships that you develop with these individuals will help to positively influence your experiences along the journey. Having an understanding of the experiences you and your predecessors may share will help increase your awareness and improve your communication about the process.

You may be picking up this book for the first time after you have completed your required coursework and you are entering the research stage of your graduate program. Ideally, you started to contemplate and plan seriously for your thesis or dissertation while completing your prior course requirements. You may have explored aspects of possible research topics while completing earlier course projects. Given that you will be required to spend much time within the research area that you select to be the focus of the remaining stages of your dissertation project, you really want to make this important decision only after conscientious, informed deliberation. Alternately, you may have found this book after your manuscript topic and research group and trip route has already been determined. Either way, remember that no time is wasted in learning about those things that can derail you from following the necessary steps in your plan, and from traveling toward your goals. Learning about "what not to do" in advance of potential mistakes is valuable time well spent, even if you never experience the same level of difficulties as others.

By design, each chapter of this book provides the reader with a concise understanding of each of the topics which contribute to a comfortable journey. Be sure to read and contemplate what you specifically need to know and understand about each topic in order to learn about new ways to gain incremental success in your travels, as well as to ensure a healthy and happy arrival at your destination. If a chapter does not apply to your program, topic, or discipline, feel free to skip around and read the chapters which seem to help you the most. The thesis and dissertation steps here may not occur in the same order as you are experiencing them, or you may need to go back and review particular sections again when changes are made. Your iterative learning and growth in understanding about what you are experiencing is just like the natural recursive process of research—as you learn new things, or realize you need to go back to relearn others, this guide will provide appropriate entry points to a variety of stages of your journey.

Each chapter also suggests additional readings to learn more, although we realize you are likely to consult many of these suggested titles regarding many different issues and topics encountered at different stages of your journey. Together, they represent a comprehensive list of books used by others who have traveled these roads before you. Use these additional resources, along with others suggested by your professors and program, as assigned travel readings along your way, especially for steps for which you struggle or need additional inspiration. Never fear, since others who have completed this unique trip know that you will too, by incrementally identifying segments of your most logical path.

This book provides actionable information and insights about the emotional, reflective, and awareness skills needed to undertake and survive the journey through this challenging and rigorous academic process. Our discussions of personal and interpersonal strategies supplement the content knowledge and evaluative abilities gained by students through research courses embedded in the typical graduate program and via the textbooks used in these courses. This book is not a style guide; the tools and sources and guidelines specified vary by institution. You will definitely want to understand the norms in your field as well as the stylistic expectations of your department, college, or university, and then diligently and meticulously follow those requirements as you learn them. When you're ready to hear the cautionary tales of what happened when someone lost their way, allow our explanations and examples help you get back on track! You are not the first, nor the last, to encounter the thesis and dissertation travel issues presented in this book, so let's figure out how to navigate them, together!

We would like to acknowledge the editorial assistance provided by Laura Daniels and Dr. Amy Fleming during the writing and revising of this book. Their commitment to the importance of this project and their dedicated work has greatly enhanced the practical value of this guide to its intended audience. The authors are also grateful for those many colleagues and reviewers who provided feedback on early versions of the book. We acknowledge and thank the many colleagues and students (our own and others') who provided inspiration for the experiences and suggestions sections of this book. We hope that our readers—including graduate students, thesis and dissertation candidates, and faculty mentors, counselors, advisors, and academic and professional supervisors overseeing and guiding this research—will let us know if and how this book may have helped on your journey. We look forward to celebrating with you a job well done!

In conclusion, we must acknowledge that it is not unusual for a traveler's anticipation, expectations, and (at times) anxieties regarding an upcoming trip to grow as a departure date approaches. This is natural as you prepare to embark on one of the most important pilgrimages of your personal life and professional career. We trust that our labors in compiling, detailing, and sharing our insights and experiences will serve you well as you embark on this new and exciting chapter of the story of your life. If these travel excursions were truly easy, everyone would have already taken them. Know that you are already quite accomplished for even embarking on this voyage, and realize that you are indeed totally capable of completing it!

Let the journey begin …

Best travel wishes!

Glassboro, NJ, USA

Robert S. Fleming
Michelle Kowalsky

Student Experiences and Suggestions: *Advice from Many Other Travelers*

As with planning any travel adventure, there is much that you can learn from others who have already taken a similar journey. These seasoned travelers, like the authors of this travel guide, have shared suggestions regarding things that you will want to do, and to avoid doing, based on their own travel experiences. You will find that their suggestions will prove beneficial as you chart your travel plans and embark on a memorable journey. As previously mentioned, many of their details have been kept confidential so that even the brightest students and most accomplished professionals could share their challenges and advice with you here. Everyone encounters difficulties as they are learning to do new things; these bumps in the road as you travel are to be expected. Previous travelers already know that it is indeed possible to stay on the path, and to focus in order to finish! We look forward to one day hearing from you too, when you are similarly sharing your insights with future travelers.

Contents

About the Authors

Robert S. Fleming holds a joint appointment at Rowan University in Glassboro, New Jersey, as a professor of management in the Rohrer College of Business where he previously served as dean, and a professor of crisis and emergency management within the Disaster Preparedness and Emergency Management program. In addition to a doctorate in Higher Education Administration from Temple University, he has five earned master's degrees, including a Master of Governmental Administration from the Fels Center of Government of the University of Pennsylvania. The primary focus of his research, teaching, and consulting has been on enhancing organizational effectiveness and resilience, with an emphasis on contemporary businesses, non-profits, public safety, and governmental entities. He is a prolific author, having published a number of books and articles, as well as a recognized authority and media source for various business, emergency management, and crisis management topics. For more than 30 years, he has been a student of the thesis and dissertation process and has assisted students and colleagues in their journeys from the initial conceptualization of their research interests to successful completion of a substantial project.

Michelle Kowalsky is a librarian at Rowan University in Glassboro, New Jersey. She holds multiple degrees as well, including a doctorate in Education from Pepperdine University. She teaches undergraduates, graduate students, faculty, and staff about the art and science of research in all subject areas. As a reference and instruction librarian and tenured professor, she has served as a Dissertation Chair and committee member, as well as a Master's Thesis Chair for the College of Education. Her background includes serving as a Library and Information Sciences faculty member, as a teacher preparation professor, as a graduate program coordinator and academic advisor, and as an academic, school, and public librarian. Her research interests focus on the interactions between libraries, technologies, and learning, and she has published and presented on a wide variety of research topics in the fields of business, education, and librarianship.

Your Commitment is Essential to Success

1

1.1 Role in Survival and Success

Achieving real success in any endeavor throughout one's life requires more than a half-hearted commitment; rather, it demands full engagement categorized by a complete understanding of the project or initiative that one is undertaking. Specifically, it demands attention to the details which will be required to complete the project successfully. While this reality is true for any undertaking, it is of paramount importance for graduate students entering the research stage of their academic programs, wherein they will be expected to complete necessary research and writing activities. Ultimately, they must produce and defend a thesis or dissertation that meets and, ideally, exceeds the expectations of their research advisor and committee, department, and university.

Reaching the important milestone of becoming ABD ("all but dissertation") after completion of required coursework and comprehensive examinations should certainly be a cause for celebration. Yet the advanced thinking and heavy workload of the thesis or dissertation process lies ahead. While throughout this book we will refer to the dissertation, the reader should realize that each topic discussed relates to the essential research processes involved in preparing either a master's-level thesis or a doctoral-level dissertation.

While it is likely that some graduate students might prefer that this final culminating experience were not required in their degree program, the reality reveals that it is the final challenge holding candidates back in their work toward a valuable graduate degree. Like any other major undertaking that you have pursued or will pursue in the future, successful completion of your institution's research requirement in a professional, compliant, and timely manner will have positive consequences. The quality of your manuscript will determine if you advance from the ABD ranks or fail to complete the degree requirements of your academic program. Should you persevere and succeed, your newly awarded degree will open many professional doors and opportunities throughout your career.

© The Author(s), under exclusive license to Springer Nature Switzerland AG 2021
R. S. Fleming and M. Kowalsky, *Survival Skills for Thesis and Dissertation Candidates*, Springer Texts in Education, https://doi.org/10.1007/978-3-030-80939-3_1

1.2 What You Need to Know

An important distinction of graduate research projects in master's or doctoral programs is that they should afford the student the opportunity to select and pursue a research topic that aligns with their individual research interests. It is important to recognize this early in your research process as you seek to identify the research topic that you will pursue in your thesis or dissertation. This should not be a lighthearted decision, given the reality that you will be expected to spend much time studying your selected research topic throughout your project and it will subsequently play a role in charting your future research and pursuits. While your research advisor and committee will likely influence the selection of your research topic and methodology, it is important that you ensure that the topic which evolves from these deliberations is one that you truly own, given its importance to your research activities for a number of future years. You will want to select a topic which leads you to develop appropriate research and scholarly capabilities, which will hold your attention over a long period of time, and which will contribute to existing knowledge in your area of interest.

The essential takeaway from this initial chapter is to understand that this will be one of the most challenging and labor-intensive journeys that you will ever undertake. Yet it can also, if properly planned and orchestrated, be one of the most rewarding and interesting activities you have experienced. Your thesis or dissertation research will often represent the most extensive individual research project of your career, and it is perhaps the longest document that you will ever author.

Ideally, a candidate would fully commit to this research undertaking, unencumbered by any other responsibilities or obligations. However, that is rarely the case given the many personal and professional responsibilities to which degree candidates must continue to devote the necessary time and attention. Nevertheless, we assure you that it can be done! The importance of developing and enacting a realistic plan for project completion through effective time allocation and management must be fully acknowledged before you proceed. And then once you've planned the work, carry out your plans as designed. Perseverance is a key survival skill for your journey.

Your success in this life-changing professional endeavor will demand complete commitment to producing a quality outcome. This commitment must be present from the time you embark on your earliest research steps, and it must continue as you engage in each of the steps of the process, right until you deliver the final version of the manuscript. The insights presented in the various chapters of this book are intended to assist you as you make and sustain necessary perseverance through the research process in order to finally reach your desired destination. You can do it, and we stand prepared to help you do so!

1.3 Student Experiences and Suggestions: *Commitment—Don't Begin Your Journey Without It!*

These recommendations relate to the essential importance of commitment before and throughout your journey. While some students acknowledge this before embarking on their research travels, others came to understand fully the importance of a genuine commitment at some later point throughout their respective journeys. The advice of one research advisor to a student to select a research topic that they were not just interested in, but also passionate about, became really useful advice. Another student thought that their faculty member's guidance was valuable when explaining how they should make their decision on a topic only after conscientious consideration of their own related qualifications and interests, not just those of their faculty advisors.

Another graduate student benefited from learning in their research methods course that it was important not to let others, including one's research advisor or committee members, unduly influence their selection of a research topic and thus proclaim the "right" topic for the student. Someone in their first research course made the mistake of following the encouragement of their research advisor and selecting a research topic that he did not truly "own," simply because they could not think of anything better. This led to minimal commitment to their research journey and numerous unnecessary frustrations and detours along the way; ultimately, they abandoned their journey entirely.

However, some gain an appreciation of the importance of fully understanding the various research process activities and the time commitment that should be anticipated to complete each. A particular student wanted others to know that the big picture of their life was an important consideration also. They found that it was important to consider one's present and likely future responsibilities, as well as the expectations of one's program and institution, in fully understanding the necessary travel commitment that you are making. Planning to allocate the required time to the various stages of your journey cannot be underestimated. Still other students encountered somewhere along the way the point when their academic travel plans were stalled and almost derailed when family and professional responsibilities made it too challenging to devote the necessary time and commitment to their dissertation journey.

We trust that these experiences of other travelers relayed throughout these chapters will impress upon you the importance of selecting a project that works for you, both at the present and to help fulfill your future goals. You will be able to fully commit to engaging in the necessary activities for that project in order to complete your journey, because you really are ready! Your many travel guides throughout this book stand prepared to assist you with sage advice throughout your journey.

1.4 Things to DO

- Identify a research topic that you have the passion to pursue.
- Develop a full understanding of the various research process activities.

- Assess your qualifications and interest to conduct the proposed research project.
- Consider current and likely future responsibilities and obligations that will impact the time that you have available to dedicate to research activities.
- Understand the expectations of your academic department, college, and/or university regarding your commitment to the research process, including any residency requirements, deadlines, and timelines.
- Be realistic regarding your ability to commit fully to learning all aspects of this process.
- After conscientious reflection and deliberation, enact each of the necessary research activities to help you complete your thesis or dissertation.

1.5   Things NOT to Do

- Let others, including faculty members, unduly influence your choice of a research topic.
- Select a research topic without taking the time and effort to determine an appropriate topic which is right for you.
- Underestimate the time commitment that you will be required to make in order to complete your thesis or dissertation.
- Fail to properly evaluate other responsibilities, obligations, and time commitments that will compete for and limit the time you have to devote to your research activities.
- Ignore the importance of involving relevant individuals before you make important decisions about your research project.
- Engage in a half-hearted, partial commitment that falls short of what is truly needed to complete your thesis or dissertation successfully.

Bibliography

Bui, Y. N. (2014). *How to Write a Master's Thesis*. Sage.
Rossman, M. H. (2002). *Negotiating Graduate School: A Guide for Graduate Students*. Sage.
Williams, K. (2018). *Planning your Dissertation*. Red Globe Press.

The Research Process

2

2.1 Role in Survival and Success

While you have no doubt conducted research as you completed various assignments throughout your academic studies thus far, you are about to embark on the most extensive research undertaking of your academic program and perhaps your professional career. The magnitude of the journey that you are about to take is similar to expanding one's limited, regional travels into taking that "once in a lifetime" trip.

Developing a thorough understanding of the research process before planning your trip and departing on this potentially life changing journey will prove instrumental to the success of this research journey. Planning your trip carefully will be invaluable in preparing you for additional research adventures throughout your professional career. Taking the time to fully understand the intricacies of the research process prior to embarking on your research journey will enable you to reach your intended destination sooner, and to avoid the many possible challenges and inherent frustrations of thesis or dissertation travel throughout your journey.

While library research may be familiar to you from previous educational experiences in college courses, the empirical part of the process may be unfamiliar, especially at higher levels of research specificity. Most people have never previously conducted the necessary level of detailed background research, nor written a formal hypothesis or research question prior to undertaking a thesis or dissertation. Therefore, they need to learn how to do it, and specifically how to organize their thoughts and work for maximum efficiency of effort. You should never feel ashamed that you have not ever done this type of high-level project before, nor feel embarrassed about not knowing what you are doing at times. None of us knew how to do this either when we first started; learning these tasks now is just part of the process. In the way that a new traveler learns the customs of different parts of the world, you too will learn the more intricate traditions and innovations of the academic and scholarly universe.

© The Author(s), under exclusive license to Springer Nature Switzerland AG 2021
R. S. Fleming and M. Kowalsky, *Survival Skills for Thesis and Dissertation Candidates*, Springer Texts in Education,
https://doi.org/10.1007/978-3-030-80939-3_2

2.2 What You Need to Know

The research process for a thesis or dissertation actually consists of two types of research. First you will perform library research. This means you will look for articles, books, and other scholarly sources which were already published on your topic. The quality and quantity of published items is important, so take direction from your committee and other professors about what kinds of sources you will need. Having a strong base of published research on your topic is essential to explaining how and why your own project contributes something new to that scholarly discourse.

Checking with a librarian who is familiar with your subject area is a very good idea. You may want to make research appointments with a knowledgeable librarian at the beginning, middle, and end of your search process. Library research will usually include database searches for peer reviewed journal articles, book catalog searches of your own and others' libraries, and use of online search engines and professional organizations to find emerging scholarship. It could also include other types of sources, some of which your own library does not currently own, but which you can borrow from other libraries or find in other repositories. Much of this library research will appear in your literature review, and possibly also in your introduction.

Second, you will perform empirical research. This will be for the methods and results sections of your thesis or dissertation, which usually describes your own project's process and findings. By designing and conducting your own study, experiment, and/or analysis, you will contribute to knowledge in your field and, ideally, become the author of one of the library articles that others will quote in the future for their own papers. In this way, experiment or investigation will soon contribute new information to the already existing literature on which you reported earlier in your manuscript.

While you may consult a published source in order to help you learn how to do your study methods or data analysis, a source like this is not the focus of your empirical research chapters. Rather, a detailed description of your own unique, rigorously conducted study is preferred, and you indeed may explain which researchers' models you employed. This explanation of the qualitative and/or quantitative steps you used makes up the main part of your thesis or dissertation chapter about methods, and which demonstrates your proficiency in conducting original primary research. Secondary sources, such as library books and journal articles, usually comprise your literature review chapter, and discuss other's empirical studies on your topic. How-to help guides and tutorial websites may help you to learn what to do in writing a dissertation, but often do not need to be quoted in your manuscript as secondary sources. It is helpful to ask for guidance from your research advisor when questions about these arise.

Research is often iterative, filled with many details that can get forgotten and even change as you are working on it. Consider everything as tentative until the final copy of your thesis or dissertation is accepted. Then you will not worry when changes need to be made, since that is a normal part of the process. Again, no time spent selecting or deselecting articles for your literature review is ever wasted; this process simply makes you more of an expert on the field you have chosen.

The same is true for time spent investigating and choosing the many details of your project's procedures. Awareness of the nuances of possible methods for exploring your topic, and enhancing your awareness of the many sources which exist on your topic, is a key survival skill for your travels. The closer your work looks to a finished product, or in other words similar in scope and quality to those journal articles or books you have seen, the less writing you will have to fix later.

Proper citation, appropriate writing style, and detailed formatting of the appearance of your paper are all very important. Learn how to properly cite and format, and then apply what you have learned to your own work as you go along. Begin to find as many sources as possible on your topic from as many different places as your librarians and advisors recommend. Then record citation and location information about those sources from the very beginning of your library research, so that you do not lose any important items when you need to refer to them later. More information on this process appears in later chapters as well.

2.3 Student Experiences and Suggestions: *Plan and then Plan Some More*

One of the most important things research advisors know and mention during the first few weeks of their courses is that the research process is an iterative one that spans a number of years as you complete your thesis or dissertation. While many faculty devote several classes to teaching "the process," other institutions have students "learn by doing" in teams or with research partners. Either way, as the student you must take every opportunity available to you to continue to learn the ways of academic, empirical, and scholarly research. Students recount that throughout the latter part of their journeys, they came to appreciate the wisdom of others in laying this essential groundwork, before allowing them to move forward.

Many students learned during those early class sessions that the steps and associated activities follow a logical sequence from the time that a student identifies an appropriate research topic through the successful defense of their thesis or dissertation. Others were not allowed to discuss the individual research topic or process until they had mastered other aspects of scholarly inquiry first. One student said their professor explicitly prepared them to expect unusual events along the way, like in a journey when you would have to make some mid-course corrections due to weather, illness, or simply the need for rest. Whichever way your research advisors choose to advise you on your journey, students advise seeking advice from many different sources in order to gain a clear picture of what lies ahead. And of course, they urge everyone to realize that necessary adjustments are just part of the process and should not be interpreted as failure.

One student was not as fortunate, and they embarked on their dissertation journey without really understanding what was involved. They assumed they would just take the classes and be finished; yet they now know that the formal structures of graduate work are only just the beginning. Independent thinking is required at increasingly higher levels as you travel through the different stages of your project. Former students suggest learning not only the overall process, but also the importance of the early steps in setting a trajectory towards successful completion of their research. One common mistake included trying to rush through the early stages of the process and then becoming frustrated and disenchanted when their research advisor and committee members suggested that it was time to slow down the momentum and address some problems. Others felt pressure to finish their work on a particular timeline that was either self-imposed or too fast for their current skill level. These students suggest seeking out different ways of thinking about the problem by talking to others and finding more information about what to do next, as well as locating peers with whom to brainstorm solutions.

Some students compared notes on their journeys when meeting at research events on or off campus. One student admitted that prior to their first public research talk, they had in some respects underestimated the preparation for and significance of a life in academics. They were initially reluctant to seek assistance when they had questions or encountered issues, and those same issues were brought up by the audience during and after their presentation. While it was a welcome surprise that others were so interested in their project, it was also clear that they should have done more work on it in advance. They realized that providing a quality product was truly important to other professionals in the field, and more accomplished researchers wanted to help improve the quality of a project, not necessarily attack the novice researcher presenting it.

2.4 Things to DO

- Take every opportunity to learn about what is expected of you.
- Determine the expectations of thesis and dissertation candidates in general, as well as the specific requirements of your department, college, or university.
- Determine what makes a good quality thesis or dissertation in your discipline, especially among recent graduates of your institution and others.
- Recognize that the research process is an iterative one and that there will be times when "mid-course" adjustments may be appropriate.

- Attend workshops conducted by librarians and current students, any dissertation preparation presentation by the institution's research office, and any and all other related information sessions offered by your department, college, or university.
- Utilize available online help sources such as thesis or dissertation support groups, recommended chat meetings, and discussion forums in your field and in general.

2.5 Things NOT to Do

- Ignore the importance and merit of taking the time to gain the necessary understanding and knowledge before embarking on your research journey.
- Deny that you are undertaking a significant project and fail to seek out and take advantage of resources available within and outside your institution.
- Be reluctant to seek necessary assistance from the members of your research committee, as well as knowledgeable others throughout your research journey.
- Limit yourself to only library resources available at your library, failing to take advantage of inter-library loan programs and visitor access to other institution's collections.
- Think you have failed in some way when your research committee suggests or requires that you make changes as you research and/or write up your project.

Bibliography

Bowden, J. A., & Green, P. (2019). *Playing the PhD game with integrity connecting research, professional practice and educational context*. Springer.

Evans, D., Gruba, P., & Zobel, J. (2014). *How to write a better thesis*. Springer.

Teitelbaum, H. (1998). *How to write a thesis*. Macmillan.

The Importance of Effective Time Management

3

3.1 Role in Survival and Success

Just as smart travelers consider in advance what will be required to ensure their successful journey, a student about to embark on their thesis or dissertation should recognize the importance of similar preparation. Whereas successful travel by car or train requires essential timing, decision making, navigation, and other abilities, successful thesis or dissertation travel also requires a fairly comprehensive knowledge and skill set, encompassing the essential areas of finding, planning, project management, and communication.

An easily overlooked but crucial skill that will prepare you to survive the thesis or dissertation process is that of time management. Without effective time management you will likely encounter many challenges throughout your journey that can potentially derail your trip or greatly diminish the pleasure of your travels. Thoroughness and time spent in preparation in advance of travel which plots out your course of action will always make you feel more comfortable in your decisions whether traveling through graduate school or traveling around the country.

The importance of effective time management must be further developed during your journey, even if you feel you already manage time and projects well. A thesis or dissertation is a new kind of project that will require you to summon all of your available skills, as well as learn a few more complex ones. This new set of proficiencies will work together with your existing knowledge to evaluate and adjust nearly every aspect of your project as it is created. While this chapter focuses on the importance of effective time management, those that follow will consider the related issues of developing a realistic timetable and work plan, and the importance of meeting deadlines as you navigate through this process.

© The Author(s), under exclusive license to Springer Nature Switzerland AG 2021
R. S. Fleming and M. Kowalsky, *Survival Skills for Thesis and Dissertation Candidates*, Springer Texts in Education, https://doi.org/10.1007/978-3-030-80939-3_3

3.2 What You Need to Know

An essential starting point in understanding the importance of effective time management is to recognize the essential aspect of writing and researching. Of all the resources that you will ever have at your disposal, or over which you have discretion in using, time is unique. Time is a finite resource; once it is used up, you can never recover it. You will never be able to request a second chance as to how you use that time. Throughout our life's journeys we face many junctures where we are required to make decisions as to how we allocate and use the limited time that we have. While the amount of time each student needs to produce a manuscript will differ, you must budget for more time than you think you need, as well as make specific plans for best use of the time you do have available.

Your earlier decision to pursue graduate studies represents a major personal and professional decision given the time commitment that it necessitates. The fact that the final step in your academic program requires you to complete a thesis or dissertation suggests that you have in some ways already committed to allocating necessary time to complete your courses and the research process that follows. Ideally, you learned some important lessons in completing your graduate coursework regarding your ability to manage time and projects effectively and efficiently. You have traveled before, but this next destination is new, and requires some different strategies.

Specifically, your new strategies must take on particular characteristics in order to be successful. *Effectiveness* relates to whether you accomplish what you set out to do, such as complete your thesis or dissertation and earn your degree. *Efficiency* considers whether or not you used available resources, including your time, in the best manner possible. The guidance provided in these chapters is designed to prepare you to navigate your thesis or dissertation travels effectively and efficiently. Time management, therefore, must be recognized as a key survival skill throughout your journey.

3.3 Student Experiences and Suggestions: *Keeping Your Travels on Schedule*

Some students report that the importance of effective time management was introduced early in their research methods courses and reinforced as they examined the research process activities. Having successfully completed their research journeys, these students acknowledge that one of the greatest challenges of thesis or dissertation travel is ensuring that you are using your time effectively and efficiently. Of course, other students had not realized before their journeys that time is a scarce resource, for which there will always be competing demands. Regardless of when they became aware of this issue, most students are quickly (or eventually!) able to acknowledge and explain the value of time in determining success.

Anyone who has successfully completed this journey will attest to the value of new insights along the way, especially acquiring new skills to help answer their project's research questions or learning new things about themselves. Many students have pointed out that writing a thesis or dissertation helped them understand their own patterns and behaviors better, including how they tend to manage or not manage their time. In comparing experiences at various points during the process, many graduate students realized that while their research interests were similar, their approaches to managing time and projects were radically different. Discussing with others how they approach work habits and balance competing demands for their time and mental energy is likely the most popular suggestion that former graduate students provide to others embarking on this journey.

Some students believe they tend to be good at the planning aspect of projects, and they always want to have a detailed plan or calendar that incorporates all activities and phases of their current personal and professional projects. Yet even those with these organizational skills say they are still learned new ways to manage new requirements. One student's approach to time management was to plan and complete one step or segment of a project before turning their attention to planning for the next phase of that project. Another tried to map out the whole basic process first, and then fill in the details of each step as they moved into a new phase of their project. As faculty, we have learned that both approaches have advantages and disadvantages and realized at the end of our respective journeys that all of these time management approaches could be successful. While some had embraced the concept of developing an appropriate plan for allocating and managing time throughout their research journey, others had realized the importance of being realistic in the time it takes to complete the various stages of this journey.

With any type of plan, it is wise to acknowledge that incorporating some break time will help increase your chances of success. Multiple students mention that they gave themselves a day off, or a few hours in their daily schedule to exercise, to relax, or to walk outside. By having this extra space added into their usual planning, and sometimes explicitly as a section in their schedule grid, the students became more realistic and determined that they simply could not work continuously on their project all day or every day. Others realized later that they were actually more productive after building into their routines some free time to think about things other than their thesis or dissertation, or to exercise or listen to music. Having extra time planned can also help with catching up on tasks when the time to complete certain activities is outside your control and in the hands of others, such as your survey participants or members of your research committee.

3.4   Things to DO

- Understand the importance of effective time management in the successful completion of your thesis or dissertation.
- Understand the time management challenges that you may face throughout the thesis or dissertation process.
- Allow yourself time to learn the process of writing a thesis or dissertation, as well as time to thoroughly research your topic and methods for investigating it.

- Ponder a work plan for completing your thesis or dissertation based on your time management history and practices.
- Recognize and commit to the importance of meeting all deadlines associated with completing your thesis or dissertation.

3.5   Things NOT to Do

- Underestimate the importance of effective and efficient time management throughout the research and writing processes.
- Fail to consult with your research advisor before developing your research plan and timetable.
- Develop personal goals or dreams that are too aggressive, or otherwise unrealistic.
- Procrastinate in determining the time/project management approach that works best for you.
- Forget to develop new time management skills as well as intentionally improve upon your existing skills.

Bibliography

Brause, R. S., & Dissertation, W. Y. D. (2000). *Invisible rules for success*. Falmer Press.

Halyna, K. (2019). *A concise guide to writing a thesis or dissertation*. Routledge.

Mewburn, Inger. (2017) *How to be an academic: the thesis whisperer reveals all*. Kensington, NSW, Australia.

Developing a Realistic Timetable

4

4.1 Role in Survival and Success

Similar to preparing a tentative time schedule for an upcoming road trip, you will want to develop a realistic plan for your research journey that allocates appropriate time to each activity. Understanding that a process is simply a sequence of activities that are enacted in a specific order and directed toward attaining a particular goal will assist you in developing a viable research plan and schedule. This plan and its scheduled activities should be challenging but also realistic. While you will be required to make significant progress throughout the research process, some activities cannot be undertaken until such time as prior activities are completed and approved at various points by those directing and overseeing your research.

You must come up with a plan and timetable that works not only for you, but also for your research advisor and for the members of your committee. Your planned activities and schedule must incorporate the time you anticipate having available to devote to your research activities as well as time for meeting other life responsibilities. While a realistic plan will enable you to complete your trip by the desired time, pursuing an unrealistic plan – or attempting to travel with no real plan at all—will likely yield a highly unpleasant travel experience. It will often result in you not realizing your travel goals of completing an appropriate thesis or dissertation project and thus receiving your graduate degree.

4.2 What You Need to Know

You should begin your planning process with the desired end in sight, working backwards from the date you anticipate graduating from your degree program. Successful research planning requires that a student fully understand each of the individual steps or activities involved in the thesis or dissertation process, and the time it takes someone at your institution to proceed through each of them. It is likewise imperative that, in collaboration with your research advisor, you develop a realistic plan for effectively and efficiently completing each activity, based on an informed understanding of how much reasonable time should be allocated to each activity.

You will want to make sure that you incorporate any *soft deadlines* with which your research advisor and committee will expect you to comply, such as dates by which they expect to receive and review your work submissions. Similarly, you will want to know and list any of the *hard deadlines* officially imposed by your department, college, or university for academic work or procedural forms which must be completed. Your plan should also incorporate reasonable allocations of time which permit your advisor and committee members to review your work and provide feedback. It is important to remember that these individuals, much like you, have other professional responsibilities and personal obligations in life that will determine when they have time to devote to review of your research project.

You will want to recognize that not building some lighter workloads or additional free days into your timetable is tempting fate, given that it would not be unusual for you or your committee members to encounter circumstances that result in delays in your progress. While you would like to assume that everything that you submit to your research committee will be approved immediately by them, this is probably an example of wishful thinking. You will want to incorporate sufficient time in your plan to accommodate the asynchronous back-and-forth interaction that is typical between a thesis or dissertation candidate and the members of their committee.

Involving your research advisor and committee members in this planning stage is important for several reasons. In addition to their guidance enabling you to develop a realistic research plan and timetable, their involvement at this stage of the research process typically results in them taking ownership for enacting their roles and responsibilities in accordance with the earlier agreed upon plan. They will sometimes need to deliver corrections or advice to you that you may not want to hear, or they may take more time than you would like in providing their comments to you. Not all plans are perfectly followed even when all parties have the best of intentions. Therefore, being realistic with yourself and others is an important survival skill for maintaining your composure during thesis and dissertation writing.

4.3 Student Experiences and Suggestions: *A Realistic Travel Itinerary*

Some students were grateful for the travel comparisons, in which they navigate each stage of their travels and develop a realistic timetable for completing each segment of their lengthy journey. Others requested different analogies related to their interests, and found them from their research advisors, online support groups, or students from other institutions. Many students reported that explanatory frameworks for understanding the tasks at hand were invaluable. They had knowledge and insights regarding the nature of the project being attempted, and the milestones or deadlines that they were expected to meet, whether imposed by their institution or by their committee. Some graduate students recommend having your research advisor and committee members review and approve your work plan and proposed timetable after it has been reviewed by your peers, in order to determine its practicality given the topic and activities required. As a new researcher, you may not have realized that you misjudged something.

Another graduate student found a way to manage their time and complete their journey while juggling family and work responsibilities. They admitted that they were only able to do so by developing a plan that worked for their situation, and by spending much time working with their family members in order to ensure the plan would be attainable. They incorporated an anticipated graduation date a year later than most other students in their class, and adjusted their goals based on their own personal timeline, not one that their peers were following. This proved to reduce their stress and conflict during the process.

Another student, with high aspirations and achievements from their undergraduate days at a college reunion, discovered that an overly aggressive or otherwise unrealistic timetable would not serve most other students well during thesis or dissertation travel. This student had minimal responsibilities and did not have to work during their time as a graduate student, and they already knew how do execute their research methods from prior work experiences in the field. Once again, most students realize, their particular thesis and dissertation manuscript must get completed in a realistic manner for their individual circumstances. Meeting other students with different situations can only help you feel more comfortable that your choices are indeed right for you.

While pursuing their undergraduate degrees, many students participated in competitive sports, via the university or with outside groups. These contexts also provide meaningful analogies for understanding how individual performance and team collaboration work together in completing a large project. Depending on their knowledge of sport and their level of play, some students viewed the thesis or dissertation process as a longer race where you needed to pace yourself in the earlier stages to have the energy left in the later stages of the race. Others found useful understandings by comparing roles of their advisors to those of coaches or team captains. Of course, for any metaphors you choose, the thesis and dissertation journey will be seen as more than one race, one match, or one game. It may be a marathon, or the road to a championship, or a multi-season preparation for sustained career goals! Regardless of the end result, every workout leads to improved performance when it matters most. Most students report one or more moments of understanding when using these analogies contributed to growth in understanding, improvement in motivation, and increased comfort in traveling the road ahead.

4.4 Things to DO

- Consult with your research advisor regarding appropriate time allocations for the various research activities.
- Ascertain all deadlines that should be incorporated in your research plan and timeline.

- Consider in advance any personal and professional responsibilities and obligations that may limit the time you have available to devote to your research activities.
- Incorporate extra time periodically within your planned schedule to accommodate unanticipated delays which may arise during the process.
- Review and reflect on your personal habits, tendencies, and preferences.
- Have your research advisor and committee review and approve the proposed timetable.

4.5 Things NOT to Do

- Isolate yourself from others as you develop your research plan and timetable.
- Develop a research timetable that is too aggressive or otherwise unrealistic.
- Avoid or forget personal and professional events which will naturally occur during your research activities over the next few years.
- Forget appropriate deadlines in your research plan and timetable.
- Ignore the significant influence that other faculty members will have on your timetable and project design and progression.
- Either underestimate or overestimate your own capacity to learn new ways of thinking and working.
- Keep general deadlines mostly in your head, instead of preparing plans more specifically on an actual calendar.
- Remain rigid or inflexible about potential changes to your intended schedule.

Bibliography

Foss, Sonja K, & William J. C. Waters. (2016). *Destination dissertation: a traveler's guide to a done dissertation*. Lanham, MD: Rowman & Littlefield Publishers.

James, E. Alana, & Tracesea H. Slater. (2013). *Writing your doctoral dissertation or thesis faster: a proven map to success*. Thousand Oaks, CA: Sage.

White, B. (2011). *Mapping your thesis: the comprehensive manual of theory and techniques for masters and doctoral research*. ACER Press.

Developing a Time and Resource Allocation Plan

5

5.1 Role in Survival and Success

While the previous chapter considered mapping out your overall travel plan and itinerary, we will now consider how that plan must be customized in accordance with your travel interests and practices. The need to make your plan into one that works for your life is similar to the process of incorporating your preferences for travel, including consideration of the time at which you like to get started each day of your trip, how far you want to travel each day, and the time when you would like to arrive at your resting stop each evening. Some travelers will prefer to get an early start each day, while others will want to depart only after getting up later and taking time for a casual breakfast. Some will have the desire and stamina to start early and travel many miles each day, while others will want to drive shorter distances each day and spread their journey over more days. You will need to learn to properly allocate both your physical time and mental energy and then follow through on your plans in order to complete these tasks successfully.

The importance of developing such insights about yourself and how you travel should be apparent, as should be the value of conducting a similar introspection before you embark on your dissertation journey. Unless you develop an informed approach to allocating your time resources and mental resources in completing your thesis or dissertation, you may be in for a less-than-pleasant travel experience. While your familiarity with the library research process will be essential, knowing yourself will be the key to navigating the road ahead successfully. Only you know how much effort it takes you to perform different thinking, organizing, and writing steps, and (if you are honest with yourself) you also know which of those steps are currently the easiest or the most difficult for you to accomplish. Therefore, careful consideration of your allocation of personal resources is an important survival skill.

© The Author(s), under exclusive license to Springer Nature Switzerland AG 2021
R. S. Fleming and M. Kowalsky, *Survival Skills for Thesis and Dissertation Candidates*, Springer Texts in Education,
https://doi.org/10.1007/978-3-030-80939-3_5

5.2 What You Need to Know

Each person is unique in many ways, including the particular collection of personal attributes that make up their personality. We each have unique talents that contribute to personal and professional success, as well as weaknesses that can hold us back. In reflecting on the various activities that you will be expected to undertake successfully in creating and delivering your thesis or dissertation, you have probably already considered your knowledge and skills in relevant areas such as searching, analysis, and communication. We trust that by now you fully appreciate that the development of a realistic plan and effective time management will serve as your guidance and routing system throughout your journey. Your success throughout your travels will be enhanced by charting a course that allows you travel in a productive manner that works best for you.

A starting point in determining the most effective and efficient way to allocate your time and other resources to this journey involves understanding your established lifestyle and patterns. This requires considering how you spend your searching time, thinking time, and writing time. You will need to review how, when and how much recreation or relaxation time you need in between these cognitively demanding tasks. While our focus will be on how you spend your waking hours of the day, also recognize the importance of a good night's sleep. Balancing all of the appropriate times for scholarship and leisure during the manuscript preparation phase is important. You will want to consider that there is a difference between *available hours* and actually *productive hours* as you analyze how to best utilize the time and energy you have to dedicate to your thesis or dissertation journey.

We all have patterns of how we use time productively, and we can probably identify when, how and why we procrastinate. The understanding that you develop regarding these important aspects of time management will enable you to determine what works best for you in terms of making the time you devote to this pilgrimage as meaningful as possible. An example would be a person who likes to get up early and is prepared to organize their day in a manner where they engage in their research activities for several hours at that time before turning their attention to other personal and professional demands of the day. In contrast, there will be others who find later in the day or evening to be their most productive time to work on their thesis or dissertation. For some, weekends may afford more time to engage in prolonged work on their research project. Watch your own habits and behaviors to figure out your productive times of day or week. You should allow for longer, uninterrupted amounts of time periodically, so that you can get into the flow of being fully focused on your project.

While understanding yourself and your situation is extremely important in determining how to allocate your time in the most effective and efficient manner, so too is recognizing some of the typical travel hazards that you will encounter during your journey and how to avoid these "bumps in the road." Recognize that a journey which may seem massive and unattainable becomes less overwhelming when broken down into a series of manageable steps or activities. Approaching your research process in this manner allows you to see that you are making the necessary progress towards your goals as you complete each and every activity. Rather than thinking about the hundreds of hours that may be necessary to complete your thesis or dissertation, focusing on the particular activity that you plan to undertake and complete this week, or over the next month, makes more sense.

The key to success in time and resource allocation is to develop and orchestrate a plan that is tailored specifically to you and enables you to make the necessary progress towards completing each of the stages that you have defined. You will want to approach every day of your work plan with a clear understanding of what you have done so far and what you ideally would like to accomplish during that day's work session. Each day you should prepare for the planned activities of the next day and be realistic in what you can reasonably expect yourself to complete during the allotted time. It is important to remember that every mile you travel, and every step you complete, brings you closer to your destination.

5.3   Student Experiences and Suggestions: *Traveling in a Way that Works for You*

Most students realize their thesis or dissertation journey involves making a number of instrumental decisions based on an understanding of both the tasks that they will need to complete during each section of their journey and their pattern of completion of past projects. A few students explained that they felt skilled in planning but then had difficulty in prioritizing items on their lists, especially when multiple items needed to be finished at once. Several graduate students suggested analyzing work habits more specifically and seeking advice from others in person or online may increase productivity when accomplishing a large project such as this.

The insights provided by research advisors and committees can be an essential starting point in enacting your plans, and many students believed their advice helped in developing realistic plans and typical time estimates for completing tasks. However, several students felt that both they and their advisors underestimated the time required to complete specifics of collecting data, analyzing results, and reporting on their findings. One student felt that their research group became more tired and less motivated as their project progressed, so they needed to allow more time for the later parts of the project than originally expected. It is important to note that this is not a failure since there is no standard time allocation plan that will work for all research projects. Estimates and plans can and do change, and many students recommend being flexible and not getting too upset about this, since it happens to most students (as well as most academics and professionals) quite regularly.

One student shared that before planning and embarking on their journey, they made a list of factors that contributed to and distracted from their productivity when working on past projects. They realized that there were days of the week and times of the day for being most productive, and that these writing periods seemed to work well, even with a few adjustments during certain seasons of the year. This student liked devoting their undivided attention to these tasks for extended periods of time, often during weekends. Yet others find out that they are most productive in the mornings, or in short bursts of writing after thinking about their topic while doing other non-research activities. Still others were clearly more productive in the evenings, often working into the night many times during their journey. And some maintain that writing just a paragraph at a time periodically throughout the day helped them write multiple pages easily. No one pattern will work for everyone, but you will be able to identify what patterns work for you, and to accomplish your tasks most easily when following them.

In many ways one of the most important things that we learned about thesis and dissertation travel was the importance of having and following a roadmap to guide your journey. Just as one should not plan to travel from coast to coast in the United States in a day or two, so too should your plan allow sufficient time for a productive and pleasurable trip. Similar to reflecting on the day's travel at the end of each day of a multiday trip, we recommend two important things. One is to take time to celebrate your progress at the completion of each activity and milestone, as well as the time to relax and prepare for the next leg of your journey. At the end of each stage of your journey we have also found that it is beneficial to evaluate how you have allocated and used time in the interest of determining if you should make any adjustments in your travel plans.

5.4 Things to DO

- Identify factors that contribute to your productivity in undertaking and managing a large project.
- Identify things that interfere with your successful allocation and management of your mental energy.
- Evaluate other responsibilities and obligations that will determine the amount of time you will have to devote to your thesis or dissertation, including the times that your schedule permits you to work on your project.
- Estimate how much time will be required to perform each activity in completing your thesis or dissertation.
- At the completion of each activity, evaluate how you allocated and used time and energy, so that you can determine if you need to make any adjustments in your approach.

5.5 Things NOT to Do

- Minimize the importance of evaluating your personal time management patterns and preferences in developing a time allocation plan.
- Underestimate the time required to complete each activity.

- Allow distractions or procrastination habits to impede your progress.
- Become frustrated or overwhelmed by focusing on the amount of work it will take to complete the overall thesis or dissertation process.
- Overlook the importance of building in time after completion of each milestone or activity to celebrate success, relax, and prepare for the next activity.
- Skip the reflection step of evaluating how you are allocating and using time at various points in the process and/or refuse to make the changes necessary to enhance your effectiveness.

Bibliography

Bolker, J. (1998). *Writing your dissertation in fifteen minutes a day: a guide to starting, revising, and finishing your doctoral thesis.* H. Holt.

O'Leary, Z. (2013). *The essential guide to doing your research project.* Sage.

Walker, Melanie, & Thomson, Pat. (2010). *The Routledge doctoral student's companion: becoming and being a doctoral student.* New York: Taylor and Francis.

Understanding Institutional Policies and Procedures

6

6.1 Role in Survival and Success

If you have ever driven a vehicle, you are familiar with the rules of the road. You may also know that various states often have different driving laws and regulations. Just as there are travel rules when taking a trip via car, bus or train, there are similar requirements that you will be expected to understand and fully comply with throughout your thesis or dissertation journey. The rules of the road in thesis or dissertation travel will likewise differ from institution to institution. These expectations of your college or university are delineated in institutional research policies and procedures, as well as in approved student policy documents and handbooks. It is imperative that you seek out and meticulously comply with all relevant policies and procedures.

Many thesis or dissertation projects use surveys, interviews, observations, or other information obtained from humans. Before you approach your human subjects and start asking them questions, or before you start observing their behavior or collecting their personal information, you will need permission to do so. Every university will require that your thesis or dissertation project be reviewed in advance, in order to make sure you are not harming any human subjects with your proposed investigation. The campus group that grants this permission is often called the Institutional Review Board (IRB), or some similar name. Other scientific or laboratory projects must be approved by chairs, deans, or other authorities in order to assure their safety as well as the availability of supplies for the duration of the work. Consider these approval groups and your direct faculty supervisors as the traffic enforcers who check to ensure you are following the rules necessary to maintain order along your journey.

The nature of some projects may not need these additional approvals at the department or institutional level. Certain kinds of documents in the public domain, or alternately, confidential processes of invention or investigation, may require different kinds of nondisclosure agreements or perhaps require none at all, depending on the topic. For example, IRB approval is absolutely required for

© The Author(s), under exclusive license to Springer Nature Switzerland AG 2021
R. S. Fleming and M. Kowalsky, *Survival Skills for Thesis and Dissertation Candidates*, Springer Texts in Education,
https://doi.org/10.1007/978-3-030-80939-3_6

projects which study humans in any way, including their characteristics, their perceptions, their behaviors, their communications, and more. Much of the doctoral student gossip at many social science groups revolves around troubles navigating the IRB process. Yet these drama-filled experiences and stories of past problems can be easily avoided. For most graduate students, doing library research and writing long papers are familiar activities, but navigating specific university research policies and proving that you are complying with federal mandates are tasks that are not as familiar to most people. Therefore, informed compliance is essential for a successful thesis or dissertation journey. In other words, become aware of the many rules which govern progress throughout your project, and then follow them closely for a trouble-free experience. Double-checking the information you receive by asking lots of questions is an easy way to start!

6.2   What You Need to Know

Some research methods or topics may inadvertently harm your human participants due to your own unconscious bias, an accidental data breach, or public revelation of some information of a very personal nature. Therefore, you need to write in great detail about how you will conduct your project by describing the types of information you want to gather, your reasons for wanting that information, a description of every part of your research method such as how you will perform data collection and analysis, an explanation of the results you expect to find, and more. Offering your full compliance with the rules when necessary, and then choosing to dispute them after an informed counterargument has been determined, is a useful survival skill which can help you weather the roads ahead.

Committee members may have questions about any or all aspects of your project, but this is a common part of the application process. If you have worded something unclearly or if you did not include specific details, you will receive a request for more information or for particular revisions. If these requests seem to be stressful to some students, this may be due to their lack of familiarity with the process. Seasoned researchers know that questions from supervisors or offices overseeing work in your field are not a personal attack, nor are they a negative critique of the idea for your project. Rather, the reviewers may simply need more information about exactly what you intend to do, so that they can prove your investigation is not problematic, especially in ways that you perhaps have not yet identified.

As part of your application to conduct your study with human subjects, you may need to develop a letter to provide to each of your human subjects as a request for their participation. By providing participants with introductory details, often called an Informed Consent Form or some similar name, you will advise your human participants of the types of information you wish to obtain from them. Your communication will contain a clear explanation of the purpose of your intended project and the risks (if any) assumed by those who participate. While this may seem at first to provide an unnecessary barrier between you and those you wish to study, it assures that you have permission to proceed from those involved without causing any hardships for them or for you.

After reading the information about your study, if your intended human subjects agree to participate in your study, they will formally agree or *opt in*, thus providing you appropriate permission to use their responses. If you are unsure if your human subjects will want to participate, check with your research advisor about doing a pilot study before committing to a particular method, a set of survey questions, or other processes. Remember that you also need to provide a way for participants to *opt out* of inclusion in your study for any reason. By carefully completing an IRB application, you will have already thought through, in advance, the reasons that your project is likely to be successfully completed as described. If your project does not involve human subjects, then you may not need to do this type of process at all, so not to worry!

6.3 Student Experiences and Suggestions: *Learning the Rules of the Road*

One student reported that their professors emphasized the importance of academic integrity in conducting and reporting on your research projects, much like rules of the road with which they would be expected to comply. Just as there are general driving regulations or border crossing rules specific to a particular state or nation, rules across institutions and even across their programs may vary.

Some students benefited from the insights of past students who had completed their journeys and came to their classes to share their travel experiences. As invaluable as this was while planning, individual students felt it was most valuable during the implementation of their plans, when selected individuals were honest about sharing both the good and bad of their travels. However, not all advice from others will apply to every situation for current students, so investigating more details is usually advisable. One dissertation candidate shared that they made the mistake of being willing to listen to anyone who had undertaken dissertation travel, and as a result received and acted upon information which did not apply to their field, or which did not align with their university's processes. Just as you might stop to evaluate certain information you hear from the news or friends, an informed assessment about the source and context of the material is useful.

Graduate students discovered that there were many credible sources of the travel guidance as they planned their journeys. Many would research the current information provided by their university, college, or department by checking to see if it was similar or different than other institutions and other students' experiences. One student said their own university made this comparative information available through workshops, handbooks, and on their website. Checking for accurate and timely information about creating a thesis or dissertation, as well as information which you will include about your topic of study, are indeed parts of the larger process. One student found that integrating the information that their university formally made available to them along with the informal advice of and conversations with others, helped to determine whose information may be inaccurate or outdated, or even recently changed. It is easy to remain on the right track by making regular inquiries about the appropriate trip-planning resources that you might need.

Other students reported that taking the time to fully understand and carefully follow the directions in completing university forms minimized the concerns of reviewers and the need for revisions. Their experiences taught them the importance of being completely honest with everyone involved in your project. There is great value in having many different people review your project proposal before you submit it. Some wayward travelers who tried to hide information from others regarding details of their intended projects, especially those students who falsified data or misled participants, were summarily dismissed from their degree programs, and others remain under investigation for potential criminal fraud. Therefore, disclosure of all aspects of your research, and confirming approval from all involved, will be important for students in all subject areas.

6.4 Things to DO

- Become familiar with how and where you can locate the most up-to-date information about the research approval process through websites, handbooks, workshops, or other means early in your research process.
- Compile and study the written directions from your department, university, or advisors about the human subjects' approval process for you to follow.
- Consult with others as you estimate how much time each of the approval steps take and ask them for insights from their experiences in also going through this process.
- Complete any forms required in your human subjects' application carefully, using provided templates and following the expected writing style.
- Try your best to follow the IRB's rules correctly the first time, in order to minimize reviewer's concerns and required corrections later.
- Be totally honest with the human subjects from whom you seek information.

6.5 Things NOT to Do

- Assume that you can avoid an IRB review for a project involving information obtained from humans, since this is rarely the case.
- Attempt to trick your participants into giving you information they would not otherwise want to share.
- Forget that human subjects have a right to stop participating in your study, or to withdraw their participation at any time.

- Get frustrated with the IRB process, especially when a correction to your work is suggested.
- Misrepresent the complexity of your project in order to get through the process faster, or otherwise try to avoid study elements which you fear may not be approved.
- Fail to fully disclose what types of information you want to collect and use, where and/or from whom, and why.

Bibliography

Calabrese, Raymond L. (2006). *The elements of an effective dissertation and thesis: a step-by-step guide to getting it right the first time*. Lanham, MD: Rowman & Littlefield Education.

Firth, K., Connell, L., & Freestone, P. (2020). *Your PhD survival guide: planning, writing, and succeeding in your final year*. Taylor & Francis.

Hjortshoj, K. (2018). *From student to scholar: a guide to writing through the dissertation stage*. Routledge.

The Importance of Meeting Deadlines

7

7.1 Role in Survival and Success

Ideally after returning from a long trip, the traveler will fondly remember the journey and treasure the meaningful experiences they had along the way. Many travelers also take the time during the trip to reflect on their travel experiences in the interest of identifying travel strategies that worked well, as well as those things they would likely do differently during their future travels. An example of this might be sleeping too long one morning and thus getting a late start on one or more days of the travel adventure. Similarly, arriving at the wrong time of day or the wrong day of the week results in a missed opportunity to see sites when they were open or to attend special events in the places you are visiting along the way.

The insights gained through such adjustments and reviews not only will serve the traveler well in their future travels, but also will enable them to provide useful travel advice and suggestions to others. While there are certainly unique differences between these two journeys, having and following a realistic travel plan and reaching milestones are the ultimate goals. Your work along the path toward those goals includes deadlines and reflections about what to fix along the way, since these are always attributes of travel success.

Seasoned thesis or dissertation travelers, regardless of whether they succeeded in reaching their original goals, will attest to the importance of understanding and meeting deadlines along the way. The importance of meeting all deadlines should be obvious, but since they are familiar parts of our past education, we may tend to overlook the true significance of firm deadlines. The potential impact that missing thesis or dissertation deadlines has on the researcher and their relationship with the research advisor and committee members should be acknowledged.

© The Author(s), under exclusive license to Springer Nature Switzerland AG 2021
R. S. Fleming and M. Kowalsky, *Survival Skills for Thesis and Dissertation Candidates*, Springer Texts in Education,
https://doi.org/10.1007/978-3-030-80939-3_7

7.2   What You Need to Know

Throughout our lives we frequently encounter deadlines that we are expected to meet, whether responding to an invitation to attend a social event, registering for an upcoming class, or filing our tax return before the deadline. Throughout your graduate studies leading up to the thesis or dissertation stage you have certainly faced numerous deadlines and successfully met them or you would not be at this stage in your graduate program.

While the deadlines that you encountered in your previous coursework afforded you the opportunity to develop your skills in meeting deadlines, you will be required to hone or perfect these skills as you embark on your thesis or dissertation travels. An essential starting point must be to understand fully the deadlines that you will face in your process, and then to comprehend the role that meeting each and every deadline will play in completing your thesis or dissertation.

Some deadlines relate directly to university processes, and therefore will not be as flexible as those for typical course assignments. The deadlines imposed by a faculty member, while establishing the "rules of the road" for a particular course, are very different than the deadlines that you will encounter in completing your thesis or dissertation. While a course instructor may have "cut you a break" by granting an extension for the due date of a particular assignment, it will be in your best interest to neither need nor seek deadline extensions as you navigate the research process.

The deadlines that you must become aware of and incorporate in your research plan and schedule will originate from two sources. Your department, college, or university will have established deadlines related to various steps within the thesis or dissertation process. Missing these "hard" deadlines will almost always delay your travel and complicate your arrival. These deadlines typically include filing and submission dates. An example of this would be missing an IRB deadline which resulted in losing your window of opportunity to collect data, or having your anticipated graduation delayed due to failing to file the form to schedule defense of your work in enough time to complete inevitable revisions. Try your best to anticipate official deadlines and prepare for them in order to avoid disappointment.

In addition to the above deadlines which should always be considered firm and non-negotiable, it is likely that your research advisor and committee members will impose certain "soft" deadlines regarding when they expect you to complete certain work and submit that work to them for review. It is imperative that you respect and seek to comply with these deadlines in the interest of affording your committee members the time they need to enact their responsibilities in reviewing your work and providing constructive feedback. Consistent punctuality is an important survival skill to display during your thesis and dissertation travels, as it is in life.

Not respecting these deadlines and your responsibility to comply with them can significantly impact your working relationship with your advisor and committee. Given that you will travel with them for the entire journey, you will want to impress them with your commitment to meeting any and all deadlines, whether established by your committee, department, college, or university. Happy travelers can weather many storms together!

7.3   Student Experiences and Suggestions: *Schedules and Timing*

In addition to striving toward a consistent implementation of their plans, certain students came to appreciate the significant relationship that exists between deadlines and a candidate's stress level. Being aware of upcoming deadlines and properly preparing in advance of them can result in a good type of stress that can both motivate and empower you. But for many students, working up to the last minute to meet deadlines, or expecting to miss them entirely, can produce real anxiety and frustration.

Some students found partners among their peers who could help them understanding the timing of deadlines and keep them aware of upcoming issues they might encounter during their travels. A few students found a process that worked for them, in which they actually held each other accountable for staying on track in their progress in advance of each and every communication with their research advisors. In doing so, they reported to each other first, and developed project charts that each used to keep up with work on their projects. Some would check in with their group to ask certain questions in order to monitor each other's progress, or just to regularly offer encouragement to each other throughout their respective journeys, even if their steps were not occurring at the same times. One group of students agreed to plan on completing each stage of their work at least a month before any related deadlines, which seemed to work quite well.

In addition to the formal university and college deadlines, most students gained an understanding that any deadlines that their research advisor or committee requested for submitting their work should be treated as formal deadlines also. Many students devised strategies to organize their work so that they could meet faculty-imposed requirements easily, and usually with time to spare. One student said they were late in submitting work to their advisor on one occasion, given that it took more time than expected to complete a particular segment of their research. Another student likewise fell behind a time or two based on their responsibilities as a graduate assistant. In these cases, notifying their advisor in advance about their inability to meet the deadline helped everyone involved to reorganize their expectations, their time and their efforts accordingly.

Through the experiences of many travelers along the way, we realized that many students had to learn about commitment the hard way. Some deadlines established by a college or university, including those related to scheduling an oral dissertation defense or the timeframe for making revisions to the manuscript are firm and not open to negotiation. Students often received harsh consequences for not meeting expectations and they heard stories of others who had similar problems and learned of the seriousness of their errors. Some students realized that deadlines established by even the friendliest research advisors and committee members should be respected as well. While their advisor and committee members were willing to extend some flexibility, failing to meet multiple deadlines or to produce the agreed-upon quality of work compromised the progress of some student's journeys. For others, their lack of motivation to complete work on time hurt their working relationship with the very people trying to help them. Everyone makes mistakes and gets sidetracked periodically, so it is important to reach out for assistance when you may need help as a result of poor planning, a lack of motivation or commitment, or even just procrastination.

7.4   Things to DO

- Recognize the role that meeting all deadlines plays in completing your thesis or dissertation, as well as on your stress level and ability to move through the process successfully.
- Identify all deadlines prescribed by your department, college, or university.
- Identify all deadlines imposed by your research advisor and committee.
- Develop and follow a work plan and schedule that provides for completion of the various research activities in advance of the dates that they are due.
- Should you anticipate having difficulty in meeting a deadline, inform your research advisor and seek their guidance.
- If you miss one deadline, learn from that experience in the interest of not missing additional ones.

7.5   Things NOT to Do

- Ignore importance of meeting all deadlines established by your committee members, department, college, or university.
- Deny the impact of not meeting deadlines that your research advisor and committee may establish on not only your progress toward completion of your thesis or dissertation, but also on your working relationship with the advisor and committee.
- Fall behind in your progress towards meeting deadlines as a result of poor planning or procrastination.
- Forget to keep your research advisor and committee members informed if you anticipate or experience any issues that will prevent you from meeting deadlines.
- Avoid making a firm commitment to complete all activities in advance of deadlines.

Bibliography

Greetham, Bryan. (2019). *How to write your undergraduate dissertation* (2nd ed). London: Red Globe Press.

McAlpine, L., & Amundsen, C. (Eds.). (2011). *Doctoral education: research-based strategies for doctoral students*. Springer.

Ogden, Evelyn Hunt. (2007). *Complete your dissertation or thesis in two semesters or less*. Lanham, MD: Rowman & Littlefield.

Understanding Why Candidates Fail to Complete Their Thesis or Dissertation

8.1 Role in Survival and Success

Perhaps it would seem highly unlikely that a graduate student, after successfully completing all of the requirements of their academic degree program leading up to the thesis or dissertation research project, would fail to complete this last "hurdle" in the journey. Yet more graduate students than one might realize, or that their academic institutions would like to admit, fall by the wayside during the challenge. Although sharing this reality with you sets a different tone than the preceding and later chapters, it is important that you realize as you begin your journey, that not everyone who embarks on this life-changing journey reaches their intended goal successfully.

The travel experiences and difficulties of past travelers may vary widely at times, but most of their difficulties share common characteristics. By understanding these potential "roadblocks" and "detours" that you could encounter during your journey, you will be able to avoid or address them, rerouting your trip when necessary. As with any trip that you will take during your lifetime, anticipating the challenges that you might encounter, and being prepared to face and resolve them when and where necessary, will ensure that you experience success.

Recognizing the most common stress points which have made other travelers decide to turn away will help you to see where your own vulnerabilities might lie. In addition to challenges related to the candidate's personality or habits, or those of the research advisor and committee members, there are a number of situational factors that could potentially prevent you from successfully finishing your project. These include changes in the candidate's current job or responsibilities that either limit the time available to devote to research activities or which no longer require an individual to complete the additional graduate degree. Changes in personal relationships and family responsibilities also can pose challenges to successful completion of a thesis or dissertation. Relocation or major life changes associated with

© The Author(s), under exclusive license to Springer Nature Switzerland AG 2021
R. S. Fleming and M. Kowalsky, *Survival Skills for Thesis and Dissertation Candidates*, Springer Texts in Education,
https://doi.org/10.1007/978-3-030-80939-3_8

either of these situations can also mean that a candidate is attempting multiple journeys at once, thus limiting their chances of efficiency in producing the necessary components.

Likewise, candidates fail to successfully complete this process for financial reasons, whether associated with the lack of needed support for their research activities or other aspects of their lives while maintaining enrolled status as a graduate student. Attending to medical or health issues that arise during this journey, whether those issues involve the student or significant others, might impede one's progress in completing a thesis or dissertation. Since life will often take precedence over schoolwork, it is important to recognize when these need your attention instead.

8.2 What You Need to Know

While there are certainly unique circumstances or situations that may impede the progress of a given student in their research travels, there are several typical reasons that graduate students fail to complete their thesis or dissertation. While use of the word "fail" might suggest that the candidate has survived the voyage up to the point that they fail to defend their thesis or dissertation successfully, it is quite common for travelers to lose their way at various junctures on their journey.

These travel problems can result from not taking the time before the trip to select a manageable topic that the researcher has both the expertise and passion to undertake. It is also imperative to secure a research advisor and committee members that share your research interest and are able and willing to commit the necessary time and guidance. This area has proven problematic for some students, especially when conflicts occur with or between committee members. Loss of your research advisor or committee members can also present significant challenges, particularly if this occurs late in your process. While it is common to experience some negative critique or opposition, many times these are natural parts of the process and should be expected.

Failure to develop a realistic plan, allocate the necessary time, re-evaluate how to manage your time effectively, or meet "hard" and "soft" deadlines (including those self-imposed) have also derailed the journey of many past travelers. Once again, a fully-engaged commitment throughout your journey is imperative. Resiliency is a key survival skill for your thesis or dissertation travels; those travelers who finally achieve a completed degree are usually those who have increased their capacity for resiliency.

While you will hopefully not experience any of these or other major problems in your journey, recognizing the potential for them is important, as is the role of thorough planning and developing a realistic timetable that allows sufficient time to complete your research activities. Allowing for some "slack time" to accommodate the road hazards you may encounter during your journey is a prudent decision which enables you to adjust your expectations and behaviors as a result. Remember, a "course correction" is not a failure of the entire journey!

8.3 Student Experiences and Suggestions: *Don't Let Bumps in the Road End Your Journey*

One student recalled that they were somewhat disturbed by one of the topics discussed during an early class meeting, when classmates in attendance were explicitly reminded that not all students who embark on this voyage avoid drowning! Professors said there was so much more to do than just following the steps, even after successfully completing their academic program's course requirements or benchmark exams. Some students saw this as bad news and thought they might quit the process shortly after it started. While this made many nervous, the rest of the session was dedicated to sharing the various reasons that candidates fail to complete their thesis or dissertations. Most students left that class meeting knowing what problems to navigate and what the most common successful experiences had in common. They felt it was better to know what to expect, even the negative aspects, in advance. With diligence and attention, they could avoid most of these problems for themselves.

Other students agreed that knowing about things that might happen along the way which could potentially derail their ability to complete their research projects was quite helpful. Many felt that early disclosure of issues allowed them to take time to develop the necessary mindset for success, or to regroup and revise plans when necessary in order to continue on their journeys. A student shared that anticipation of challenges along the way helped them to resist the inclination to think that they were the only one who had ever encountered problems. Another student was able to stay on their intended path despite encountering several minor bumps in the road and one major roadblock that they had heard about previously. This student knew that others had successfully navigated through these problem areas in order to finish their journey.

Collegial working relationships developed with research advisors and other faculty members early in the process were important for some students during their later journeys, particularly when they encountered travel challenges late in the process and needed someone new with whom to brainstorm ideas. While keeping your research advisor and committee updated about important breakthroughs or roadblocks is important, it is even more crucial to open lines of communication if you experience developments in your personal or professional life that present challenges to your progress. One candidate, who assumed that the issues that they experienced were unusual and embarrassing, chose not to bring problems to the attention of their advisor. For months, they struggled with their problem, which was not an academic one, without the help and support of their school. It is important always to remember that your research advisor and committee members, along with your program and institution, desire to see you succeed. They probably have available and confidential resources to help you address your situation, so asking your faculty members, campus offices, or online help desks for assistance is always a good idea.

Similar to reflecting on the day's travel at the end of each day of a multiday trip, we recommend two important things. One is to take time to celebrate your progress at the completion of each activity and milestone, as well as the time to relax and prepare for the next leg of your journey. Whether you disagree with the advice you are given, or you have an argument or make a series of communication mistakes, or you are upset at the level of support you are receiving, keeping the lines of communication open among everyone, even if this seems difficult at times, will help you to maintain forward progress. Kind words, apologies, and positivity are appreciated by everyone. At the end of each stage of your journey it is beneficial to evaluate how you have progressed, including what you did well and what you could improve, in the interest of determining if you should make any adjustments in your travel plans. Most likely, you will be quite proud of yourself for learning new things and navigating new territory. Take some time to compliment yourself on a job well done thus far, and remember that although all progress takes work, it is totally possible!

8.4 Things to DO

- Anticipate potential challenges to completing your thesis or dissertation.
- Recognize and acknowledge that developments, circumstances, or situations will occur that have the potential of compromising your ability to complete thesis or dissertation requirements successfully.
- Regroup and revise your plan as necessary when you encounter these challenges.
- Keep your research advisor, committee, and department "in the loop" regarding significant developments that arise in your personal and/or professional life that are challenging your ability to complete your thesis or dissertation.
- Realize that the working relationship you have developed with your research advisor and committee can be invaluable as you seek the best way to proceed.

8.5 Things NOT to Do

- Assume that you are the only student that has ever encountered these particular problems during the research journey.
- Feel that this is a problem or issue that you must deal with on your own.
- Neglect to keep your research advisor and committee aware of the issue(s) you are dealing with and their impact on your progress.
- Forget that your institution probably has provisions to help you address the situation you are facing, such as granting you a leave of absence
- Fail to resume your research activities when you have resolved the involved outside issues.

Bibliography

Kelly, Frances Jennifer. (2017). *The idea of the PhD: the doctorate in the twenty-first century.* London and New York: Routledge.

Lipson, Charles. (2018). *How to write a BA thesis: a practical guide from your first ideas to your finished paper* (2nd ed). Chicago: University of Chicago Press.

Miller, A. B. (2009). *Finish your dissertation once and for all!: how to overcome psychological barriers, get results, and move on with your life.* American Psychological Association.

Focusing on a Manageable Research Topic

9

9.1 Role in Survival and Success

It is not uncommon for a novice traveler planning a long trip to develop a plan that attempts to visit more places, take in more sights, or do more things than are realistically possible. This urge to "cram in" as much as one can is a frequent tendency of some individuals who are new to the art and science of travel planning. Whether their ill-advised plan results from the excitement and enthusiasm to travel to new and exciting places or the perceived reality that they might never have the opportunity to engage in such an adventure again, they develop a travel plan that almost always results in their great travel expectations not being fully realized.

Unfortunately, the same inclination also exists with many thesis or dissertation travelers as they plan their first great adventure. The fact that most have not taken such a journey in the past, and the perceived reality that they will likely never do so again, drives them to select a research topic that is not suitably delimited and manageable. This often proves to be problematic once the thesis or dissertation traveler embarks on their journey.

Selecting a research topic that is not properly narrow in scope is a mistake that many have regretted later. A topic or method that is unmanageable could best be described as an "albatross" that will burden you throughout your thesis or dissertation travel. Managing your selection of project characteristics, while weighing the pros and cons of each choice you are making, will help you determine what aspects are manageable and what aspects are unwieldy (too many parts or steps to do at once), overly ambitious (life's work rather than one study in a series), or overwhelming (too big of a project given the time and resources available). The ability to focus your topic in scope and breadth in a way aligns with the intended format of a thesis or dissertation is an important survival skill.

© The Author(s), under exclusive license to Springer Nature Switzerland AG 2021
R. S. Fleming and M. Kowalsky, *Survival Skills for Thesis and Dissertation Candidates*, Springer Texts in Education,
https://doi.org/10.1007/978-3-030-80939-3_9

9.2   What You Need to Know

The selection of a research topic is perhaps the most important decision that you will make as a thesis or dissertation traveler. In addition to "driving" all of the remaining activities of the research process, it will also dictate much of what you focus on over a number of years. The importance of selecting a manageable topic by limiting its scope is also reinforced in three later chapters, the first of which will consider identifying a research area in which you have sufficient interest. The latter two chapters consider the process of identifying and refining a research topic.

While you should look to your research advisor and the members of your committee for guidance in selecting a topic and identifying appropriate research questions, it is imperative that you are actually the one to determine the research topic that you will study. While it should be a topic that you are both qualified to study and passionate about, it should also be a topic that is neither too small nor too simple for a thesis or dissertation. It should also not be too large an idea to explain or too large a problem to solve via one project, study, or experiment.

The fact that you are embarking on this novel journey (that you will likely never take again) should not result in a decision to do everything all at once. If you do not focus your research topic appropriately, then you will live with the consequences of that unwise decision. Similarly, you should not allow your advisor or committee members to persuade you to take on a research project with an unreasonably large scope. Lastly, you should recognize that the more passionate you are about a topic, the greater will be the inclination to frame your research topic much more broadly than you really should.

While this may be the only time that you will conduct the research associated with a master's thesis or doctoral dissertation, you will have many future opportunities to conduct further research and publish in your area of interest after you complete this current journey. Look to your research advisor for their guidance as you select a research topic of sufficient difficulty but which has clear boundaries. Over time you will realize the wisdom of selecting a manageable research topic, often through hearing about the challenges that others have faced as a result of not doing so.

9.3   Student Experiences and Suggestions: *Exploring Your Travel Interests*

A starting point in planning any successful trip is determining the destination to which you desire to travel. While that will obviously be to meet the thesis or dissertation requirements of your program, it is also important to plan a journey that will benefit you in terms of the skills that you will be qualified to share at the completion of your travels. Some students felt that they took too long to ponder, deliberate, and ultimately select the perfect topic that aligned with their research interests. Others seemed to know right away and seemed to follow their passion to explore a particular topic further in order to meaningfully contribute to the existing body of knowledge in that area. Most students' process was somewhere in between these extremes, and the speed at which they produced work did not necessarily align with either the complexity of their undertaking or their ultimate success. Your thesis or dissertation topic will become clearer as you learn more, so let the journey transform your thinking!

One student pointed out that their research advisor and committee members were extremely helpful in encouraging them to take more time to identify a research topic or method that would be useful for the current project and likely beyond. Students in various fields mention that their programs require them to publish before undertaking their independent thesis or dissertation topic, in order to understand how graduate level projects can drives one's future research stream. Other programs expect the final thesis or dissertation manuscript to be the initial publication of one's professional career. Either way, you have likely collaborated on several research ideas which served as a basis for conference presentations and journal articles. Some students enjoyed having a variety of ideas from which to choose, and others hoped to try out specific ideas in the professional literature in advance of committing to a particular trend or line of inquiry. Taking the necessary time and expending the energy to brainstorm possible research topics before selecting the ones that they were passionate enough about to pursue for several years makes great sense.

Selecting a topic that interests you and is sufficiently original in scope and difficulty given the degree that you are pursuing should meet corresponding expectations of your department, college, or university. One student failed to delimit their topic to one that was both appropriate and manageable within the established time limits to complete their degree program. It was reported that this happened against the sound advice of their research advisor and was driven by a mindset that this would be the only time they would ever have the opportunity to explore their research interests with the available resources and work space. Had the student pondered their objectives in more detail, they would have completed their doctoral degree much sooner and with less frustration, allowing them to move on to conducting additional research related to their research interests and potentially even secure funding to develop a bigger and better study in the future.

Part of the graduate student learning process is to discern which rules apply to them, which directions are non-negotiable, and which actions matter most to their subject field and future career plans. Some students discovered that they became experts in complying with the expectations of their university for candidates completing their dissertation, as well as prioritizing which aspects of their research were most viable at their own institution and in their own discipline. While some aspects of thesis and dissertation travel are common, others may diverge slightly or can differ significantly. Successful students quickly figured out what aspects of a project were best for fulfillment of a degree, and which aspects of their life's work would happen after the degree was obtained. These students checked their understandings and assumptions with others who were more knowledgeable in the field and who were farther along in the research process, enabling them to prioritize which of their ideas could be used in the short term and which would be possibilities for the future.

9.4   Things to DO

- Understand the importance of selecting a topic whose scope and difficulty are appropriate based on the degree that you are pursuing and the expectations of your department, college, or university.
- Seek the guidance of your research advisor and, perhaps, potential committee members as you deliberate your research topic.
- Brainstorm the various research topics that you are considering.
- Select a research topic that corresponds with your interests and, ideally, your passion.
- Delimit your topic, as appropriate, consistent with your research interests.
- Secure approval of your research topic from your research advisor.

9.5   Things NOT to Do

- Assume that this is the only time that you will ever have the opportunity to conduct research in your area of interest.
- Ignore the importance of seeking guidance from your research advisor and others, including authors of the published literature.
- Forget to focus the scope of your research topic by identifying what it is and what it is not.
- Commit to a research topic that will likely prove unmanageable and difficult to complete within the prescribed time limits for completion of your graduate degree.

Bibliography

Biggins, John. (2011). *Succeeding with your master's dissertation: a step-by-step handbook* (2nd ed). London: McGraw Hill.

Levin, P. (2011). *Excellent dissertations! maidenhead*. McGraw-Hill Open University Press.

Wisker, Gina. (2019). *The undergraduate research handbook* (2nd ed). London: Red Globe Press.

Identifying an Area of Research Interest

10

10.1 Role in Survival and Success

The most enjoyable and memorable trips are planned in advance in accordance with the personal interests of the traveler. Taking the time to identify your travel interests will enable you to make good decisions regarding where you will travel and what you want to see and do during your trip. Some students may be reading this chapter earlier in their process, and some may need to revisit it later as they change course. Many will agree that it is difficult to see all of the many places to see and events to attend when visiting a large, exciting city; you may need to return more than once in order to confirm that you have experienced all of a particular area's offerings. Travel experiences in academics similarly illustrate the importance of charting out the unique travel adventure that is right for each traveler, even if multiple travelers are visiting the same city. You will want to begin your thesis or dissertation journey by identifying the research area that corresponds with your passion, but then also clarifying an aspect of your interest which can be explored within a thesis or dissertation manuscript.

Choosing a disciplinary area can seem like an overwhelming task at first, especially since it may feel like you will be forever linked to that subject once your thesis or dissertation is published for the world to see. However, identifying an area of research should be relatively easy once you engage in introspection about your interests and career path. Just as you can review your past trips to determine what you liked and disliked about them, consider your past work and what you like about different disciplines of study. As you ponder more and more specifics of your idea, after researching, thinking, and engaging with others in your field, you may realize that you likely already know the answers to many of these questions. As you are determining areas of study about which you are enthusiastic, it may be helpful to make a ranked list of ideas, and also indicate those subjects, fields, or trends that are important in your field but which you don't particularly like. Decision making is a survival skill which is only undertaken after proper identification of all of the

R. S. Fleming and M. Kowalsky, *Survival Skills for Thesis and Dissertation Candidates*, Springer Texts in Education, https://doi.org/10.1007/978-3-030-80939-3_10

possibilities. Make an informed and reasoned choice based on your consideration of all the options, including a review of those you have rejected.

Next you might consider what career path you will take after you receive your graduate degree. Your analysis of the academic travels that you enjoy the most will likely impact your choice of paper topic, since you will want to ensure that your work helps you to get the type of job that you desire. Do you want to manage a small nonprofit, or work for a multinational company? Do you want to be a school administrator, or a college professor? And if the latter, do you want to work at a research university or a community college or continue your career abroad? Only you can determine the life goals which your degree completion can help you achieve. If you need ideas, background research on the job market or disciplinary trends may help you choose. What areas have others been proposing or publishing about at your institution, at similar institutions, or elsewhere in your subject field? On what topics does your discipline really need more research-based practice, knowledge, or details? What types of expertise are employers seeking? Remember that your academic travels can be in either an established or a new field at this point; in the early stages of consideration, you are merely choosing an area (or maybe two) which best matches your interests. In other words, you are confirming that you will not travel to all of the other locations, at least not for the next few years, because now you have to focus!

10.2   What You Need to Know

Just as when traveling with a family or group, others will try to influence your selection of a thesis or dissertation topic, or provide unsolicited advice on what you should do. These travelers could be more experienced doctoral students, faculty advisors, or even family and friends. Listen to their concerns, but resist the temptation to pick a certain topic just because it will please others. Your choice of a travel locale for sustained research is a highly personal one, and only you know which subjects will continually engage you and feed your intellect. As long as you have confirmed your general area of study, any further details you can provide should help others understand what you are trying to do, especially those who have not been through a thesis or dissertation process themselves. Ideally, as you keep telling both friends and other academics your travel ideas, you will experience increasing clarity and confidence in your choices.

As you have certainly done when planning a non-academic trip, remember that it is OK to change your mind! You don't have to feel obligated to remain with the first idea you had, or the idea which others thought might be easiest. Many thesis or dissertation topics are of equal difficulty for a traveler who has never attempted one before, so not to worry. Create a project that showcases and reflects your best abilities, and everything will work out just fine. Travelers who are good decision makers always have reasons for choosing certain options over others, and can explain those choices clearly and easily.

Possibly, knowledgeable others may also be giving you valuable feedback throughout your travels, even though you may not realize it. Experienced research advisors and committee members are able to identify right away any topic that is unfocused, unpopular, or quite frankly, impossible. Bounce your ideas off of a variety of faculty members at your own institution, as well as those you meet at professional events and conferences, to evaluate their reactions to your plans. You can even tell fellow travelers about some of your already-rejected ideas, just to get confirmation that you're on the right track in eliminating them as possibilities.

When deciding travel plans, you nearly always consult both friendly resources (people you know) and objective resources (online reviews or guides) before making a decision. Include in your feedback loop those who do not know you personally, such as professors from other colleges; they will be able to focus solely on your research idea as you describe it, rather than on your shared history as a student in their course, or on their relationship with others at your institution. Just as with traveling, innovative ideas or popular topics are both options in the early stages of selecting a research area, so try to keep an open mind about the possibilities. There is still much to learn before undertaking research on any topic, even when traveling in areas with which you may already feel comfortable.

10.3   Student Experiences and Suggestions: *Selling Others on a Specific Location to Visit*

Ask anyone who has completed their thesis or dissertation journey, and they will advocate the importance of correctly identifying your area of research interest early in your journey. While you will have the opportunity at an appropriate point later in the research process to identify and refine your research topic, you will want to do your best at this juncture to articulate a more specific description of your research project and justification of the choice of topic that you will be required to live with for several years. Most often, graduate students who have been through the thesis and dissertation process, and even those who have become faculty members themselves, can easily articulate their successes and failures in selling their research ideas successfully to others.

One student had a good sense of their intended research topic early in their coursework, and with limited refinement, ended up actually pursuing that topic in their final study. This student's peers felt that they truly internalized the idea of further advancing their discipline through rigorous study and publication. Yet many of those peers had only basic outlines of their current work and research trajectory, so the appropriate choices became clearer to the rest of these students only later in the process. They explained that they learn best by doing, rather than by watching. You too should decide on the most important details after significant research and conscientious contemplation, so that you do not become frustrated with a project that is too narrow to be meaningful or too broad to manage effectively.

Those who know your personal behaviors well, such as family and friends, and those who know your academic behaviors well, like fellow students and your professors, will easily see when you are not excited about your project. They may also sense a disconnect between your interests and the current project you are trying to complete. If you notice that you have progressed too far into a project that is degree-worthy but which no longer speaks to your passions or identity, all is not lost. You can improve the rest of the world after your thesis or dissertation is done and your degree is awarded! Simply view your project as a showcase of your theoretical knowledge or your technical skills in preparation for the real work which will begin thereafter. This can serve to motivate you to finish the academic exercises in order to get on with your exciting plans ahead.

Knowing and being able to articulate your research interest persuasively will be important as you identify appropriate faculty members to serve as your research advisor and committee members, and later as you seek research collaborators in your field. These individuals will expect that you have taken the necessary time to select a research area that has the potential of contributing to the existing body of knowledge, rather than selecting a seemingly easy project that would allow you to race through a project without yielding its intended value to you or your profession. Students who acquired the habit of diligence in defining the scope and sequence of their potential research areas gained invaluable skills in convincing faculty members to join them on their journeys.

10.4   Things to DO

- Determine what topics would motivate you for the next few years.
- Select a research area that lets you help others in a broader sense, rather than a project that will just help a small group of people in your own town or state.
- Explore the discipline in which you are interested by researching its published literature in detail as well as other people researching in the area, which will enable you to make an informed decision.
- Seek to learn how projects and papers on your potential topic are created, completed, and communicated.
- Realize that not everyone knows their intended thesis or dissertation topic right away.
- Recognize that it is better to take your time to identify the right research area at this juncture, rather than regret your choice later.

10.5   Things NOT to Do

- Become frustrated as you seek to identify your research interest.
- Commit to a narrow idea or methodology too early in your decision making process.

- Follow the crowd in pursuing the same topic that your department, research group, or program suggests that all of its students study, rather than finding a particular aspect of that topic which speaks to you personally or suggesting a well-thought-out alternative.
- Suggest a research area that will take your entire lifetime to study properly, or that would require Nobel-prize funding to complete.
- Fail to realize that your thesis or dissertation is simply your *first* project as an academic, and as such it is meant to display your research skills and aptitude to take on future projects.
- Think that your thesis or dissertation must contain the sum of your life's work.

Bibliography

Brause, Rita S. (2012). *Writing your doctoral dissertation: invisible rules for success*. New York: Taylor & Francis.

Single, Peg B. (2009). *Demystifying dissertation writing: a streamlined process from choice of topic to final text*. Sterling, VA: Stylus.

Thomas, Gary. (2017). *How to do your research project* (revised ed). Thousand Oaks, CA: Sage.

Roles and Responsibilities of a Research Advisor

11

11.1 Role in Survival and Success

Rather than taking a journey alone, many travelers will decide to have a companion accompany them on their trip. This is often the case when one is embarking on a long trip or traveling to a destination to which they had not traveled before. The value of having a seasoned travel companion is obvious, given the role that their travel experience can play in enhancing both the success and pleasure of a journey. Ideal travel companions exchange their expectations, information, and feedback clearly and kindly, in order to improve the experiences of everyone.

The same is true in thesis or dissertation travel. Given that you likely have not engaged in such travel before, nor have experienced the scope and length of the academic journey that you are about to undertake, you most certainly will need experienced travelers to guide you. The thesis or dissertation process at your college or university will recognize this and require you to have not only a research advisor but also committee members to assist you in mapping out your trip and in navigating the many steps and challenges that separate you from your destination.

Given the integral role that these travel guides will play in your experiences, it is prudent to study the roles and responsibilities that your research advisor and committee will assume during your journey. Most certainly, their expertise in prior thesis or dissertation travel will enable you to move with confidence on this challenging journey. The quality of the professional working relationships that you develop with these individuals will enhance your travel success, as well as increase the pleasantness and efficiency of your journey.

© The Author(s), under exclusive license to Springer Nature Switzerland AG 2021
R. S. Fleming and M. Kowalsky, *Survival Skills for Thesis and Dissertation Candidates*, Springer Texts in Education,
https://doi.org/10.1007/978-3-030-80939-3_11

11.2 What You Need to Know

A research advisor, often referred to as a thesis or dissertation chair or committee member, is the faculty member that your college or university has designated to lead the work of your thesis or dissertation committee. Specifically, this professor will assume primary responsibility for assisting you throughout the research process, and this important travel guide may or may not be selected with consideration of your input as the traveler. As such, this faculty member has a responsibility to assist you in charting your travel course and in guiding you throughout your journey. Many words have been used to describe the role of a research advisor including coach, guide, consultant, mentor, supervisor, and teacher. Categorizing this role as a travel advisor or guide helps you to see that you are on the journey and responsible for arriving at the destination successfully, yet your travels can and should be greatly influenced by a more knowledgeable other. Although this role is viewed differently across institutions, some commonalities may appear across universities, among nations, and between subject areas.

While you may have taken your last formal class before entering this stage of your journey, you will want to recognize that you will have many opportunities to continue to learn while under the tutelage of your primary research advisor. In addition to gaining valuable insights that will contribute to making appropriate progress in your journey, you will also have the opportunity to learn things from your advisor that will prove beneficial if you have the opportunity to serve as a research advisor for a thesis or dissertation candidate in the future. If that seems too far off in the future, just remember that you have already benefitted from others who have shared their travel advice with you; paying it forward is a natural outcome once you have an experience to share!

You will want to develop an understanding of the roles and responsibilities of a research advisor early in your journey, prior to determining which particular faculty members or doctoral-level experts you would like to accompany you on your thesis or dissertation travels. It is imperative that you fully comprehend the customary and appropriate roles and duties that this person should be expected to enact as they support you throughout the research process. Similarly, it is important to determine which responsibilities should not fall to your research advisor. For example, daily questions, uninformed decision making, or carelessly prepared submissions would generally be considered annoying to your principal research advisor or committee members during this process. Much of the learning about how to do a dissertation can be found in other sources more readily. Instead, "do your homework" on advisor's background and skills before asking, deciding, or preparing a proposal for them.

Many of these tasks are your responsibility as a graduate student at the highest level, and managing daily project operations is not something your research advisor should be asked or expected to do. Failing to follow up on the faculty members' design suggestions, or failing to fully research on your own and in advance each area which impacts your project can also negatively impact the working relationship between you and your advisor. Both parties must have a clear understanding of their individual roles and responsibilities, as well as activities for which they share responsibility. The working relationship that you develop must be an adult-to-adult one, rather than a parent-to-child relationship. An advisor who makes their working expectations clear provides valuable information to help you learn how to become a quality travel companion.

Understanding your research advisor's role and your own responsibilities during each and every stage of your journey is an essential survival skill. With good information about your fellow travelers, you will be prepared to embark on a successful journey that begins with agreeing on your research topic and culminates with the oral examination that in most instances is the main task over which your research advisor will preside. In addition to working with you throughout your journey, your research advisor will expect to be kept up to date regarding your progress at appropriate times, and will provide certain directives about the pace and quality of your progress as well. As you can see, mastering the art of both speaking and listening in equal amounts, in a symbiotic partnership with your support team, will result in a most enjoyable journey.

11.3   Student Experiences and Suggestions: *Research Advisors as Travel Guides*

Over the course of their research journey, many students found invaluable the guidance of their research advisor, or main mentor, even if they didn't always understand that individual's directions. By the end of their programs, many graduate students report that they had a much fuller understanding of the importance of selecting the appropriate faculty member to serve as a research advisor, and the constraints and difficulties of those performing these roles. A few students stated that their research advisors shared their visions and philosophies, and thus easily agreed to take on a leadership role in their journeys. However, they also realized that many highly talented and dedicated faculty researchers may not also have the same level of talent to be advisors. Experiences of brilliant content analysis but nonexistent procedural support are unfortunately common experiences for students in dealing with their research committees, yet many of these struggles are thankfully not apparent in the students' final manuscripts.

Students noted that certain important takeaways from their courses included discussion of the appropriate roles and responsibilities of a research advisor, as well as which requests were unreasonable to expect from an advisor. Discussions with more advanced students, and attention to the stories which circulated around the departments, enabled many candidates to learn that in addition to their responsibilities to their advisees, research advisors have responsibilities to their department, institution, and profession as well. Often, less experienced faculty members were struggling with many of the same issues themselves, and simultaneously ensuring attributes of scholarship rigor and quality applied to their own work as well as to that of the students they were supervising.

Students were also sometimes surprised to learn that their research advisors had numerous other demands on their time and that questioners needed to be respectful, appreciative and patient with faculty members. One student who gained a reputation for being unreasonable in their expectations, believing that their advisor should reply to detailed requests on the same day and ideally within a few hours, failed to realize that teaching class sessions and responding to candidate questions were only a fraction of their responsibilities at the university. Of course, some students remarked, certain faculty members made juggling their multiple academic and family roles look easy. Yet most gained new appreciation of and insight regarding the many required responsibilities of a professional academic career involving teaching, writing, presentation, service, advising, and supervising, which were in addition to any personal responsibilities outside of the university.

A different graduate student, in contrast, became a faculty favorite by always contributing to the goals of the department, participating in events when possible, and remaining upbeat despite setbacks. One student felt that they demonstrated an appreciation of their advisors' time by always turning in their best work in a timely manner and allowing the faculty member to determine a timeframe for feedback based on when the submission arrived within their own schedule of work. By understanding that the advisor needed time to conscientiously review and comment on their work, and by remaining positive instead of needy, this student felt they received better feedback than expected. They explained to a new group of graduate students in a peer information session that they were always professional in their expectations and dealings with their advisor; that they never felt ashamed or like it was a bother to reach out to their advisor when they needed guidance or direction; and that they strived to always give the benefit of the doubt to others, even when they were disappointed, in hopes of receiving similar treatment themselves. Apparently this advice worked well, since this candidate became a popular dissertation advisor as well, many years later!

11.4 Things to DO

- Recognize the responsibility that your research advisor has to you, as well as to your department, institution, and profession.
- Fully understand the roles and responsibilities of a research advisor prior to considering potential faculty members that you would like to serve in this important role.
- Learn from your research advisor how to be a good citizen in shared scholarly pursuits, so that you can help future students through your advice or as a member of their committees.
- Recognize that your research advisor has other personal and professional responsibilities, including working with other advisees.

- Do your part to contribute to an effective working relationship and progress towards completion of your thesis or dissertation.
- Rely on your research advisor, as the chair of your committee, to communicate with other committee members and involve them on your behalf.

11.5 Things NOT to Do

- Develop unrealistic expectations for your research advisor.
- Expect your research advisor to discuss your project with you daily, or even weekly.
- Contribute to role-related issues, including role ambiguity and role conflict, by not asking questions which clearly delineated roles, responsibilities, and expectations in advance.
- Submit less than your best work at all times.
- Continuously seek guidance and assistance from your research advisor.
- Attempt to reach and communicate with your advisor at inappropriate times and through inappropriate means.

Bibliography

Joyner, R. L., Rouse, W. A., & Glatthorn, A. A. (2013). *Writing the Winning Thesis or Dissertation: A Step-by-Step Guide*. Thousand Oaks, CA: Corwin Press.
Nygaard, L. (2017). *Writing your master's thesis: From A to Zen*. Sage.
Parija, S. C., & Kate, V. (2018). *Thesis writing for Master's and Ph.D. program*. Singapore: Springer.

Selecting Research Advisors

12

12.1 Role in Survival and Success

If you have ever taken a long trip with a companion, particularly one that spans a number of days, you will realize the importance of having the "right" travel partner. While traveling with the right person usually results in a great trip, travel with the wrong travel companion can increase the challenges or frustrations of your trip, as well as complicate reaching your destination according to plan. Engaging in pre-travel discussions that lead to consensus on such things as the planned pace of your journey and the places you plan to visit along the way, are of obvious importance.

Given that your thesis or dissertation travel will involve one of the longest journeys that you will ever undertake, selecting the right travel companion as your research advisor is certainly among the most important travel decisions that you will ever make. You will want an individual who, in addition to being qualified to guide you through this challenging journey, is also interested in the research you propose to undertake and willing to sign on as your travel guide. Revealing your honesty about your own skills, and displaying a willingness to continue a dialogue about what you still need to learn, can help everyone in your process learn what is still needed for a successful completion.

While not finding the right travel companion for a reasonably short road trip is something that you should be able to live with, failing to select an appropriate individual to guide and champion your research journey can prove problematic later in the process. Given that you will be required to work under the guidance and direction of your research advisor for the duration of your journey, selecting a faculty member with whom you can develop an appropriate working relationship is imperative.

© The Author(s), under exclusive license to Springer Nature Switzerland AG 2021
R. S. Fleming and M. Kowalsky, *Survival Skills for Thesis and Dissertation Candidates*, Springer Texts in Education, https://doi.org/10.1007/978-3-030-80939-3_12

12.2 What You Need to Know

It is important that you acknowledge the significance of this early decision and the impact it will have on the rest of your journey. While you may receive guidance and suggestions from others, including your academic advisor, as to who would be the best person to have as your research advisor, it is important that only after conscientious consideration and deliberation you decide who you feel would be the best person to serve as your tour guide on this life-changing journey. While it might be that your academic advisor would be the most appropriate person, that is usually not the case in that regardless of their particular qualifications as a researcher, you will want a research advisor who shares your research vision.

Likewise, while you might be inclined to seek a popular member of your institution's teaching faculty, you should recognize that we all have talents and interests and that some great teachers are the last people you would want to supervise your research journey. You will learn that, similar to teaching, research is an acquired skill that comes with experience and time. This would suggest that you might want to recognize that a new faculty member with no or limited experience serving on a thesis or dissertation committee, much less chairing one, while willing to serve in this capacity might not have the travel experience that you should desire in a research advisor. You will likewise want a faculty member with demonstrated skill in facilitating the thesis or dissertation process by working with students and the other committee members.

You will want to identify a faculty member whose past personal research or that of the research projects that they had supervised aligns with your research interest. A shared vision and passion will enhance the success and pleasure of your journey together. You may have interacted with a faculty member earlier in your program who had expressed an interest in your research area and perhaps even the willingness to consider serving on your committee if your intended research topic was compatible with their interests. Therefore, being honest with yourself about your alignment with a potential research advisor—either in personality, work ethic, background knowledge, or availability—is an essential survival skill.

You will want to identify and "interview" several faculty members who could be appropriate to serve as your research advisor assuming they were in a position to make the necessary, extended time commitment. Given that you will need them to commit to working with you for a number of years, it is important that they realistically consider whether they are in a position to take on this role. A faculty member may have various practical reasons for indicating that they are not available to serve as your research advisor, including an upcoming sabbatical, plans to assume additional responsibilities, current advising load, and perhaps even contemplated retirement. During this "interview" you will want to get a sense of whether your individual styles would be compatible and whether taking this journey together might make sense. If you should ask someone to serve and they turn you down, you should accept this decision as an informed one and not seek to understand their basis in making it.

You will also want to gain insights about each person's track record as a researcher and thesis or dissertation travel guide through other means. Appropriate things to consider as you "thin the herd" of potential candidates is the reputation, expertise, and style of each. You will want to discover and seriously consider the number of advisees that they currently have, the number of students who have completed their thesis or dissertation under their supervision, and ideally the percentage of their advisees that complete their thesis or dissertation. An additional consideration is how long it typically takes students under their supervision to complete the thesis or dissertation.

Once you have identified the faculty member that you want to serve as your research advisor, you will want to make the case to them and hopefully secure agreement to join you in this journey. Assuming the faculty member responds affirmatively, you will need to follow your institution's procedures for officially appointing this person as your research advisor.

12.3   Student Experiences and Suggestions: *A Travel Guide Who Speaks Your Language*

Many students commented about the importance of identifying the right advisor for themselves and their work. They spent many a late night in the student lounge crafting arguments aimed at convincing a particular individual or committee to agree to guide them. In some ways, this may be more difficult than choosing the institution at which to study for your advanced degree. For some students, this decision is made for them, depending on their academic abilities or interests, or their specialized needs for methods, funding, or equipment. Whether they got to choose their research advisors or not, students say that their best efforts were spent in learning more about the advisors, and that learning to speak their disciplinary language like a peer became instrumental to their later success in navigating all types of research journeys.

One student used a strategy of interviewing the potential faculty members at their own university, and then making appointments to speak by phone to other faculty who had similar subject area interests at other institutions. Although many of their successful meetings benefitted from introductions in advance, often explanatory inquiries which showed strong knowledge of the research area were enough to persuade a reply. Through these short question and answer sessions, the candidate was able to determine which faculty members shared their vision and interests. They were able to have a lighthearted discussion about the future of their topic and the field, and for faculty in their home department, get an idea of the professors' current and likely future responsibilities in case they might have the necessary time to devote to supervising the student's upcoming project. After practicing all of these contacts, the student developed a presentation for future students explaining the ways to connect with other academics with whom you can develop a productive working relationship, either for student level projects now, or with a view toward career collaborations later.

Never engage in satisficing when making important decisions that will drive your future research activities, publication outcomes, and contributions to your discipline. Perhaps others will not know that you may be settling for a thesis or dissertation topic that does not excite you, or one that a faculty member convinced you was the next new trend in your field but now potentially is not. At this point in your progress, not only can you feel confident to know that your choices were not ones you would ever make again, but also you can finish what you have started, even if it is not perfect. Even if you have made some irreversible decisions, you can still complete your project, knowing that you have certainly created the best product possible given the circumstances. Although some students eventually completed their dissertations with lackluster topics, loss of interest in their topics along the way contributed to a more challenging journey and became visible to others via their mediocre final products. Many students indeed learn the most about being a top-quality academic well after they celebrate their final day as a student researcher. This surely makes for a great cautionary tale to tell other students when you are the guide!

After completing their respective journeys, two students decided to conduct a post-trip analysis and comparison of their dissertation travels. This was seen as a way to decompress, to celebrate, to review and to reflect. Both candidates concluded that the success of their journeys was, in large part, a result of having each other—someone who figuratively spoke their language and understood the environment, much like a local travel guide. They both agreed that they not only needed each other as support, but that they also needed more experienced travelers to show them the way. They said the professors and advisors who helped the most were those who could explain methods and topics and problems in ways they could easily understand. These advisors usually had the best records of teaching in one-on-one situations, of communicating clearly equally in writing and in person, and of graduating students with some regularity each year. Yet personality and inspiration were also instrumental characteristics for those in supportive roles, and students felt strong connections to the particular faculty members who exhibited styles which were complementary and not necessarily similar to their own. As with most important considerations, taking the time to determine the characteristics which are needed in guides for your research journey will help you make good decisions on companions for academics as well as for life.

12.4 Things to DO

- Review your institution's process and procedures for appointing thesis and dissertation research advisors.
- Identify a number of potential faculty members who you think might be appropriate to supervise your thesis or dissertation journey.

- Prepare in advance of scheduled "interviews" with potential committee members to identify the things you need to ascertain to make an informed decision about skills, knowledge or other qualities which will serve you well.
- Consider the faculty member's current advising responsibilities and the impact that this could have on their ability to dedicate the time and attention necessary to your research project.
- Ensure that the faculty member you select has research interests that align with yours and a shared vision regarding your proposed research topic.
- Ask in an appropriate manner, including affording sufficient time for the person to contemplate taking this journey with you.

12.5 Things NOT to Do

- Underestimate the importance and lasting implications of this critical decision on your research journey.
- Fail to take the time to determine appropriate selection criteria and meet with all candidates under consideration for roles on your committee.
- Underestimate the importance of a faculty member's track record in successfully supervising past advisees.
- Decide without purposeful, conscientious deliberation who would be the ideal candidate to ask to be your research advisor.
- Be coerced into accepting a faculty member as a research advisor primarily based upon their availability and desire to chair a research committee.
- Forget to express your gratitude whether or not the person accepts your invitation.

Bibliography

Cassuto, L., & Weisbuch, R. (2021). *The New PhD: How to Build a Better Graduate Education*. Johns Hopkins University Press.

Kelsky, Karen. *The Professor Is In: The Essential Guide to Turning Your Ph.D. Into a Job*. New York: Crown, 2015.

Walshaw, M. (2012). *Getting to Grips with Doctoral Research*. Palgrave Macmillan.

Working with Your Research Advisors

13

13.1 Role in Survival and Success

An essential starting point in planning any trip is for the travelers to arrive at a mutual understanding regarding the destination to which they intend to travel, as well as the route of travel that they will take. Before departing on the trip, it will serve both parties well to reach agreement regarding each person's role(s) including such essential activities as map reading and driving. As the travel progresses, each will usually learn more about their travel companion, including their personality, preferences, and expectations for their journey together.

Similar advice is also beneficial regarding the thesis or dissertation journey you have committed to take with your research advisor. Understanding your respective roles and responsibilities during this journey is of utmost importance. Similar to the map reader who provides necessary guidance and directions to the driver, your research advisor's role is to provide the necessary guidance that you will require to complete your thesis or dissertation. You should plan to do the actual driving by following the expert advice of the seasoned traveler who, fortunately, has agreed to take your great journey with you.

Developing an appropriate working relationship with your research advisor, wherein each traveler understands and proficiently enacts their role and responsibilities, will in large part determine your travel success. It is important to recognize that successful thesis or dissertation journeys are realized when a candidate affords their research advisor the opportunity to lead and facilitate the process and shape the project in the direction of its best outcome. Your flexibility in learning new ways of thinking and doing, while following the lead of a more experienced educator (even if you have significant experience yourself), is an essential survival skill.

R. S. Fleming and M. Kowalsky, *Survival Skills for Thesis and Dissertation Candidates*, Springer Texts in Education, https://doi.org/10.1007/978-3-030-80939-3_13

13.2   What You Need to Know

The success of your thesis or dissertation journey will in large part be determined by the nature of the working relationship that develops between you and your research advisor. While a positive working relationship will enable you to make the appropriate progress towards your destination, a negative one will most certainly make the journey more challenging, and potentially compromise your ability to arrive at the desired destination. By realizing the importance of developing a synergistic working relationship with your research advisor from the day you embark on your travels and throughout the journey, you should be able to engage in the behaviors that characterize a true professional researcher. It is important always to remember that your research advisor was willing to sign on for the journey and, like you, desires to see your travels together succeed.

Many of the "bumps in the road" that thesis and dissertation travelers encounter arise from role-related issues, including role ambiguity and role conflict. While *role ambiguity* involves party members having a different understanding of their role and that of their counterpart, *role conflict* results when one party decides not to enact their expected role. By taking the time before you and your research advisor embark on your journey to discuss and clearly articulate the individual roles and responsibilities you each will be expected to perform, as well as to check periodically on those that you will enact together, you will significantly reduce the likelihood of having role-related issues cross your travel path.

It is imperative that both of you understand the reasonable expectations that you should have for each other during your journey. Complying with these "rules of the road" will be expected and should be delineated clearly. These would include seemingly unimportant logistical matters, including expectations regarding how and with what frequency you will typically communicate and interact. Your advisor should let you know the best time(s) to contact them as well as the preferred method of communication. Learning the preferences of your advisor, along with the style of dialogue of scholars within your discipline, will help you reach your destination more easily. Delays are not necessarily an indication of poor work or a negative response!

While you will also engage in work with the other members of your thesis or dissertation committee at appropriate points during your journey, the fact that your research advisor may help coordinate those interactions will be appreciated. Often, you will usually be awaiting feedback from one source which reports on the collective opinions of your committee. It is indeed preferable that you are usually only awaiting one person's response, rather than a response from each individual member of your committee. Although travelers along the same route will necessarily experience their journey in a slightly different way, this is not necessarily problematic, and differing perspectives often enrich any project. Do your best to consistently demonstrate that your research advisor was correct in their determination that you would be a worthy traveler to join in the thesis or dissertation journey.

While following the advice should result in a successful trip and development of a respectful, long-lasting relationship with your research advisor, unfortunately there are times where a candidate's working relationship with their advisor weakens. Unattended travels often result in unfinished journeys, and sometimes it becomes highly unlikely that a student will complete their thesis or dissertation under the continued supervision of the current research advisor. There can be various reasons contributing to this unfortunate reality. Ideally, both the student and the research advisor recognize the need for a change and their institution has policies and procedures which, while rarely needed, provide for replacing the advisor, or if appropriate appointing a co-advisor. Should your travels suggest this change, ask your department or institution for advice before making any of these decisions.

13.3   Student Experiences and Suggestions: *Your Shared Journey*

Students noticed that the quality of the working relationships that they established in their travels definitely affected the degrees of success and stress during their thesis or dissertation journey. Some noted that the earliest relationships were the best, since advisors knew them longer than most, but others credited enhanced connections late in their journey which helped provide new perspectives. Groups of classmates found that it was useful to establish ground rules for working with their research advisors so that everyone knew what to expect and how to behave for difficult interactions. Many students explain that understanding their advisors' expectations for how they should anticipate interacting with them, and asking for explicit details if they are not offered throughout the research process, were vital steps which made the journey easier.

Most students felt it was important to agree with their advisors on a timetable for their travels at the outset of the project, so that students could deliver each submission on or before established deadlines. One student, whose advisor was not very communicative, learned the importance of being patient after submitting their work for review. Although the advisor read and commented quite quickly after getting started, and their feedback was invaluable, getting a place in the busy advisor's schedule was problematic. Most students struggle with allowing their advisors the necessary time to review and comment on their work, but some eventually realize that the advisors may feel the same when anticipating reading their students' submissions. One approach included staying in contact with advisors and being honest in sharing with them any issues they encountered or concerns they had, even if those requests were not immediately acknowledged.

Certain research advisors expected that students would bring any problems to them in a timely manner, rather than sharing them with other committee members or outside parties. If this is requested of you, it will be essential in developing mutual respect and trust between you and your research advisor. One student made the mistake of talking to committee members and other faculty first, sharing multiple complaints, rather than working things through with those who could solve their problems. Their error in judgment negatively impacted what had been a previously positive working relationship with their research advisor. Some students reported that their advisors fell ill temporarily, experienced deaths in the family, or endured other very personal issues which affected the amount of time or energy available to work with their candidates. Students may have been upset initially, but were later pleased that they worked on other tasks while they waited for replies, allowing inevitable problems to be solved elsewhere before returning to the work at hand.

Perhaps the most distraught students were those who procrastinated. One student would continually avoid work, promise to deliver work on time, rush through what was requested by the research advisor, and then submit nearly every submission late. The student admitted that they were struggling with multiple personal and academic issues at the time, but just did not know how to break the cycle of poor performance and could not afford to pause their program due to requirements imposed by their job. When the advisor did not respond as anticipated, they argued and insulted and threatened everyone, becoming more anxious and depressed as the months passed. As this student recounted the story of their journey at a workshop, we all learned the value of campus resources and professional help. The student eventually resolved their issues and embarked on a new start with their advisor after seeking help from the university's wellness center and talking through problems with a counselor. This allowed the student to reorganize their efforts, understand their own reactions to situations, and receive regular support in order to complete their project. We must all be grateful to these courageous travelers who have shared their problems as well as their solutions so that our own journeys can be more informed!

13.4 Things to DO

- Agree on an established timetable and strive to meet each deliverable and deadline.
- Be honest with your advisor regarding issues that you encounter that are impacting your progress.
- If you have a concern about your advisor or progress talk to them rather than other committee members or outside parties.
- Recognize and address potential issues, including conflicts, in a timely manner and work through any issues together.

- Be patient and give your advisor the time that they need to enact responsibilities properly.
- Keep in contact with your advisor and intentionally seek to develop a positive working relationship based on trust.
- Be professional and appreciative of your advisor's work at all times.

13.5 Things NOT to Do

- Procrastinate, or forget what motivates and organizes you best.
- Feel that you should always wait to hear back from your advisor before moving forward on your research activities.
- Make promises regarding deliverables and fail to keep them.
- Undermine your research advisor by going to other committee members for advice without their awareness of these requests.
- Avoid bringing any issues or concerns that you have to the attention of your advisor.
- Mislead your advisor regarding your progress or any other aspect of your research project.

Bibliography

Carter, S., & Laurs, D. (2014). *The routledge doctoral student's companion: Developing generic support for doctoral students: practice and pedagogy*. Taylor & Francis.

Finn, J. A. (2005). *Getting a Phd: An action plan to help manage your research, your supervisor and your project*. Routledge.

Guccione, K., & Wellington, J. (2017). *Taking control of writing your thesis: A guide to get you to the end*. Bloomsbury.

Roles and Responsibilities of Your Committee

14

14.1 Role in Survival and Success

Rather than travel alone or with a single travel companion, some travelers will decide to have additional travelers join them on their trip. While doing so can prove advantageous, there can also be a downside to traveling with a group if the roles and responsibilities of each traveler are not agreed to before departure, and adhered to throughout the journey. Any traveler who has failed to work out such understandings before a trip will likely attest to the wisdom of so doing.

While you would never undertake your thesis or dissertation journey alone, neither would you and your research advisor embark on this adventure before identifying appropriate travelers to take the journey with you as members of your research committee. In addition to meeting the requirements of your college or university that you have a research committee chaired by your research advisor, the addition of these individuals to your travel party will further contribute to your travel success. All members of your travel party should be able to understand, respect, and properly enact their prescribed roles and responsibilities, and ideally, each of them will have a positive and verifiable record of having done so via recommendations of others.

14.2 What You Need to Know

The importance of each member of your research committee understanding their role, and also of you thus having a similar understanding, cannot be overstated. If all members of your travel party understand, respect, and enact these designated roles, you are prepared for a successful journey. Otherwise, you may discover that the "bumps in the road" that you encounter may actually result from the internal workings and climate of your research committee. With the assistance of your research advisor, you will want to ensure that you do all you can to avoid ambiguities or conflicts regarding the roles and behaviors of the various committee members.

A research committee is usually comprised of the research advisor, who serves as its chair, and additional faculty members selected based on their qualifications, interest, and availability to serve on a particular research committee. Faculty members serving on a research committee have obligations to the student, to the research advisor, and to their college or university. They are entrusted with the responsibility of ensuring quality in their program, its research activities, and the resulting theses or dissertations of its graduates. Maintaining collegiality with these gatekeepers along the entire timeline of your journey is an essential thesis or dissertation survival skill.

Typical functions of a thesis or dissertation committee include reviewing and approving the research proposal, providing advice and assistance throughout the research process, reviewing and approving the final manuscript draft, and conducting the oral examination. As you can see, your committee members will interact with you from the time you begin your journey in the proposal stage to the time you defend your thesis or dissertation, and potentially beyond as colleagues in your field of study. Committee members will be expected to ensure that your work meets the highest standards of scholarship, so respect and collegiality in all of your dealings with them is of the utmost importance.

Committee members will usually have roles similar to those of the research advisor, but will have less responsibility than the advisor. While most institutions have general guidelines regarding the functioning of research committees, your research advisor and committee members will usually have discretion in the assignment of roles and responsibilities to committee members. Committee members will typically follow the leadership and guidance of the research advisor chairing the committee.

The key thing to remember is that your research advisor is responsible for facilitating your overall journey and that they will engage in appropriate delegation of responsibilities and authority to other members of your committee. You will therefore want to take the time to clarify with them the roles and responsibilities that have been assigned to each committee member and their expectations regarding how and when you should interact with the other members of your research committee. Learn more about your advisor's views and plans regarding the pace and content of communications with committee members, and then follow the advice you have received.

14.3   Student Experiences and Suggestions: *Understanding the Roles of Your Travel Guides*

While your research advisor will provide primary and ongoing guidance during your research journey, they will be assisted by several other faculty members who have agreed to serve on your research committee, and perhaps other faculty who may advise them. One student regrets that they did not treat their main research advisor as the lead travel guide on the project, and instead involved multiple other advisors from their own and other institutions in their study. The faculty chairperson felt disrespected when the student did not follow directions, so the student's travel slowed down unnecessarily until this misunderstanding was resolved. Another student did not realize that particular university rules had changed from the time a more senior student mentor and friend had progressed through the same program. As you can see, it is important to learn the boundaries of your particular colleagues and mentors, and to evaluate the nature and extent to which each of them can and should directly provide you with appropriate help.

Another candidate encouraged other students not to question the advisors since they had previously served, often together, on previous thesis and dissertation committees. They suggested different ways to interact with potential advisors in advance of any research travels, to make sure each of the committee members knew how the chair expected to interact with them. While it may be too risky to try to find out which faculty members do not get along with each other, it is certainly possible for candidates to have good relationships with each of their committee members or supervisors, even if those members do not have productive relationships with each other. The advice offered by multiple voices in the department and university, and among alumni, can be invaluable and can provide insightful guidance about communication styles.

Most students are prepared to understand the roles and responsibilities of their various committee members and to consistently follow the direction of their research advisors and committee members. However, others explain that constructive debate and questioning of their advisors' suggestions was encouraged and often expected. This may be the most difficult aspect of your conceptual work to discern. Procure advice from other candidates, both past and present, as well as the norms in your department and discipline. And, of course, trial and error is a useful strategy as well! Investigate how and when it is appropriate to bring dissent and debate into your workflow, and then follow the guidance that your research advisor has defined. Learn the subtle differences between arguing about conceptual, theoretical, or methodological issues and disputing the reasoned decisions of more experienced researchers at various times during your journey.

Students have spent much time discussing among themselves which faculty members they felt would be appropriate to join their journeys as committee members, and which advisors they wish were no longer involved in their project. Faculty may sometimes share these same feelings, but ideally their professionalism does not reveal these details. Students need to avoid sharing these details publicly once their projects are underway. While many advisors possess all the requisite knowledge and skills that committee members should possess, given the nature of the research topic and the extent of the project, not every individual possesses every skill in equal amounts. Just as some students work well together in supporting their respective journeys, some faculty work better together in various combinations as well, as the group provides complementary skills. If there is an imbalance in your current committee, this is not necessarily problematic. Remember, new combinations of individuals can work well together as each member grows and contributes in their own unique ways. That is the true meaning of contributing to a team!

14.4 Things to DO

- Study guidance documents provided by your department and institution to ensure that you properly understand the requirements.
- Meet with your research advisor before embarking on your journey so as to understand the roles and responsibilities of each member of your research committee.
- Learn how your research advisor, as committee chair, expects you to interact with them and other committee members.
- Seek clarification from your research advisor any time you are unsure of which member of your committee to approach regarding a particular question or issue.
- Follow the guidance of your research advisor as you engage in interactions with committee members.

14.5 Things NOT to Do

- Fail to take the time to understand the designated roles and responsibilities of the various members of your research committee.
- Disrespect your research advisor by not following the guidance that they had provided regarding the respective roles and responsibilities of committee members.
- Ask or expect committee members to do things for which they are not responsible or the most qualified member of your committee to handle.
- Assume that committee members know each other well, or even like each other.
- Assume that committee members are familiar with each other's research or all of the research you will need for your own project.
- Expect that you and your project are your research advisor's or committee members' only responsibilities.

Bibliography

Roberts, C. M. (2010). *The dissertation journey: A practical and comprehensive guide to planning, writing, and defending your dissertation.* Corwin Press.

Robertson, M. J. (2019). *Power and doctoral supervision teams: Developing team building skills in collaborative doctoral research,* 2nd edn. New York, NY: Taylor & Francis.

Wisker, G. (2012). *The good supervisor: Supervising postgraduate and undergraduate research for doctoral theses and dissertations,* 2nd edn. London: Palgrave Macmillan.

Working with Committee Group Dynamics

15

15.1 Role in Survival and Success

Although you may have known your travel companions fairly well before your trip, it would not be unusual to discover that their behaviors might change during the journey as a result of their interactions with each other. While the thoughts and actions of your travel companions will ideally align, many travelers find this not to be the case. Like any group, your travel party may become cohesive and a pleasure to be a part of, or it may deteriorate into a dysfunctional group. You want to do all within your power to ensure that your own behavior does not influence any of the potentially negative outcomes of group travel.

While it would be unfortunate to have a serious problem on one of your trips, the good news is that most trips last a fairly short time regardless of the group dynamics that may arise. As a result, you will always have the opportunity to consider what you learned this time around, and to make changes in assembling an appropriate collection of travelers for future trips. That may not be the case with your research journey since you may or may not have an ideal mix of committee members for your project. But don't worry. Whomever is on your research team will be capable of contributing improvements to your thesis or dissertation journey, thus making it a better project.

You may even be able to anticipate and prevent possible undesirable group dynamics which have the potential to delay or derail your journey. The ability of committee members to function effectively under the direction of your research advisor can often be ascertained by consulting with your advisor and their current students, and by looking at their past accomplishments in serving on thesis or dissertation committees. Past history, in this case, is usually a fairly reliable predictor of future performance and behavior. Naturally, that advice would be applicable to you as well.

© The Author(s), under exclusive license to Springer Nature Switzerland AG 2021
R. S. Fleming and M. Kowalsky, *Survival Skills for Thesis and Dissertation Candidates*, Springer Texts in Education,
https://doi.org/10.1007/978-3-030-80939-3_15

15.2 What You Need to Know

You will want to recognize that it natural for a newly-established group to go through a series of stages of group development that can include brainstorming, decision-making and reinforcing behaviors. Deliberations regarding how the committee should function should result in consensus regarding how the committee will operate and carry out its tasks. Although adjustments may be made to the rules of how your group will work together, taking the necessary time to ask questions and to work through this process together prepares your research committee to lead and guide your thesis or dissertation journey successfully. Thankfully, it also helps you learn what to expect during both brainstorming and approval processes.

It is also important to acquaint yourself with the potential problems that you could encounter and be prepared to work with your advisor to prevent them and effectively and efficiently resolve any issues that should arise. While preventing undesirable group dynamics should be your goal, it will also be important to recognize and resolve in a timely manner any issues that do arise. In the regular routine of life, people make mistakes, have bad days, or experience stress. Maintaining and even increasing your patience and tactfulness, as everyone's emotions escalate and dissipate over the course of your project, is an important survival skill.

Many of the potential issues that could arise can be avoided through the proper selection of your research advisor and committee members. However, other issues involving unexpressed or unmet expectations can likewise compromise the effectiveness of your committee. The importance of you and your committee members "being on the same page" regarding your work processes, both individually and together, cannot be overstated. You should fully understand and commit to enacting your responsibilities properly, in accordance with the expectations of your committee. When in doubt, ask for clarification, especially regarding timelines and manuscript quality.

Keeping your journey on track and progressing in a timely manner is an essential role of your research advisor that can only be achieved through the cooperation of all members of your travel party. Differences in time orientation can not only delay your travel, but also negatively impact the working climate within your committee. Should committee members not focus on the task at hand, travel can likewise be delayed often leaving you and other committee members frustrated. At other times, delays can be caused by committee members who have differing points of view regarding the research project or certain committee or university processes. Effective and timely communication is necessary to maintain the interest, involvement, and engagement of all committee members. Your research advisor will want to ensure that each member of your committee has adequate opportunities to participate fully in your journey and to develop the desired level of commitment to your work.

15.3 Student Experiences and Suggestions: *Working on Travel Logistics*

You have likely discovered that successful travel with a group of travelers could perhaps be accurately described as both an art and a science. While each may have their unique ways of doing things, as well as individual preferences and behaviors, you will want to learn how to interact positively with each individual, as well as with the overall group. Some students realized early in their project that each member of their research committee truly wants to do their part to make the journey a success. As one student explained, if that was not the intention of your committee members, that faculty member would not have signed on to travel with you at all. Some students wished they had done a better job of honoring the early requests of advisors, especially when they were unsure of the details. If they could do it over again, they would have asked more than once for additional explanations of how things would work.

Several students reported that their courses promoted group development among members of their class or cohort to demonstrate ways a group could become highly cohesive and productive. Many reported that they learned about the sequence of stages that groups typically experience when forming, brainstorming or crystallizing. Some candidates pointed out that it is not unusual for a newly-formed group to experience various issues of conflict which can undermine, at least initially, the ability of its members to work together effectively and efficiently. It is not unusual to experience trouble in any new undertaking, and in most cases, these concerns were resolved through clear communication of expectations and by describing the standards by which the committee would agree to operate.

Some committees and teams do not need to interact on every aspect of a project, and certain individuals may only provide feedback on particular aspects of the planning or on the final manuscript. Many research committees become increasingly cohesive and productive over time, but of course students have examples of those in which harmony was unfortunately elusive. A few students nevertheless point out that solving interpersonal problems among faculty is not actually their responsibility. While all realized that selecting research committee members who had a demonstrated record of working together in this role made all the sense in the world, often this is not possible due to faculty availability, workload, methodological considerations, or various other reasons. While some students took these types of rejections personally, most realized that the project would still remain their own regardless of which faculty participated, so guidance in the identification of appropriate strategies for moving forward was welcome from any and all sources.

Other students recognized how fortunate they were in having great research committees to guide their travels over the entire course of the journey. Most candidates do not have such ideal experiences, much like the distribution of experiences in real life. Still others found that faculty interest and expertise may have been in more narrow or specialized fields than their proposed thesis or dissertation project, so the scope of possible contributions of advisors in accordance with their own knowledge, skills, and abilities was only learned by all much later in the process. As a result, one student's advisor recommended that they not ask or expect committee members to review details that they had not already agreed to, in order to avoid potentially creating conflicts between committee members and their areas of influence on the project. Although most students remembered that they received conflicting and often opposite feedback on a particular aspect of their study, it was usually the research advisor who had the final decision on how to solve these dilemmas, either with or without the help of others. Most, however, quickly learned that problems were resolved in one way or another when they brought their concerns about research committee or team dynamics and functions to the attention of their research advisor or supervisor.

15.4 Things to DO

- Recognize that it is not unusual for a newly-formed group that has never previously worked together to experience group dynamics that can compromise its ability to function effectively and efficiently.
- Bring any concerns that you have regarding the functioning of your committee to the attention of your research advisor.
- Follow the guidance of your research advisor in reaching out to individuals to invite them to join your research committee.
- Recognize the vested interest that your research advisor has in assembling a committee capable of working well together and enabling you to reach your destination.
- Understand that your travel success will only be fully realized by affording each committee member the opportunity to contribute in their own ways throughout your journey.

15.5 Things NOT to Do

- Fail to recognize the importance of interpersonal and group dynamics.
- Engage in behaviors that have the potential of creating conflicts within your committee.
- Assume that you already know the talents of each committee member or exactly how, when, or what they might contribute your project.
- Forget that your research advisor is in a much better position to make an informed decision in this matter than you likely are.
- Interact with the members of your committee in ways that are not aligned with the roles, responsibilities, and procedures delineated by your research advisor and institution.

Bibliography

Bryant, M. T. (2007). *The portable dissertation advisor*. Thousand Oaks: Corwin Press.

Lunenburg, F. C., & Irby, B. J. (2007). *Writing a successful thesis or dissertation: Tips and strategies for students in the social and behavioral sciences*. Sage.

Sumerson, J. B. (2013). *Finish your dissertation, don't let it finish you!* John Wiley & Sons.

Identifying a Research Topic

16

16.1 Role in Survival and Success

Once you have narrowed your trip choices and selected a particular location toward which to travel, the next thing you would want to do is to determine the specific attractions that you want to visit at that location. Visiting every available attraction at a locale will likely not appeal to you, or even be possible given available resources. But as long as the location you chose corresponds with your true interests, then your decision is likely to result in an enjoyable trip. The same is true in thesis or dissertation travel, in that you will want to refine your research topic to a specific area that corresponds with your goals and passions. To do anything less would be like following the travel agenda of someone else who does not share your interest, and thus your enthusiasm, for the journey.

Your thesis or dissertation research topic might be one which defines the rest of your career in academia, or it may be simply your first attempt at sophisticated research. For some, completion of a thesis or dissertation will set up a productive research stream of projects for years; for others, a thesis or dissertation merely helps them realize that a particular area of investigation is not appropriate for a lifetime of research. Either way, your dissertation topic needs to be one which ideally helps you do two things: (a) to determine a disciplinary area of your interest with which you are comfortable being associated and possibly maintaining expertise; and (b) to help you practice, with skilled guidance, a research method which is commonly used in that discipline. A topic that is too narrow or too broad will not work well for thesis or dissertation research, since it will not help you prepare the appropriate type of deliverable. Similarly, a topic that encompasses your life's work within your first paper does not set the stage for continuation of that line of investigation over time.

As you narrow down the sub-discipline for your project to select a narrower aspect of the larger subject area in which you want to work, you will likely find multiple ideas which interest you. In this case, you can either choose one of those topics to the exclusion of others, or you can combine two topics in a unique way. Your topic must enable investigation and analysis in enough detail for you to write a one-hundred- to two-hundred-page double-spaced document about it. Look for others' completed dissertations from your institution and others for ideas on length and scope. While you likely cannot cover all of your favorite topics in one manuscript, try to choose the one which affords the option of reporting on a cohesive single project.

When faculty remind their students that their work should be original, they mean that the specific subject matter of your investigation, and the means by which you are studying that subject matter, has not been previously studied by others. Your topic does not necessarily need to be amazingly groundbreaking or wildly innovative. Your topic just needs to be something specific that has not been researched quite in that way previously. The easiest way to determine this is to do exhaustive research in library databases, on the free web, and among the conferences and professional organizations in your field. Although the destination and landmarks may seem fuzzy at first, clarity is valued when describing thesis and dissertation concepts, thus making it a survival skill which is sharpened over and over again as your project moves forward. Clarity of expression and plans solves many problems throughout the process of researching, writing, and communicating. Clarity in explanation of your project idea and its benefits and boundaries will be appreciated by all and throughout the entirety of your journey, and by readers of your manuscript both now and later.

16.2   What You Need to Know

Some faculty members have described the process of selecting a topic as an individual internal quest, and others see it as arriving at a shared conclusion after much discussion. However you arrive at this step, you will certainly consult many sources such as books, articles, and websites before deciding. Taking your time in deciding is actually an important part of the process, and understanding how you might go about reviewing your options is a necessary step. An analogy which some have found helpful is likening the process of finding a thesis or dissertation topic to wandering in the woods. First, you need to determine which forest (major discipline) is most attractive to you. Likely, this will be the subject matter with which you have already identified when you meet people and provide the answer to their question about which field or subfield you have chosen. As a follow-up question, others will then ask what your thesis or dissertation was about, so determining a coherent answer to those questions will take some practice.

In your travels, you will then wander in that forest (in other words, you will research that subject's literature), in order to select some trees to spend time examining. The trees (particular topics in that subject) will be many, and the amount of literature on each of these topics will vary. Don't let that bother you, since you will easily get an idea of which topics you like to spend time reading about, and which frustrate or bore you easily. Later, you will select a tree (topic) and commit to sitting on one of its branches (your favorite idea, which can potentially become a thesis or dissertation project).

Your particular project idea (the branch) is thus situated within a particular topic (the tree) in your field of study (the forest). The leaf on that last branch is the particular angle that you choose, or the particular lens through which you will study that topic, thus making your dissertation a unique leaf, in good company of a forest of many other researchers who spend time working on projects in this discipline. Analogy or not, the process of thorough research and thinking has many stages, and you will spend varying amounts of time at each stage, even going back to revisit them periodically to justify your choices and remember how you arrived at your present location. This is a journey of exploration, so allow yourself enough time to fully experience and enjoy the ride.

16.3   Student Experiences and Suggestions: *Selecting a Travel Destination*

While it might seem that you will soon be ready to embark on your thesis or dissertation journey once you have identified an area of research interest that is only the beginning of your research journey. Many students who have little difficulty determining their general area of interest later realize that selecting their precise research topic is a much more challenging task. Some students report second-guessing their selections of topic, research questions, study methodology or even attempting the project at all. These misgivings are natural and a periodic review of your choices and direction may indeed be healthy for you as well as your project.

One student said that a professor played a key role in preparing them to select appropriate research topics, without doing the choosing for them. Others said that their research advisors assisted them in narrowing their topics and determining ways to make their project unique and not a repeat of one already completed. Another student praised multiple professors who had suggested that it was never too early to start thinking about a potential research topic, and felt they had many people to talk to before finally deciding. Of course, students who had to do some choosing and narrowing in coursework felt that they received more formal feedback on their choices. Yet students in disciplines where apprenticeship in research groups became their discussion forum confirmed that they arrived at more or less the same point in their thinking, perhaps through less formality and more frequent revision of ideas through conversation.

A cohort of graduate students found out that one of their members worked in their university's library. Their classmate introduced them to multiple library staff members and to the various library sources, including online databases through the library's website that they all used extensively throughout their program. As a result, certain students found new sources of encouragement from these information professionals to select research topics that will make a meaningful contribution to others, and to have their initial project serve as a catalyst for their future research as well as that of other researchers interested in testing the same types of ideas.

Another student pointed out that while most thesis and dissertation candidates aspire to explore a topic that has not been studied previously, it was important not to become overly concerned with originality in selecting a research topic. Any topic can be studied in multiple ways, so the project itself may easily be seen as one which was not completed in quite the same way by others. At a workshop, one particular thesis student offered themselves as an example of how becoming so preoccupied with selecting a unique research topic can delay embarking on and completing one's research journey. They explained to the incoming class of students that they simply must start somewhere, and that putting their thoughts down on paper as well as memorizing a 10-word summary of their research idea would be helpful. This is much like an individual who spends so many years figuring out the right travel destination and plan that they miss out on many great travel experiences they might have had in the interim. Any student can make an original contribution by studying a new aspect of a topic, a unique set of study subjects or materials, or by using a different research method. Talking these things through with others has been shown to provide great practice and to gain welcome feedback.

16.4   Things to DO

- Start early in thinking about a research topic, and leave yourself lots of time to research in many different places including libraries that provide a new set of resources and perspectives on your subject area.
- Choose a topic that helps others in your field or community.
- Select a topic of societal interest so that your efforts are widely read and your suggestions have an opportunity to help others.
- Determine that your topic/method combination has not yet been seen in the literature of your field, and has not yet been presented at any of the usual conferences in your field.
- Discuss your potential research topic with other graduate students, people in your discipline, and even academics in other fields.

16.5   Things NOT to Do

- Worry too much about being overly original with your research topic.
- Fail to realize that it is actually very easy to be original by studying a new aspect of a discipline, or by studying a common aspect with unique participants, or by using a different method than others who researched before you.
- Fail to recognize that thorough research and thinking takes many months and often many years.

- Rush to complete your research project.
- Feel guilty if you change your mind regarding your research topic.
- Continue with a bad research topic or one that you have lost interest in.

Bibliography

Boland, A., Cherry, M. G., and Dickson, R (2017). *Doing a systematic review: A student"s guide*, 2nd edn. Thousand Oaks, CA: Sage.

Murray, T. R., & Brubaker, D. L. (2008). *Theses and dissertations: A guide to planning, research, and writing*. Sage.

Oliver, P. (2012). *Succeeding with your literature review: A handbook for students*. McGraw-Hill Education.

Refining Your Research Topic

17

17.1 Role in Survival and Success

As you continue to plan your journey, you will recognize the need to further refine your travel interests beyond simply visiting the usual sights. You would want to determine your specific interests in stopping to review particular places. As you further refine your travel agenda, you are likely to spend your time experiencing well-known destinations, as well as follow paths to new or interesting locations with which you were not previously familiar. Accordingly, take the time to conscientiously review these and then deliberately limit your research interests to those destinations which help to form a manageable thesis or dissertation topic.

You have likely already spent much time investigating your topic and choosing your specific area of interest for a dissertation project. Continually revising, rewriting, and refining your research topic proposal is a natural part of the research and writing process. After completing a written draft of your proposal, you should set it aside for a short while. Give yourself some time away from your topic (maybe a week or two, but not more than a month), and then return to review your paper with "fresh eyes." This should not diminish your excitement at accomplishing all that you have thus far; instead, allow it to energize you as you confirm which parts of your proposal are solid and which need some attention. No matter how sophisticated your original thoughts were on a research topic, refining each part of your proposal is a necessary step to ensure clarity of expression and maximum efficiency in communication, in order to create an effective roadmap for you to follow as you move forward in the process.

Next, you will check all of the important details of your trip to see if they still reflect the journey of your intended thesis or dissertation study. Is your main discipline clearly defined, and the subfield of your choice clearly justified? Are you still investigating a problem that is important, and is your purpose for doing all this work clearly explained? Does the topic you want to study align with the methods that you are suggesting? Are your intended participants or existing data or documents still available for analysis? Lastly, do you still want to do the project as

© The Author(s), under exclusive license to Springer Nature Switzerland AG 2021
R. S. Fleming and M. Kowalsky, *Survival Skills for Thesis and Dissertation Candidates*, Springer Texts in Education,
https://doi.org/10.1007/978-3-030-80939-3_17

described. Theses and dissertations need decisions made about a great many details which make up the overall project and manuscript, and remaining cognizant of the need to get through all of these details will help you complete a long journey by keeping up your energy and working steadily toward your goals.

These structural issues will be most important to check so that you don't proceed with an investigation that is not likely to actually work or that has changed so much that you now dread doing it. Check again to determine that you have articulated a convincing argument about why you want to study this topic. Is it actually feasible to conduct this particular project, given existing personal or institutional constraints of time, availability, costs, approvals, and the like? If you are feeling confident with the basic what/how connections (in other words, what will you study and how you will study it), then it is time to examine more of the details you are providing in each section of your paper. Remember that continually asking and answering questions about the direction and nature of your journey helps you to more easily correct your course of travel along the way.

17.2   What You Need to Know

Your thoughts will evolve with every day you spend working on your thesis or dissertation; therefore, you must consider all of the parts of your thesis or dissertation idea which need revising, whether those aspects are small or large. First, check on the way you are expressing your topic. Can what you are studying and how you are studying it be expressed in one complete sentence and does that sentence make sense to most people? As you are telling others about your intended topic, does it feel like you are reciting the thesis statement of your whole project, or just part of it?

Ideally, one sentence should capture your project's essence, at least for most audiences. If you can't state your project idea in one sentence, you may be trying to do too much in your project, or you haven't streamlined the purposes of your study. As you are telling others about your intended topic, if you need to use more than one sentence to do so you may be describing your research questions, rather than the goal of your entire project. Try to disaggregate each of these parts of your thesis or dissertation, and practice reciting them as discrete parts. While all of these questions and answers may seem tiring, they are indeed beneficial to both your long-term and short-term travel plans.

In your particular discipline, you will learn particular ways to state the questions which your research will attempt to answer. These research questions will govern the flow of your arguments as well as the systematic collection of data. If there was ever a time to learn more about the process of writing a dissertation, it is in reading about others' ways of defining their research questions and in soliciting feedback on your own research questions, early and often. Many times, the specific wording of a research query may direct your project in a particular direction, and it is necessary to check and double-check that the questions you are attempting to answer in your project can actually be provided by the methods you are outlining. Many of the recommended books provided throughout these chapters offer advice about creating research questions in many subject areas, and some of your professors may recommend even more resources. A recursive view of the writing, editing, and justifying your research questions will likely be taken, both now and later, with multiple iterations of their wording critiqued by nearly all of your advisors. You may find that online discussion groups and more senior graduate students nearing the end of their programs can provide helpful feedback during the brainstorming and drafting phases of narrowing your project's scope.

By refining the specific language you are using and the depth of explanation you are offering, your document will offer a cohesive argument for how and why you want to undertake this project. By making time to revise throughout your thinking process, instead of waiting to make changes all at the end, you will save precious time and energy for when you need it the most. Some students may view suggestions about changing their topic or even any part of their written draft as a defeat or a criticism; try not to take changes personally. The revising and rewriting process is actually a central part of ongoing academic life, so finding comfort in reviewing your work regularly will benefit your productivity in both the short term and in the long run. Endurance during the thesis or dissertation journey, and in your academic life thereafter, is an important survival skill.

17.3 Student Experiences and Suggestions: *Travel Plans Should Be Clear but Flexible*

A graduate student recounted a particularly important point emphasized by a professor that they seemed to recall periodically when struggling to finish their writing. They explained that while deciding on a research topic is always an important milestone in one's research journey, it is important not to view that research topic as something that is so fixed that it may not be subject to modifications should they become appropriate later in your research journey. One of their classmates adopted a rigid mindset regarding their topic before they even fully developed the idea for their study. They became stuck on one particular idea and never became comfortable enough to take the multiple opportunities offered to revise it. As a result, their project proposal was denied, and they had to start fresh with a new topic and work more closely with faculty in order to design a stronger study that advisors would be able and willing to support.

So, regardless of how much you are in love with your topic and how supportive your research advisor and committee members have been, you should always remain open to appropriate revisions that will strengthen your research proposal as well as the resulting value of your research project. A doctoral student described a situation where their committee members were more experienced in their study's method than the lead research advisor. While this seemed awkward at first, both the student and their advisor eventually learned new techniques from the other faculty who were along for the journey. In this seeming reversal of roles, the senior researchers helped to suggest adjustments to the project which neither the student nor their chairperson could have anticipated. Happily, the recommendations were carefully followed and later commended when the results were presented publicly.

Students in certain disciplines were asked to refine their projects continually as they engaged in a dialogue of learning over a longer period of time. They were already revising their initial research plans while preparing their written proposals. Other students' programs asked them to revise up until a particular benchmark phase, after which only minimal changes would be allowed. Either of these processes can work well, since students in both scenarios had ample time to rethink a number of aspects of their planned journeys, albeit at different stages in the process. New ideas found in the literature, or new discoveries presented at conferences, or even newsworthy media items had the potential to greatly enhance some students' research proposals, although at some point, they did not radically change their research topics. Some students stayed with the topic and method that they had selected initially, while others made useful changes in restating their research questions based on thinking further about what it was that they specifically wanted to study during their research journey. Many research advisors and committee members proved to be quite supportive of these improvements, as long as they were thoroughly justified.

One student shared that as they worked on their research proposal it became clear that while they were still committed to the same research area and topic, they had not articulated their research questions in a concise, clear, and understandable manner. The student was so proud when they reached a point where they could persuasively, in a single sentence, share the intent of their research project with academics in the field and receive an approving response. Another student felt the need to stick with the original research topic that their advisor and committee members had agreed upon and thus did not take the opportunity to push toward a much more exciting and valuable research journey in their area. Nevertheless, most students find that their area of interest, their particular topic of interest, and their expressions of the questions to be answered through their project all come together at one stage or another. You may need to return to some of the chapters in this book in a different order than presented here, or perhaps review this advice at multiple points in your journey. We encourage you to remain flexible in your thinking and agile in your actions as you work on developing a sound research proposal based on a well thought out research project.

17.4 Things to DO

- Complete as much researching, writing, and revising as you can early in the process, since later parts of the research will consume much of your time.
- If you have already made a presentation about your topic, such as in a class or an academic poster, be sure to revise these items as well.

- If your revised manuscript is too different, or much better than your previous work (which is likely), just label those early files as "old draft" or "version 1," so you can archive them and continue to edit your best, newest version.
- Realize that revisions are not the end of the world, and what you write now might be much better than what you wrote three months ago.
- Go with the flow in order to offer a consistent and conscientious effort, since slow and steady tends to win the race.

17.5   Things NOT to Do

- Make revisions just to placate emotions (either your own or others').
- Procrastinate on any of the steps you know you must complete but which seem difficult.
- Avoid answering important questions about your project, even simply to yourself.
- Forget to make multiple physical and digital backups of your work.
- Assume that one revision is enough.
- Fail to recognize that spending the quality time necessary to create a polished manuscript now will result in less work to do later.

Bibliography

Alvesson, M., & Sandberg, J. (2013). *Constructing research questions: Doing interesting research*. Sage.

Clark, I. L. (2007). *Writing the successful thesis and dissertation: Entering the conversation*. Prentice Hall.

Thomas, R. (2019). *Little quick fix: Turn your literature review into an argument*. Sage.

Identifying Literature Review Sources

18

18.1   Role in Survival and Success

Seasoned travelers recognize the value of pre-trip planning. The quality of the time one spends before embarking on a journey can greatly enhance the success of any trip. Review of travel guides and related materials enables a traveler to learn from the experiences of others in charting their route of travel and the sights they desire to visit along the way. Advance planning minimizes later learning about places that one could have visited had they known about them prior to the trip. The same is true as you plan your thesis or dissertation journey.

Perhaps similar to reviewing travel guides and the like, you will want to conduct a comprehensive literature review regarding your research topic. You will want to discover the "journeys" of researchers whose earlier travel interests are similar to yours. You will want to benefit from their travel lessons and incorporate them as you plan your journey. It is important in thesis and dissertation travel to become familiar with those prior research journeys that will inform the various aspects of your thesis or dissertation journey.

While there will always be some travelers who fail to take the time to research and plan their travels properly but are able to make the best of it as they travel, this mindset should never be the case in thesis or dissertation travel. It is imperative that you fully recognize the importance of conducting a comprehensive literature review prior to charting your thesis or dissertation journey. Keeping an open mind about the fluidity of disciplinary boundaries as well as the potential merits of (and possible improvements on) others' published work is a definite research survival skill. Acknowledge that your own library, institution, or country might not have all of the most relevant sources. Consider that even those journal articles you do find useful may not include in their bibliographies every item that you may ultimately need. The insights that you will gain in thinking in new ways will prove critical throughout the thesis or dissertation process, both as you defend your own choices and as you describe those you did not choose.

© The Author(s), under exclusive license to Springer Nature Switzerland AG 2021   95
R. S. Fleming and M. Kowalsky, *Survival Skills for Thesis
and Dissertation Candidates*, Springer Texts in Education,
https://doi.org/10.1007/978-3-030-80939-3_18

18.2 What You Need to Know

A strong literature review is an essential element of your thesis or dissertation research. Your literature review should cover all of the seminal literature on your topic. The insights gained from conducting a comprehensive literature review will enable you to establish the parameters for your research project, including why you are doing it, why you are designing it in a particular way, and the underlying assumptions that form the context for your research. While it might seem that you would want to limit your literature review to fairly recent sources, going further back in time will enable you to establish a theme to distinguish your work from similar topics that evolved later. You will be able to determine the importance of particular articles by checking citation counts and chaining bibliographies of famous articles to see who they quoted.

Much like a traveler would keep a journal of places visited, you will want to keep a record of the search terms and limiters you choose on the different search screens (like subject headings, dates, keywords, relevance vs. newest date, etc.). It is important to utilize multiple resources provided for your subject area, given that the database content of different vendors may not overlap. You will therefore want to supplement your database and web searches with multiple search engines, tools, and finding aids, along with virtual discussion groups and reports of meetings in your field. Each of these resources will contain different content, offer varying means of access, and use diverse search result algorithms. In searching multiple library databases and articles from various journals you may want to consider not limiting your sources to U.S.-centric on English-only sources, unless your research topic necessitates it. Your literature review can also be enhanced through review of professional publications, association publications, related blogs, and news which references research articles. Seasoned travelers take recommendations of places to visit, either online or in person, from any and all reputable sources!

18.3 Student Experiences and Suggestions: *Using Previous Literature as a Travel Roadmap*

Many students have been reminded by many of their professors that a comprehensive literature review plays a vital role in successful trip planning and travels. One student stated that they had greatly underestimated both the importance of a comprehensive literature review and the time required to review the literature related to their topic properly. The student was surprised to learn that other students spent weeks and months devoted to the literature review stage of their projects, rather than only a week or two. Others realized that most of their early work was in searching and reading previous studies in their field, which actually took less time than writing about them. Of course, some items took longer to read than others, and graduate students in multiple subject areas will reveal that they needed help understanding some of the literature that had been published or presented on their topic of interest. Whatever it takes to become an expert in your field, every hour and day you dedicate to your literature review and background research will prove beneficial later, easing your travels.

One research methods professor had given a student a sequence of helpful advice regarding the essential time and identification of related works by others who had studied the topic and methods previously. The student learned that they should review all seminal literature related to their research topics and never to delimit a literature review to simply identifying a specific, minimum number of articles needed. They explained that using the same searching keywords or limiting the review of the literature to only sources listed in related theses or dissertations or published articles was not enough. Comprehensiveness and full understanding was the goal, the student explained, so that when students were asked about particular literature they were familiar enough to confirm why they chose to or did not choose to use those items to inform their current project. Ideally, the previous literature which exists in your discipline will help you determine previous areas which have been traveled and those which need a new road added to the map!

Sadly, another student reported multiple missteps in this stage of their project, and they worked too quickly, explicitly not seeking broad familiarity with the large quantity of literature in their area. As expected, this led them on rocky dissertation travels. In a false spirit of efficiency, the student had quickly and narrowly selected a particular list of articles that they had found, and created a ready answer about how other research was not related to their own topic or project. Their peers were astonished that the student, who was fortunate enough to have heard previous advice on how candidates needed to become immersed in the dialogue of their field in order to become a scholar themselves, was too stubborn to comply. In thinking that they had found a shortcut, the student instead was directed by their research advisor and committee members to do much more work to prove that they actually read and understood a wide range of related articles before making any decisions. This delayed their journey by nearly another year, and the rest of their class moved onward in the program without them.

In following the guidance of university librarians and research methods professors many students were able to find the information that they needed as well as access more materials that may not have been obvious on their first research attempts. Students took many trips to their university's library to meet with the staff or take workshops about searching strategies and tools for research at the graduate level. Other students used the library's website to access the full text of journals and to obtain online help when preparing the literature review sections of their manuscript. Most students reported that they needed to check on their scholarly resources even later in their processes, in order to capture new items every few months as they were published, or to access a new electronic database or emerging search tool in their field. A particular graduate student who worked in their school's library suggested to everyone that they should utilize multiple library databases and not limit their literature search only to the most convenient or the most frequently cited sources. Students who did not have a central library or place to find quality literature utilized the extensive collections of other libraries and professional organizations, and they used interlibrary loan services to secure articles and other materials of interest. At most institutions, there are numerous additional members of the library staff and other research offices who have various specialties and will be ready and willing to guide students at any stage of their project.

18.4 Things to DO

- Recognize the importance of conducting a comprehensive literature review.
- Be sure to include all seminal literature in your literature review.
- Utilize multiple library databases, tools and finding aids related to your research subject area, and seek advice from many sources.
- Keep a record of the databases, search terms and limiters that you use in your searches.
- Do not limit your literature review to the most convenient sources.
- Search catalogs of other libraries and utilize interlibrary loan to secure articles not available at your library.

18.5 Things NOT to Do

- Rely solely on the bibliographies of other thesis or dissertation projects, or on the most common tools.
- Fail to identify a comprehensive collection of articles that fully address your research subject.
- Focus on identifying a given number of sources, rather than the sources that will inform your planning and execution of your research project.
- Assume that all of the possible articles that you will need are available at your library.
- Underestimate the importance of identifying appropriate sources and the time necessary to conduct a literature review properly.

Bibliography

Balker, J. (1998). *Writing your dissertation in fifteen minutes a day: A guide to starting, revising, and finishing your doctoral thesis*. Henry Holt and Company.

Dunleavy, P. (2003). *Authoring a Ph.D.: How to plan, draft, write, and finish a doctoral thesis or dissertation*. Basingstoke: Palgrave Macmillan.

Walshaw, M. (2015). *Planning your postgraduate research*. Palgrave Macmillan.

Identifying Research Questions

19

19.1 Role in Survival and Success

Before embarking on a trip, it is customary to make a number of decisions related not only to the desired destination but also to other aspects of your journey. While the subsequent decisions will certainly be important in determining the success of your journey, the initial decision regarding your intended destination and reasons for traveling there will clearly be the most important one that will drive your various subsequent actions. For this step in the thesis and dissertation process, you will likely spend much brain power creating and revising research questions which govern your investigation of a particular topic in a particular way. Employing all of your best critical thinking powers, and stretching your brain in new and challenging ways during research question development, is an essential survival skill which needs your full attention.

You will quickly discover that the same is true in recreational travel or thesis or dissertation travel, as new destinations and new information change your current ways of thinking. Rather than selecting from a known list of familiar items, you will be required to identify new and unique research questions that your project will address. It is imperative that you recognize the critical importance of this step in the research process. The decisions that you make in framing your research questions will have impact throughout various stages of your research journey. You will want to "own" these research questions given the role that they will play in your extended research journey and for a number of years of your life. Taking the time to fully consider and deliberate on potential research questions will enable you to make a meaningful contribution to the existing research and body of knowledge in your area of research interest. Determining those that you have the passion to pursue will make your thesis or dissertation journey both more pleasurable and productive.

© The Author(s), under exclusive license to Springer Nature Switzerland AG 2021
R. S. Fleming and M. Kowalsky, *Survival Skills for Thesis and Dissertation Candidates*, Springer Texts in Education,
https://doi.org/10.1007/978-3-030-80939-3_19

19.2   What You Need to Know

Your research questions serve as the foundation for your research project and it is crucial that you devote the necessary time and contemplation to correctly articulate the purpose of your research project and the exact questions that it will answer. In using your critical thinking skills, you will recognize the importance of this essential early step in your research journey, and you will also want to appreciate the consequences of not taking the time and effort to properly frame the research questions that will determine the various aspects of your thesis or dissertation journey. While it might seem that writing research questions is not that difficult, you must not adopt that misguided and uninformed mindset. In fact, they are a small set of words which determine the breadth and depth of your impact in the research field of your choice.

Writing research questions successfully will require that you dedicate the necessary time to draft and revise the various questions, typically with the assistance of your research advisor. Failing to take the necessary time to "get it right" at this juncture in your thesis or dissertation journey will be a mistake that you will come to regret later in the research process. While you will want to review the research questions posed by past researchers, you should ensure that the research questions that you select align with the rest of your project and correspond with your literature review, purpose and problem statements, data collection/analysis methods, and availability of participants or sources of data. No time spent revising and studying others' frameworks is wasted; early contemplation can prevent mistakes and major revisions later in the process.

You will want to identify a reasonable number of research questions; typically two or three. If you have more than two or three you are likely writing more than one thesis or dissertation. Your research questions may or may not contain a "hypothesis," depending on the nature of your research design. They must use wording which definitively suggests that the "data" you wish to gather in order to address a particular topic is actually collectable and measurable. It is important to determine the research questions that properly correspond with your research interest. Some students just want to do the project and don't care what the research questions are. This lack of alignment will negate the value of your project. Some students write great research questions but then do not like the project that they have to do in order to answer them. You do not want to fall into either of these snares in your thesis or dissertation journey.

Your research advisor can be a valuable resource as you frame your research questions, and you should seek their guidance throughout this important step of the research process. Also take time to ponder if the research questions you have written are the ones that you want to answer. Rather than taking the easy way out and running with research questions suggested by others, including your research advisor or committee members, ensure that these questions are ones about which you care and with which you can live. You should also know that professors will often help students re-write their research questions if the study does not work out properly; after all, it is your first attempt at this complex task. Do your best to offer a set of questions which properly reflects your skill, interest, and project parameters.

19.3 Student Experiences and Suggestions: *What Do You Want to Learn Through Your Travels?*

Students say that they often struggled to articulate what they wanted to learn in their programs, since it is indeed difficult to articulate a goal for new learning when you are not sure what the options might be. Faculty would say that research questions pinpoint the specific purpose of your project, in that they go beyond the general reason for your journey articulated in the research topic that you have selected and delineate the actual things that you desire to experience and learn about as a result of that project. Yet most students said they felt like they needed quite a bit of help in composing their questions and actually understanding the ways that their research methods might produce the answers. While many thesis and dissertation travelers pursue related interests to each other when charting their journeys, your individual travel agenda should be distinct, and should be designed to enable you to learn specific outcomes about your topic.

Many students in a variety of fields complained that conceptualizing and writing research questions, while one of the most important steps in their research journey, was definitely one of the most challenging aspects of their project. Several sought help from more senior students who had written research papers before, and had them review early drafts of the first half of their project. Those you consult can definitely advise you on whether your research questions align with your methods or discipline, yet only you can know if your research questions properly correspond with your research interests. Some students worked in collaboration with their research advisors at regular intervals before they were satisfied that the student had properly crafted their research questions. Often faculty other than the student's research methods professors were available for these consultations, since they enjoyed discussing emerging scholarship. Other professors emphasized that students' research questions would drive every aspect of their research journeys, as well as serve as the standard by which their project would be deemed useful.

One student discussed their impatience with trying to arrive at the right research questions or even put forth more than the minimum amount of work before receiving feedback, since they felt that revisions were going to be required no matter what kind of work they offered to their advisors. This misstep is a common one among thesis and dissertation travelers eager to complete their journeys. The student who took the easy way out for each deadline ended up angering their research advisor, who felt that their time was wasted in reviewing mediocre and often poor work. Another student feared their advisor's negative feedback so much that they just copied the research questions which they discovered in a related dissertation, hoping those would be automatically approved. As you can imagine, these students' random guesses at what the advisor wanted could not approximate the type of quality product which would have been produced through careful reading, analyzing, and writing. Advisors were not only disappointed, but they stopped the students' progress and sent them back to attempt various stages of their projects again. The students ended up doing the originally required quantity and quality of work anyway, but now they were working under more stressful circumstances because they had upset their advisors!

One student felt they were fortunate that their advisor entertained debate about the research questions for their project from multiple committee members as well as the student themselves. Although other students who did not go along with the research questions that faculty members had suggested encountered difficulties, others felt they had influence over the wording, even if they had no idea how they might fulfill the goals of the research at the time. Others simply trusted their advisor to not provide inaccurate or misleading directions for such an important journey. In all of these scenarios, the students realized at the end of their research journey that the improvements suggested actually helped to narrow the scope of their project and to in most cases make data collection and analysis easier to perform. A few students were able to admit that there were too many questions to be answered with one project, so they could leave some of the answers to be found by others, while keeping as part of their current project the aspects that most intrigued them personally. Advisors are skilled in helping to limit your investigation to a manageable number of questions, and to convince you to leave additional inquiry for future research journeys, either by you or others.

19.4   Things to DO

- Recognize that research questions are difficult to write.
- Allocate the necessary time to develop a set of research questions that correspond with your research interest.
- Ensure that your research questions align with the rest of your project.
- Seek the assistance of your research advisor as you develop your research questions.
- Review the dissertations of previous students at your college as well as those of others who addressed similar topics or used similar methods.
- Assess the strengths and weaknesses of your research questions in comparison to those of other researchers.

19.5   Things NOT to Do

- Fail to limit your research questions to a manageable number (usually two or three).
- Fail to recognize the importance of your research questions throughout the research process and to the resulting value of your research contribution.

- Copy someone else's research questions word for word, since they will likely not have the necessary internal alignment with your own project.
- Be persuaded to accept research questions suggested by others, including your research advisor or committee members, which do not fully align with your research interests.
- Forget to check the wording of your research questions to ensure that you are stating what you actually want to study and that your intended method will enable you to collect the necessary data to answer those research questions.

Bibliography

Badenhorst, C., & Guerin, C. (2016). *Research literacies and writing pedagogies for masters and doctoral writers*. Leiden, Netherlands: Brill.
O'Leary, Z. (2018). *Little quick fix: Research question*. Sage.
Thomas, D. (2016). *The PhD writing handbook*. Palgrave Macmillan.

Developing a Research Design

20

20.1 Role in Survival and Success

In planning your journey, a fundamental decision is always the means by which you will travel. While you may often travel by car, there will be times that taking a train or a plane is a more appropriate way to travel. Among the factors that will influence your decision will be the sights and experiences that you want to take in along the way, the time you have available to complete the journey, and the information you currently have available to carry out your itinerary. In similar fashion, the purpose of your research project and the problem that you want to address must be a key factor in selecting an appropriate research design.

Once you have determined the destination to which you plan to travel and articulated it in your research questions, you will need to begin the essential task of mapping out your travel plans. In thesis or dissertation travel this will involve developing a research design for your project which specifies a model of how you will carry out the tasks necessary to arrive at the answers to your research questions. The research design is the single most important part of your thesis or dissertation since it is the substance of the new contribution that you alone are making to the field of study and the existing body of knowledge.

Your research design will serve as a road map for your research journey. While simplicity is desirable in many things, you will want to ensure that your research design incorporates sufficient rigor. This should not be confused with complexity. Research designs which are not rigorous will make your project appear less significant and useful to others. Before developing your research design you should review those of past research projects of local and famous others. Look for literature which talks about how to use a particular design in your subject area or field, and for previous projects which used that design toward successful outcomes. While you might not quote these sources as part of your methodology chapter, they will help you to discuss in a more sophisticated way the merits and limitations of the possible options for studying your topic.

© The Author(s), under exclusive license to Springer Nature Switzerland AG 2021
R. S. Fleming and M. Kowalsky, *Survival Skills for Thesis
and Dissertation Candidates*, Springer Texts in Education,
https://doi.org/10.1007/978-3-030-80939-3_20

20.2   What You Need to Know

A starting point in the selection of an appropriate research design for your project is understanding the various research designs from which you can select. One or more of the possible options in your field may align with your research project, but you will likely need to select the one design which is most useful for the task at hand. There aren't an unlimited number of research designs; most fall into the qualitative or quantitative categories, and are either human-subjects or secondary-data driven. Study these options in methods books, journal articles, and tutorial websites, and then discuss them with your research advisor before selecting an appropriate research design for your project. Since you do not want to get the broad category of research design wrong, given trends in your field, conscientiously consider each before selecting or rejecting each of the potential options.

You will want to review the work of other researchers before reaching a decision on the research design that you will utilize. Look for both strong and weak examples of your design as executed by others. Your review should also include student theses and dissertations, conference proceedings, and published research outside of your geographic area. These comparisons will help you self-evaluate your own project in advance, so that you know where you are falling on the quality spectrum. In addition to choosing some designs which you like, keep track of those which you have dismissed and why you did so. This will enable you to better justify your research design selection with reasoning based on your research topic.

You should realize that your research advisor and members of your research committee have the right of first refusal for the design you are proposing, and you should expect that they will heavily critique your proposed method and all of its details. Lots of questions and criticism on these points are not necessarily signs of poor work, since advisors will be able to troubleshoot with you some of the problems with these processes before you embark on your thesis or dissertation journey. If you respect the process, an important survival skill, then you have checked on the research designs of those who have tested other options before you and have noted their contributions to your thinking.

20.3   Student Experiences and Suggestions: *Adjusting the Plan but Continuing to Travel*

One student recalled a serious conversation with their advisor, who said that sound research design will determine not only a research project's ability to answer stated research questions, but also the resulting contribution of the candidate's thesis or dissertation to the overall scholarly conversation. Most graduate students recall being intimidated by such statements, especially when they felt pressure to produce an award-winning or professional-quality manuscript. It is therefore imperative that you develop and implement a research design that will enable you to answer fully the research questions that you plan to explore during your travels, without worrying about orchestrating the next major discovery in your field. Although it sounds simple, agreeing to make your project the best it can be is really all that you are required and able to do. Even for famous scholars, maintaining quality in their research projects is ongoing work, whether or not the study or experiment or investigation was a success. The real goal will be to complete your thesis or dissertation travel to the best of your ability, and to learn as much as you can from the experience. Accolades or critique can arrive later, but at least your project will be done!

Some students felt significant anxiety when crafting or carrying out their project, and especially when it was being publicly reviewed near the end of their journey. Although it is quite normal to anticipate some negative feedback on every project, those who have made it through these processes would encourage you to work closely with your research advisor as you develop and refine your research design. One student kept checking in with their advisor even though they were not forthcoming with much guidance. Thankfully, the advisor eventually made sure that the student's proposed research design conformed to the rigor and other expectations of their discipline, even if this meant continually delivering what the student perceived to be bad news. Later the student figured out that the research design that they initially had in mind would have been perceived as falling short of the expected style and the usual difficulty level in their field. In this case, the advisor who seemed reluctant to provide positive feedback was actually helping to shape the process so that it attracted fewer criticisms later.

Many students tentatively followed the guidance of their advisor and knowledgeable others without always knowing why that guidance was provided. Certain students avoided later travel issues precisely because they received corrections early in the development of their ideas. Listening to negative comments on work that you had spent much time and effort on, especially if large portions of that work is dismissed, can agitate or distress even the best students. However, this is part of learning to work at a higher level of complexity. You would have produced a more sophisticated product if you knew how to do it already! Only multiple rounds of academic critique can ensure that large projects become properly formed and that new learning takes place. Some graduate students have commented that they wanted to abandon their entire journey toward an advanced degree because they could not tolerate the negativity expressed about their work. We can assure you that all scholars have experienced this feeling, but they stayed on course, and that has helped travelers from diverse backgrounds and contexts to reach their destinations successfully.

A few students who shared similar research interests inadvertently found another reason to abandon their journeys, which was quite uncomfortable. In working together on research, several students each selected a similar design and argument that they discovered during a literature review that they had worked on together. In fact, some of those very details had been used by several other researchers who were published professionals, with apparent success. In a rush to procure usable content, the students did not fully consider how that background theory and design would actually fit their individual projects. So the whole group submitted similar sounding manuscripts and were subsequently accused of academic dishonesty related to copying others and not doing their own work. The students were embarrassed and apologetic, and a few wanted to quit their program that day. In retrospect, the group recognized that they were fortunate to have each other as sounding boards during their journeys. The lesson they learned was serious and their restitution was quite involved, but eventually each student rewrote a fresh proposal with the support and encouragement of the others. Rather than selecting a simple, easy, or popular research design, taking the time to discern for yourself the right context, argument, and research design for your particular project will definitely ensure safe travels ahead.

20.4 Things to DO

- Recognize the importance of the research design in determining the extent of the contribution that your research will make to the field.
- Ensure that your research design incorporates the necessary rigor required by your discipline.
- Consult with your research advisor and committee members in determining an appropriate research design for your project.
- Ensure that the research design that you select properly aligns with your project in a manner that will enable you to answer your research questions completely.
- Document both why you selected a particular research design and why you did not select other available designs.
- Pilot test your method if possible, to see if you are able to implement that design effectively.

20.5 Things NOT to Do

- Adopt a research design simply because a number of other researchers have used it.
- Fail to consider all of the research designs that may align with your research project.
- Rush through the review of available research designs utilized by other researchers who have done related projects and who are in related fields of study.
- Avoid communication with your research advisor and committee members during this important decision.
- Attempt to do the simplest design you can find, or alternately, attempt to utilize a research design that you do not yet fully understand.
- Forget to align your research design process with the research questions you hope to answer.

Bibliography

Booth, W. C., Colomb, G. G., & Williams, J. M. (2016). *The Craft of Research*, 4th edn. Chicago: University of Chicago Press.

Alexandru, C., Sakshaug, J., Atkinson, P. A., Williams, R. A., & Delamont S. (Eds.). (2021). *SAGE Research Methods Foundations*. Thousand Oaks, CA: Sage.

Trowler, P. (2016). *Doing Doctoral Research into Higher Education... and Getting It Right.* London: CreateSpace.

Identifying Data Collection Methodology

21

21.1 Role in Survival and Success

One of the highlights of many journeys is collecting things of interest that one encounters along the way, and some of these will be items we had not seen before elsewhere. Very often, the items we collect as reminders of our travels remind us about something new we have learned or seen. Having a strategy in place to decide which items collect and keep, or those simply to admire from afar, will help any traveler carry back home the most important and interesting items representative of the places visited. Similarly, you will want to have a sound plan for collecting data during your research journey, and of course, a plan for storing reminders of good ideas you just could not carry with you on this particular trip but which you could use in the future.

Reaching the desired destination in your thesis or dissertation journey successfully will require you to collect necessary data during your journey. You will need to develop a data collection plan before embarking on your journey. This should begin with identifying the various data collection methods available for you to use and conscientiously evaluating each in terms of its alignment with the purpose of your research project. You will also need to determine the physical steps for obtaining and storing your data, and for finding it again later to count and categorize. For some of you, the quantitative part of the thesis or dissertation may be frightening. However, we assure you that this only makes you nervous because it is unfamiliar. In fact, descriptive and inferential statistical techniques are indeed possible to learn, as many before you have done. Collecting research data via strict rules and procedures is likely something most students have not done extensively before, nor in such detail.

You must select a data collection methodology that will yield the necessary information to answer all of your research questions fully. While that may sound rather simple and easy to do, some students do not take the time necessary to evaluate potential data collection methods in enough detail to truly select the collection processes which best align with their research project's aims. In short, your

R. S. Fleming and M. Kowalsky, *Survival Skills for Thesis and Dissertation Candidates*, Springer Texts in Education, https://doi.org/10.1007/978-3-030-80939-3_21

data collection method must actually produce the information needed to answer all of your research questions, and in turn that information must help solve the research problem that you described. Using the correct data collection methodology is therefore essential for the structural integrity of your project.

21.2 What You Need to Know

Your data collection strategies must align with your problem, with your field of study, and with your access to participants and/or to documents/data. You will want to learn as much as you can about how others have approached data collection in your field generally and with regard to your related topics of interest specifically. Then, you will want to see how those in other fields have utilized your intended processes. Learning about all of the possible data collection strategies helps you understand others' research on your topic, including that which was produced using a method other than your own. You should recognize that the time spent reviewing all of the possible options is beneficial. Recognize that effective data collection methods are detailed, rigorous, and more complex than those that you may have previously used in other projects.

As was the case in selecting a research design, you will need to understand fully the data collection method that you select, and you will need to be capable of employing it successfully. It is also important to determine if you will require permission to use a particular data collection method or to be granted access to particular data sources. Specifically, you will need to collect all necessary data to answer fully the research questions that you posed earlier in your research journey. If you do not have permission to use a particular data collection method, or to query individual participants, then you might need to revise your research questions. This is something that you will want to think through before seeking approval from your advisor, your compliance board, or your university's institutional research group.

If your thesis or dissertation is in a humanities field, checking with your chair and committee about the scope and focus of your research project is key. Sometimes it can seem overwhelming to research and write a new perspective in a well-studied area. If you experience difficulty in finding or procuring your necessary primary sources, or in learning new technologies to perform your critique, be sure to identify these challenges early and often so that you can seek the help of knowledgeable others who may not be in your current social network. Acknowledge that it may seem scary to use a new digital technique and subsequently request review by others who have a deeper understanding of the topic but not the technology. However, if your project's goals are clear and your methodology strong, this will not be problematic. Working through your fears is a survival skill which certainly correlates with completion and success!

21.3 **Student Experiences and Suggestions:** *Documenting Your Travels*

When working on sections of a complex project, and on a particularly long manuscript, students often forget how they arrived at a particular decision or option for their journey. Some can't quite recall how they eventually chose their topic or even what made them enroll in their program in the first place. But not to worry, since these are natural reactions brought on by growth. Students' reasons for staying may not be the same as their reasons for starting, and other things may have changed in their lives over the course of their research. Nevertheless, it can be quite useful to collect and archive information about your thesis or dissertation experience along the way that you will later be able to analyze for reflecting on personal growth or in solving problems which arise in later stages of your work.

One student noted that just as they prepared to uncover the answers to the research questions that necessitated the project in the first place, multiple faculty members started questioning aspects of their study's logistics. The student said that this made them very nervous since data was already being collected but questions still lingered about its intended methods and design. Other students recounted similar critiques which arose well after certain stages of the study were already underway and could not be changed except by starting the project again from the beginning. Some students described that their way to deal with this issue was to go back to their notes and recall why certain options were chosen instead of others, and to remind others of their reasoning at the time for backing certain decisions. Since everyone is learning continuously, it is no wonder that new issues are uncovered as everyone becomes more familiar with the project at hand, or as they are able to observe what is happening as it progresses, or after they have had more time to ponder the possibilities.

Students who navigated through these surprises successfully usually kept track of their journeys, some by writing in a diary and others by listing on a calendar, to help document the path they had actually traveled, especially if the road was slightly different than the one intended. Some students admitted that they were initially looking for the easiest data collection process that would be acceptable, until their research advisors convinced them that the long research journey that they were about to take deserved better than such a minimalist approach. In journaling about their reactions or in online conversations with others, they had a record of the reasoned steps in determining what actions they were taking regarding their project. Another student kept track of times that a certain committee member attempted to address significantly different research questions than their study had planned. And even more students compared their experiences with others in their program and within their discipline, essentially documenting to someone else the rationales behind various decisions made by them or their advisors.

The smallest of documentation for reasons why a particular action was not taken proved to be useful as well for some graduate students. Certain students kept folders or files describing what their project "was not," in other words, lists of features of similar studies along with explanations of why those similarities were not pursued. A few students kept lists of fellow candidates they had met and the advice they provided, noting how much they appreciated and benefited from the documented cautions and solutions of past travelers who were willing to share their experiences. Nearly all candidates could point out ways in which they would do things differently if they were planning their journeys again. While some regretted not considering all available data collection methods before selecting one, and others found comfort in their methodology but not their topics, periodic reflections on their travels helped to solidify their learning and inform their future thinking.

21.4 Things to DO

- Consider all available data collection methodologies before selecting the one that you will utilize in your research activities.
- Review the data collection methodology used in related research projects.
- Recognize the merit of considering the methodologies utilized by recognized researchers in your field.
- Ensure that your data collection methodology is capable of producing the information necessary to answer all of your research questions fully.
- Identify which data collection methodology you have selected for your research project, crediting its source when appropriate.

21.5 Things NOT to Do

- Fail to recognize that selecting anything other than the ideal data collection methodology will compromise your overall research project and its potential contribution to the field of study.
- Attempt the minimum acceptable data collection process.
- Select a data collection methodology that you are not confident will produce the necessary information to answer all of your research questions completely.
- Simply adopt a data collection methodology because someone you know or have read about has used it.
- Forget to involve your research advisor and committee members in this important decision.

Bibliography

Calabrese, R. L. (2006). *The elements of an effective dissertation and thesis: A step-by-step guide to getting it right the first time*. Lanham, MD: Rowman & Littlefield Education.

Carter, S., Kelly, F., & Brailsford, I. (2012). *Structuring your research thesis*. Palgrave Macmillan.

McGregor, S. L. T. (2017). *Understanding and evaluating research: A critical guide*. Thousand Oaks, CA: Sage.

Identifying Data Analysis Methodology

22

22.1 Role in Survival and Success

During a trip it is not unusual for a traveler to consider departing from their original travel plan in a serendipitous way. Depending on the way you travel, you may have some flexibility to make adjustments to the original travel plan. In retrospect, some travelers may discover that the changes that they made from their original travel plans actually enhanced the success and enjoyment of their trip, while others may discover that those well-intentioned diversions prevented them from fully attaining their original travel goals. Some travelers will be instantly agitated or upset in learning about a significant change in destination, altered planned route, or different time frame.

While the same tendency can arise in thesis or dissertation travel, having a well-conceived research plan and following it is an essential element to your successful journey. This is true for all of the aspects of your research project; your adherence to the plan is imperative, especially for the data collection and analysis steps that you have selected. Attempting to change your methodology halfway through your project, or even near the beginning of your project, will be problematic. Unlike traveling on a trip, you cannot be spontaneous when selecting which route to take for your data analysis methodology. These steps will need to be described in detail, approved in advance, and yield the type of information that you can successfully analyze in order to answer your research questions. You definitely don't want to leave these important procedures to chance.

Identifying a data analysis methodology in advance of the collection of data, and even testing a pilot version of your idea with sample data, helps to make a clever idea into a strong project proposal. This prevents bias and ensures that you have properly thought through (visualized) all of the facets of your intended research project. Even if the best, most complete and detailed data is collected, a weak or haphazard data analysis strategy will not show the value of the hard-earned data that you spent all that time collecting. The incorporation of some kind of statistics, and encouraging random samples for this reason, is a modern requirement even for most

© The Author(s), under exclusive license to Springer Nature Switzerland AG 2021   117
R. S. Fleming and M. Kowalsky, *Survival Skills for Thesis and Dissertation Candidates*, Springer Texts in Education,
https://doi.org/10.1007/978-3-030-80939-3_22

qualitative studies. Enacting steps not in the approved plan is often unwise, and must only be undertaken after careful consideration and encouragement from your research advisor.

22.2 What You Need to Know

Choosing a data analysis methodology may seem daunting at the beginning of a project, especially if it is your first attempt at sophisticated statistical calculations. However, no time is wasted in early pondering of the future analysis steps you might use in the project, or on conceptualizing what the collected data might look like once you have it. Making a knowledgeable choice about your methods of collection and analysis, and assuring that they align with each other and with your research questions and topic, are essential travel options to investigate early and then commit to decisively. By specifying your process in great detail, and procuring your research committee's advice in carrying it out as described, you will create a high quality project whose value and rigor is instantly recognizable to others in the field.

An important starting point in determining the most appropriate data analysis methodology for your thesis or dissertation research is to recognize that no one automatically knows how to do sophisticated data analysis steps or how to use number-crunching tools. Take some time to learn about the analysis options for the type of data that you are collecting. Seek the guidance of your research advisor and committee members in making this important decision, and especially in changing it, since it will impact both your research process and the value of your project's outcomes. Taking time to learn new techniques, and more importantly to increase your willingness to learn some new tools, is a survival skill not only for thesis and dissertation journeys, but also for life.

You will want to discover the data analysis tools that others have used or are currently using. Seek out training and/or mentoring for data analysis early in your program. It's never too early to figure out how to make data become knowledge. There may be another researcher that you could assist/apprentice in order to observe how they are using data. It is imperative that you recognize the importance of the data analysis activities in your research journey, especially since these data analysis processes may take the longest time to complete among all of the stages of your thesis or dissertation journey. How, why, when, and what your data says will be the focus of your oral defense, and will include your defense of any changes that were made, so it's important to get it right.

22.3 Student Experiences and Suggestions: *Using Trip Data to Inform Your Journey*

In most research methods courses, students learn that sound data analysis is a prerequisite to successfully addressing their research questions. As a result, the candidate would produce a thesis or dissertation capable of making a meaningful contribution to the existing body of knowledge in their field. Yet most graduate students feel that they did not spend enough time learning about how to deal with the complexities of their research methods. Many would report later that they did not feel they mastered any one process well enough that they could repeat it easily, or even teach it to someone else. As essential as designing and implementing an appropriate data collection methodology is, a failure to properly analyze the data that you have collected can seriously derail your research journey. Some students realized their projects reflected weak data collection strategies, while other students felt inadequate in their data analysis skills, and still others felt lost in trying to interpret their findings. Since these are natural misgivings for novice researchers, their remedies may lie in looking more closely at what solutions others have found.

One student explained that they took a lot of time off their study's activities, at the urging of one of their research supervisors, in order to research how others in the same field dealt with potential flaws in their own projects. Although this seemed at the time to pause their forward momentum, they later agreed that proceeding further without the benefit of the hindsight of others would have wasted time and energy. While some students scoured the literature for ideas of how to fix problems, others continuously asked peers at their own university and elsewhere for advice and assistance. Students already familiar with the various available data analysis techniques and tools were able to serve as mentors or tutors, and to help determine the best ways forward. Some students were explicitly warned by their advisors that they should not ask others to help collect or analyze their data, even in an emergency. Yet asking for recommendations and brainstorming issues would certainly be useful in searching for the answers to everyone's research questions. The time and effort that many students devoted to learning the quantitative and qualitative tools that others have used enabled them to select and defend the proper data treatments for their respective research projects.

Most students recommend talking to individuals who have successfully used various methodologies even outside of their own subject areas. Librarians helped other students find published articles in top journals which used common procedures successfully and then reported on them clearly. A few students had the experience of using their methods multiple times during their thesis or dissertation journeys, yet others had never seen their research process utilized at all prior to their own solo project. Either way, the learning curve for experiencing something unfamiliar was still a trip which had to be taken at some point in the journey. Most students who had no idea of where to start followed the guidance of their research methods professors and supplemented their learning through meetings with advisors or tutoring from another graduate student with the necessary expertise.

Another graduate student labored on their journey for way too long because they rushed to make quick decisions on both data collection and analysis, and subsequently endured the consequences. Later they encouraged their classmates to take the time to make informed decisions regarding crucial aspects of their research project and to recognize that not every decision about a project is equally important to its outcome. Certain students had to question the role that their research advisor and committee members were playing in these decision making instances, especially when their advice seemed vague or mismatched to other parts of the conversation. The students likely had not seen similarities in their work to other students' projects, or they were not as familiar with all of the background literature detailing potential discrepancies. One student was at first angry and then quite appreciative when an advisor uncovered a conference paper which held details essential to the most difficult aspects of the student's study. Although the paper existed several months prior, neither the advisor nor the student were looking for more literature at that point in their project, and both were lucky that many weeks of extra analysis were avoided because they came upon several conceptual and operational explanations related to their current problems. Any and all new work can indeed inform your own project, both before and after it's completed!

22.4   Things to DO

- Recognize the importance of sound data analysis in determining the value of your research project upon its completion.
- Familiarize yourself with the data analysis methodologies others are using in their research projects, even if their topics are not in your field.
- Find out what statistical tools others are using in their research, and then spend some time learning how to use them.
- Recognize the importance of incorporating statistical analysis in your research.
- Identify a data analysis methodology in advance of collecting data.
- Try to analyze your data in as many ways as possible.

22.5   Things NOT to Do

- Fail to recognize the essential importance of selecting the correct data analysis methodology.
- Make a quick decision on a data analysis methodology without taking the necessary time to identify and consider those methodologies that lend themselves to your research topic and purpose.
- Fail to consult with your research advisor and committee members before selecting a data analysis methodology and statistical tools.
- Attempt to rush the data analysis step.

- Change your data analysis plan without the agreement of your research advisor and committee members.
- Leave relationships or details unexamined or unaddressed.

Bibliography

Bloomberg, L. D. & Marie, V. (2015). *Completing your qualitative dissertation: A road map from beginning to end*. Thousand Oaks, CA: Sage.

Gosling, P. & Lambertus, D. N. (2011). Mastering your PhD: Survival and success in the doctoral years and beyond (2nd ed). Berlin: Springer-Verlag.

Vogt, W. P. (2014). *Selecting the right analyses for your data: Quantitative, qualitative, and mixed methods*. Guilford Press.

Securing Support for Your Choice of a Research Topic

23

23.1 Role in Survival and Success

While earlier in planning your trip you will have identified the traveler(s) who have signed on to travel with you on your great journey, it is important that all involved travelers fully understand and agree to not only the planned destination, but also the specifics of the route of travel. Failure to agree on such matters has the potential of compromising the success of a trip, as well as the pleasure of all travelers. While some may think of support as financial or emotional, here we also think of it as ongoing cooperation. If some travelers grow weary or bored with the trip, this may not mean that they disapprove of the direction or destination. Likely you will do what you can to ensure information, emotions, and suggestions are shared well in advance of choosing the trip's features.

The same is true when it comes to thesis or dissertation travel. While you will have diligently completed a great many of the preceding steps before asking for formal approval of your research topic, "good ideas" are just that until they become actionable plans on paper. Ideally you will have selected your research advisor and committee members based on their knowledge of and interest in your topic. Working with a research advisor with a compatible personality and a shared passion for your research topic will prove beneficial as you navigate the sometimes challenging travel to a successful defense of your thesis or dissertation. Cultivating cooperation among your participants, advisor, committee, and peers is a survival skill well worth your time.

23.2 What You Need to Know

It is essential that you approach your thesis or dissertation in the same manner that you would undertake any important work project. Effectively and efficiently completing the various steps of the research process and defending your thesis or dissertation, while certainly a challenging undertaking, will provide the necessary

© The Author(s), under exclusive license to Springer Nature Switzerland AG 2021

R. S. Fleming and M. Kowalsky, *Survival Skills for Thesis and Dissertation Candidates*, Springer Texts in Education, https://doi.org/10.1007/978-3-030-80939-3_23

springboard for your future professional opportunities. Your thesis or dissertation travel will be a lengthy and rigorous undertaking. Understanding the long view from the start, and securing the necessary support from your research advisor and other committee members for the duration, will certainly contribute to a satisfying process and a top quality outcome.

It is important always to remember that your research advisor is your guide throughout your thesis or dissertation travels. Some advisors may tend to steer candidates toward particular topics based on their individual research interests, or in the interest of producing research synergies with respect to the larger research agenda of a research group, department, or university. If this is the case, it is imperative that you, your research advisor, and other committee members are "on the same page" regarding the intensity of your research interest and timing of your research outcome, commencing with the time they signed on to join you on your research journey. Fully understanding and embracing the fundamental purpose of thesis or dissertation research, while cooperating with faculty on larger goals, will ensure that you select and refine your research topic and frame an appropriate research design which aligns with your entire team's idea of a worthwhile trip.

You must approach your research project as an explorer in search of discovering new and important insights that can be shared with others interested in your field of endeavor. This is not just a way to please yourself by occupying your time on an enjoyable perusal of available information. Your thesis or dissertation journey should be viewed as one of the most challenging and important work projects you will likely ever undertake. Recognize however, that some potential research topics are just not in fashion, or are just not easy to design, or are just not good topics for empirical research. As such, these ideas will have less support from your research advisor or committee members. Your research project must be capable of making a meaningful contribution to your field of study and serve as a basis for the work of future researchers. Approaching your project in such a business-like manner will garner the support of your research advisor and committee members to guide, support, and champion your research topic and plan.

23.3 Student Experiences and Suggestions: *Meeting or Avoiding Travel Companions*

Before you embarked on your research journey, you agreed to sign on for multiple years of academic planning, and you met others who had similarly signed onto your journey as your professors, your classmates, or your tutors. You may have quickly realized that the ease, enjoyment, or timeline of certain aspects of your journey would be based on your positive or negative interactions with your various travel companions. One student was grateful that other members of their program's cohort had a complete understanding of their proposed research plans, while others valued the opportunity to persuade their group of critical peers of the merits of their intended research proposal. Others were less successful in finding friends to share parts of the journey with them, and some students regretted befriending others whose issues took time away from productivity.

One student had a particularly uncomfortable conversation with one of their advisors, who believed they were on the journey that the student initially proposed, but then was surprised to hear about a new topic for the first time months later. Another student tried to coordinate their research on a larger topic with others who would all contribute research on aspects of a shared interest. Unfortunately, they were surprised to learn that not only had some of their initial group of collaborators dropped out of the program before finishing their proposals, and that newer graduate students had been added to the team, necessitating travel back across ground that had already been covered. And of course, many students complained of their needy classmates, some of whom talked incessantly about non-project issues or complained loudly about various project requirements. Many of these students had to distance themselves from the troublemakers in their group and learn to protect their time toward research productivity.

Even among students who completed their thesis or dissertation successfully there are complaints about advisors' and supervisors' behaviors or reactions. Most students were caught off guard at one time or another by a comment or action that they did not understand. Although students may not agree with the assignments or decisions of their advisors, most said they were just interested in getting their project done, so they went along with most of the advice provided. Most graduate students eventually realized that it really was their own responsibility to ensure that their projects met expectations, regardless of what they may have been told along the way by travel companions with varying degrees of knowledge and commitment to their work.

Some students were unprepared to learn that their committee members were not really very excited about their projects, due to either the nature of the topic, the student's need for help, or even some other reason unrelated to the current situation. Although experiencing a lack of enthusiasm on the part of your research advisor or committee members can certainly be frustrating, students found that kindness and patience was repaid in the interest of enhancing the value of a project which would carry all traveler's names on it. While students throughout time have complained that faculty were not providing enough help, faculty also have complained that students often needed too much help. Indeed, crafting a thesis or dissertation is hard work, and at times everyone involved can become annoyed with each other. But though the continuing support of others, when and where they are most available and effective, most students are able to navigate through any variety of difficulties.

23.4   Things to DO

- Recognize that your research advisor and committee members have a responsibility to their department, university, and profession to oversee thesis and dissertation projects that yield a professional and valuable contribution to the existing body of knowledge.

- Recognize the importance of your research advisor and committee members being fully committed to the value of your research project and thus willing to devote their often limited time to guiding your research journey.
- After securing their agreement to serve on your research committee, keep your advisor and other committee members "in the loop" as you refine the initial research topic on which they agreed to work with you.
- Rehearse any contemplated changes regarding your research topic with your research advisor in a timely manner.
- Remember that while others may have thoughts and suggestions regarding your topic, you are the one that will "own" that topic throughout and beyond the research process.

23.5 Things NOT to Do

- Be disappointed if your first choice of a topic is not wholeheartedly supported by your research advisor and/or committee members.
- Forget that suggestions of your research advisor or committee members are frequently based on their experiences in helping other candidates through the research process.
- Give up on a research topic totally based on not receiving the initial full support that you desired and anticipated from your research advisor and committee members.
- Select a research topic that you are not really interested in or passionate about in the interest of working with a particular faculty member as your research advisor or a committee member.
- Fail to prepare to present a compelling case for choosing the research topic that you are passionate about pursuing.

Bibliography

Shore, B. M. (2014) *The graduate advisor handbook: A student-centered approach.* Chicago: University of Chicago Press
Wisker, G. (2008). *The postgraduate research handbook: Succeed with your MA, MPhil, EdD and PhD (Second edition).* Palgrave Macmillan.

Developing a Research Proposal

24

24.1   Role in Survival and Success

In planning a major trip, the astute traveler recognizes the importance of engaging in necessary advance planning, including making a number of important decisions regarding intended travel supplies, routes, and timing. Obviously, it is important to develop a travel plan that appeals to all travelers making the trip, and it is likewise important to plan a trip that is actually possible to do. While the travel plans for a major, previously untaken trip will and should often be challenging, it is important that the resulting travel plan also be realistic given time, resources, and other realities. Many aspects of the trip need to be fully evaluated and determined well in advance.

Similarly, it is important to engage in informed, conscientious consideration and decision making when planning your thesis or dissertation journey. You will need to determine if your research topic is researchable, and your analysis should consider if necessary data, information, sources, or support will be available to the researcher. An important consideration will be the ability to conduct the desired research while affording appropriate protection of human subjects. It is also imperative that you conscientiously and realistically consider if the proposed research project can be completed during the time you have available.

It is important always to remember that a thesis or dissertation project should be developed in order to have the potential of making a meaningful contribution to the field or profession. Your thesis or dissertation will be attached to you forever as one of your first published works, and often as your most comprehensive research undertaking. It is important not to skip or omit steps, since the rigor and quality of this long-term project often suggests to others what they might reasonably expect in the quality of your future work. Building rigor into your proposal at the outset will avoid problems defending weaker designs later in your process. Therefore, assuring that good decision making about the quality of your research product is demonstrated early and often is an important survival skill that will help you ultimately satisfy important quality checks and produce a worthwhile manuscript.

© The Author(s), under exclusive license to Springer Nature Switzerland AG 2021   127
R. S. Fleming and M. Kowalsky, *Survival Skills for Thesis
and Dissertation Candidates*, Springer Texts in Education,
https://doi.org/10.1007/978-3-030-80939-3_24

24.2   What You Need to Know

While the task of developing your research proposal falls upon you as a thesis or dissertation candidate, you will want to benefit from the guidance and direction of others in conceptualizing your research and developing the actual research proposal. This will certainly involve seeking guidance from your research advisor and other members of your research committee, as well as from others working in the discipline. You will also want to ensure that the content and format of your research proposal conform to the expectations of your institution. On this measure, cooperation is key, since checking in with your team and your discipline regularly will enable you to design and write in a manner similar to the most successful others in your discipline.

Review of past thesis and dissertation projects can reveal valuable insights as you prepare your research proposal. This can involve looking at the research proposals of others in your department, college, or field, as well as at their resulting thesis or dissertation products. You will want to ask a number of questions early and often as you develop your research proposal. Is there a reason why no one has done your topic before? Perhaps it is politically incorrect, or it was done years ago with boring results that failed to contribute in any significant way to the field of knowledge. You may discover that another student in your program or at another institution is already conducting similar research.

Reach out to these individuals to see if they are willing to share their research proposals with you. Ideally, they will be willing not only to do so, but also to share the feedback they have received on their proposal. The resulting insights that you can gain through such collegial sharing can prove invaluable as you prepare and refine your research proposal. You may also have the opportunity to attend public presentations of recent candidates and graduates, which can help you begin with the end in mind. However, you will want to use only the best parts of what you find from others. Copying the style of weaker students will dilute your own work; therefore, take advice and models from only the most successful ones, as identified by eventual publication of their thesis or dissertation or recommendations from your research advisor and committee members.

24.3   Student Experiences and Suggestions: *Collect Some Souvenirs of Your Travels*

Most students learned in graduate courses that at various times throughout one's career others will look to your thesis or dissertation in evaluating your ability to conduct quality research. This idea motivated some students, who strove to demonstrate their expertise as researchers capable of producing high-quality projects that made significant contributions to their discipline. This was particularly intimidating to others, who felt additional pressure to become famous in the field from work in their first independent study. And yet others saw their first published manuscript as a requirement to join the faculty of the university of their choice.

The learning sequences which different programs use in training their graduate students to be competent researchers vary by institution as well as by discipline. Some students published their work as part of a team soon after entering graduate school, while others spent five years refining a publishable project which may not have been accepted into an academic journal on the first try. At various stages in their studies, most students say that they became more confident in their abilities to prepare proposals that would clearly articulate their planned research journeys. This confidence was based on having carried out either one or many projects, and on having dedicated the necessary time to undertake and complete each of the steps, just like a professional traveler!

Students in many disciplines have kept files or documents of their work throughout their program, and especially past papers and ideas that did not result in their thesis or dissertation manuscript. One student had maintained a running list of future projects that they would undertake once they were on the job market. Another student copied rejected sections of their dissertation or pages which led in the wrong direction for the current topic, saving them for possible later use. These remnants of their thinking are like academic souvenirs of their journey, along with pilot study publications or preliminary articles which validate methods or instruments. Whether purposeful or not, students who collected pieces of their unfinished work, rather than discarding them, found that they had some ideas and writing to start with for their next projects. Many graduate students describe that their coursework or early investigations led to multiple pages of manuscripts that were started but which soon had to be abandoned so that they could work on other targeted tasks which would result in a completed thesis or dissertation.

Students who did not save previous work, course papers, or literature reviews on topics that were not ultimately used for their main project sometimes felt that they did not learn much during their training. One such student could not remember at graduation time most of the topics of the papers they wrote for graduate courses over the previous five years. While it is possible that this student lost interest in those previous topics entirely, keeping a few past papers as souvenirs may have helped them reflect on their learning or create arguments for future choices more easily. Another doctoral student whose research proposal was not approved several times, underestimated the importance of keeping those previous research proposals, noting that they had to recreate some aspects from memory when attempting their next research project upon landing a new job. Students who found the idea of souvenirs helpful were ones who built upon their previous work and effort in conceptualizing particular aspects of their topic or method. When professional writing becomes a routine part of your next job, connections to your previous thinking, reflection on your prior writing, and potential themes along your research agenda gained by reviewing your saved souvenirs can help propel your thinking forward.

24.4 Things to DO

- Remember that your thesis or dissertation will serve as an indicator of your ability to conduct quality research and will thus have professional implications throughout your career.
- Recognize the importance of producing a high quality thesis or dissertation.
- Select a research topic and methodology that are realistic based on your capabilities.
- Select a research project to which you will be able to dedicate the necessary time required to produce a quality project within established deadlines.
- Review the research proposals of others and the feedback that they received on their proposals should that information be available.
- Define your research project in a way that will contribute to its value to others.

24.5 Things NOT to Do

- Select a research topic or methodology that is not feasible to complete successfully.
- Forget to consult with your advisor and committee members early in the process.
- Attempt a research approach without ensuring that you already possess or can acquire the necessary skills to undertake and complete the research project successfully.
- Assume all published research is of equal quality and rigor.
- Model your research based on the style of weaker researchers.
- Fail to recognize that your research proposal will drive all of your subsequent research activities.

Bibliography

Booton, C. (2018). *Applying theory*. Crossline Press.
Carter, S., Guerin, C., & Aitchison, C. (2020). *Doctoral writing: Practices, processes and pleasures*. Springer.
Locke, L. F., Spirduso, W. W., & Silverman, S. J. (2007). *Proposals that work: A guide for planning dissertations and grant proposals*. Sage.

Securing Approval of Your Research Proposal

25

25.1 Role in Survival and Success

Any experienced traveler will tell you that a crucial final step before departing on any journey is to secure any necessary pre-travel approvals. In the case of a trip where you are traveling with others that would include reaching agreement on all of the essential details of the trip including the hotels where you plan to stay, who is making the various travel arrangements and procuring confirmations, and how the costs of the trip are going to be shared. Approvals, both informal and formal, are important indicators that plans for the trip are progressing as expected. Naturally, these can be updated as new information is learned or discovered, but the basic parameters of any successful journey likely will have been viewed and reviewed at regular intervals by all travelers involved.

A similar step is necessary before you embark on your thesis or dissertation journey. While this represents the last step in the research planning phase, it serves as the prerequisite for going forward in the research process. Before actually beginning to conduct your research, you will be required to secure the necessary confirmations from your research advisor and other committee members regarding your planned research project. This will include not only the agreed-upon research topic, but also your planned research design and methodology. You will also be expected to secure any approvals required from your department and/or university.

While it might seem that securing such an approval should be automatic at this point in your research journey, your research advisor and other committee members would not be doing you a favor were they just to "rubber stamp" your research proposal. Their review and concurrence regarding your planned research methodology will prove just as essential as their earlier consideration and support of your research topic. In addition to ensuring that your proposed research project is "doable," your research advisor and committee members have a responsibility to ensure that the difficulty level of your proposed project is appropriate given the type of academic degree that you are pursuing. Checking and double-checking your work against best practices is a survival skill which will set you up for success in school and in life.

25.2   What You Need to Know

While it may seem that securing approval of your research proposal is an unnecessary step or a requirement that delays your ability to actually getting down to working on your research activities, such a mindset at this juncture and throughout your thesis or dissertation journey will not serve you well, and will potentially delay your successful completion and defense of your research project. By signing on during the research proposal approval process, all members of your research committee, particularly your research advisor, are validating the merit of your research undertaking and attesting to the appropriateness of your planned research design and methodology. To honor everyone's time, check and double-check before submitting your work.

Your success will be enhanced by the guidance offered by your research advisor and other committee members before they are willing to sign off on your research proposal. You should be seeking their wholehearted support and commitment, rather than merely a willingness to "approve" your research project. If your research advisor and other committee members are not enthusiastic about your proposed project, it typically means the project has been done before and thus may not deliver new or intriguing results. They may also find that it is too simple or too complex to carry out or that there are inherent problems with the design of the premise, sample/participants, or data collection instruments.

Realize that in seeking approval, you should demonstrate both the value of your research initiative and the appropriateness of the research design and methodology that you are proposing. Ideas that are not thoroughly expressed or processes that are not fully described in the proposal are difficult for committee members to support. Respect the fact that your research advisor and committee members will expect that you articulate a strong, appropriate research methodology for a research project that will produce useful results that contribute to the existing body of knowledge and practice. Their hesitation about your proposal and any alternate suggestions are likely based on questions of rigor, completeness, and alignment of purpose. Utilize the feedback from your research advisor and committee members in making appropriate revisions to your initial research proposal. Your attention to these types of quality indicators in advance will help your project move forward more smoothly.

25.3   Student Experiences and Suggestions: *Requesting Authorization to Travel*

Universities define their review methods in a variety of ways, but most students say that their capstone project was reviewed by multiple levels of experts before it was formally accepted. Some students must procure permission to propose a conference talk, while others must request authorization to embark on subsequent stages of a project in progress, especially if these activities require funding. Many students must have their research advisor, a chairperson, or supervisor review their research proposal and sign a form or letter indicating their agreement about the proposed research study. Nearly all students say that their research committee members and advisors wanted explicit evidence of every student's knowledge and skills as a researcher, especially before they signed any formal agreements. Some students said that they needed to show proof that they had already performed the particular research methods required to complete their proposed thesis or dissertation project successfully, while others said that they had to detail a plan for acquiring new skills in writing, data analysis, or technologies used by their specific fields.

Several students stated that they had to provide evidence that their project has a sound design, and that it would be feasible to complete within a reasonable time. Another group of students used the literature in their field to confirm that their project was of the proper type, scope, and length. Still other students sought feedback from the authors of published articles in similar areas to help confirm that their proposal plans were satisfactory, or to justify changes if feedback initially suggested that they were not. One student said their advisor explained that any faculty member would actually be remiss in signing off on a marginal research proposal, or one without strong evidence of success and a thorough peer review. Instead, the professors' purpose should be to assist students by defining appropriate revisions that will enhance both the success of your research journey and the value of the resulting thesis or dissertation that chronicles it.

Other students recounted how hard they had labored in preparing their research proposal, which was then not enthusiastically embraced or endorsed by the members of their research committee. Some students' advisors wanted a publishable-quality manuscript for the first reading, while others accepted drafts that contained clear outlines but which needed more sophistication in argument or analysis. A thesis student who had the good fortune of having their initial research proposal approved without changes compared their experience with a friend who was completing a project in a related field at a neighboring university. While one student was advised to make only some minor changes to the proposal they had submitted, the other received tentative approval and was asked to provide much more substance to their argument and discussion, nearly a dozen additional pages of content. At whichever point your revisions are requested, it is important to remember that they would not be requested at all unless they improved your particular project, or your overall journey, in some way!

A particular student said their committee wanted to be reassured that the student would be able to gain access to proposed study participants before formally approving their proposal. In retrospect, the student realized that the faculty members had anticipated potential issues that the student might have encountered. A different student admitted that it was challenging to recognize and appreciate the feedback provided by the members of your research committee, since their reviews always resulted in a lot of extra work. It is understandable to be disappointed if your proposal is not immediately approved, or if you have been told that you are not yet finished but have quite a way more to travel. Students who finish the process successfully explain that you must not allow yourself to become discouraged or defensive in receiving feedback on your proposal. They note again that if advisors were not interested in seeing you succeed in your thesis or dissertation travels, they would not have agreed to become one of your reviewers at all. By the end of your journey, your committee members will also be expected to affix their names to your research project, so it is in everyone's mutual interest to ensure that it is the best it can be.

25.4 Things to DO

- Recognize the important, value-added role that your research advisor and committee members have in approving your research proposal.
- Understand that it is not unusual for a proposed research project to receive tentative approval since some parts may be too difficult based on a candidate's current skill level, due to the availability of necessary data, or because the proposed project cannot be completed in a reasonable time.
- Ask questions early and often about why a project is good or bad as proposed.
- Recognize that if this is the first time you are preparing a research proposal you will likely make some mistakes and not necessarily get it right the first time.
- Be appreciative of all feedback and suggestions received from your research advisor and other committee members.

25.5 Things NOT to Do

- Become discouraged when your initial research proposal is not approved.
- Become defensive if your initial research proposal is not fully approved.
- View feedback received on your research proposal as a critique of you personally, rather than of the research design that you are proposing.
- Abandon your proposed research and topic rather than determining necessary and appropriate revisions that you will need to make to your research proposal.
- Fail to communicate your appreciation, through both words and actions, to your research advisor and other committee members for devoting their scarce time to conscientiously considering your research proposal and providing useful and constructive, well-intentioned feedback designed to assist you in designing a viable research plan.

Bibliography

Mauch, J. E. & Namgi, P. (2003). *Guide to the successful thesis and dissertation: A handbook for students and faculty.* New York: M. Dekker.

Moffett, N. L. (2019). *Creating a framework for dissertation preparation: Emerging research and opportunities.* Hershey, PA: IGI Global.

Oltman, G., Surface, J. L., & Keiser, K. (2019). *Prepare to chair: Leading the dissertation and thesis process.* Rowman & Littlefield.

Improving the Literature Review

26

26.1 Role in Survival and Success

If you have ever planned a trip many months before the actual departure, you have learned that some things related to your route of travel or desired destination will have changed with the passage of time. An example would be the opening of a new interstate highway that will enable you to reach your destination sooner or the discovery of major highway construction projects that will most certainly extend your planned travel time or the mapped route of travel that you follow. You might also discover that there are new attractions that you would like to visit during your travels or that a restaurant where you had intended to eat has closed. Taking the time to again research your ideas closer to your time of departure will almost always prove beneficial.

A similar reality exists in thesis or dissertation travel. Additional research on your topic may have been conducted and published since the time that you completed your initial literature review. New tools may have arrived or new enhancements of the usual methods may have been espoused by the field. You will likewise want to take the time to do another round of literature searching in the interest of enhancing your knowledge and ability to engage in a project that, in addition to addressing your research interest, will make the desired significant contribution to the field. You may find that much has been published on your topic in recent months while you were attending to other research activities.

26.2 What You Need to Know

Begin your second literature search using the database search terms which were most successful earlier. In other words, repeat your process as before with the same keywords and subject terms that you recorded in your original search. While you will want to run the same database searches as before in order to isolate new items,

© The Author(s), under exclusive license to Springer Nature Switzerland AG 2021
R. S. Fleming and M. Kowalsky, *Survival Skills for Thesis and Dissertation Candidates*, Springer Texts in Education,
https://doi.org/10.1007/978-3-030-80939-3_26

you will also want to re-sort your database results by relevance in addition to using options which re-order your results by the newest dates available. Check the resulting new articles for potential additional terms or alternate keywords which describe your topic, and then search for articles using those new terms. The most clever thesis and dissertation students will consult their campus librarians and subject liaisons for objective feedback on the strategies and sources they are using, thus saving time. Actually consulting experts on research is indeed a valuable survival skill for thesis and dissertation students in all subject areas. Many have reported that their university's librarians were their "best-kept secrets" to searching more efficiently and effectively, although these research consultation services are actually available to all students free of charge.

If you've been using library databases exclusively up to this point, you will want to check a web search engine to pick up press releases or news reports about newer studies. Some of these details may not have made their way into peer reviewed journal articles yet, due to the length of most publication cycles. Now is the time to use tools which have different search algorithms (for example, use both EBSCO and ProQuest databases, or try both Google and Bing). Many databases also provide 'cited by' links, as does Google Scholar. The use of "chaining" your sources in this way, by searching for others who have also quoted these items, can contribute to a greatly enhanced literature review. Chaining your sources involves discovering "who cited what," and then tracking down other articles which also cited your most useful items. You will also benefit by carefully looking through your bibliography for the main works you are discussing in your literature review, and then citing newer sources which also quote them.

You will want to ensure that your literature review is comprehensive and that you have not missed any important research activities or discoveries related to your topic, particularly those taking place since the time of your initial literature review. You will want to check for international counterparts doing related studies, since much relevant research is not published in the United States, nor solely in English. Investigate the published literature in every library database you can find, as well as in conference proceedings and university theses and dissertations from your institution, in others from around the U. S., and in those by students in other countries, especially those known for your topic or discipline. This will help to ensure that you have a comprehensive literature review.

26.3   Student Experiences and Suggestions: *Visiting with Experts Along the Way*

Most students said they spent countless hours with the resources of their university's library, whether seeking articles from the library's web pages or attending workshops or consultations with researchers on the library's staff. Students whose institutions did not have this type of central location for accessing published literature followed up on leads from their professors and found articles using free academic search engines, by tracing the work of noted authors in their fields using their publication lists, or by interviewing other graduate students at their school for ideas on where to look for more information. Several students mentioned visiting other universities' libraries as registered guests so that they could locate even more literature they did not know about earlier.

Other students mentioned that they did not use the library building or print resources in their searches, but rather followed online a network of leaders in their fields. While these tactics may vary across disciplines, it is worthwhile to determine the best practices used in your subject area. One student even located peers who were students researching the same topics to exchange searching ideas and discuss repositories where items may be found or where requests could be made. A few students mentioned that successive rounds of literature searches helped them to not only revise and improve their initial literature reviews, but also to gain numerous insights based on the work of other researchers whose work was published in the past few months, including many recent thesis and dissertation projects. Other travelers are therefore a quality source for information at multiple points in the thesis or dissertation journey!

One student realized quickly that it was very important to keep track of ongoing research that could easily be missed while they were dedicating their time and effort to other aspects of their projects. Another concurred, noting that former students were asked about recent research related to their research topic during their oral defense and even when presenting at academic conferences. It was easier to produce a satisfactory answer about ongoing work of others if all possible repositories of information were investigated, even if access to the full text of certain publications or data sets were not readily available. One graduate student relied on the help of a friend in their class to become aware of the available search tools and holdings of their university's library, which were not necessary to use at lower levels of study. Other students maintained that their prior training required use of an extensive regional and national network of college, university, and public libraries. Yet some relied on trips to the physical library building, to access resources which were not online. Several students noted that materials in certain subject areas and from particular major publishers would never be put online, so requesting a refresher in using both small library collections and those locations with extensive print holdings was still necessary to produce a thorough analysis of the literature. Many students appreciated meetings with expert searchers who helped them find items available to graduate students online, but which they had never realized were available.

Yet another student shared at a workshop the techniques they used to determine whether work on their topic was being published in other languages or by other graduate students elsewhere around the world. Some encouraged new students to not limit their search activities to traditional library databases or to the first few pages of search engine results. Another student likewise encouraged peers to contact a variety of librarians in order to benefit from their useful suggestions of more sophisticated strategies and sources beyond the obvious. Not every student continued to build on their literature reviews throughout their journeys. Lack of thorough searching was apparently evident to their research advisors and committee members, several of whom commented that they were unimpressed with the students' reviews. Some realized that they needed to make more than cursory changes to their first draft of literature analysis, but most by the end of their journeys realized that their travel success was unquestionably enhanced by periodically taking time to actually stop and read the literature they found.

26.4   Things to DO

- Recognize the importance and value of conducting more literature searching at multiple points during your project.
- Incorporate any relevant information revealed through additional literature searches.
- Supplement traditional library database searches using web search engines which may point to additional scholarly works in different ways.
- Focus too narrowly on most recent articles, rather than relevance, in conducting searches.
- Seek to discover potential new search terms or alternate keywords.
- Use "chaining" in conducting literature searches for new items, even if you ultimately choose not to use them.

26.5   Things NOT to Do

- Fail to recognize the importance of conducting a secondary literature search.
- Forget to allocate time periodically to learn and use the capabilities of various search tools, including their different search algorithms.
- Engage in a cursory initial or secondary literature review, or limit your sources to those from a previous course paper or proposal.
- Rely exclusively on databases or full-text sources only available through your own institution's library.
- Ignore the importance of international research related to your research topic, including those studies not published in English.

Bibliography

Efron, Sara Efrat & Ruth Ravid. (2019). *Writing the literature review: a practical guide*. New York: Guilford Press.

Galvan, José L. (2016). *Writing literature reviews: a guide for students of the social and behavioral sciences* (Revised ed). New York: Taylor & Francis.

Smith, P. (2017). *Doing a literature review*. Palgrave Macmillan.

Starting Your Empirical Research Process

27

27.1 Role in Survival and Success

As interesting as the many months of travel planning may have been, the real excitement begins as you depart on your long planned and anticipated journey. During each stage of your travel, you will come to realize fully the importance of all of your pre-trip planning, especially at times when you experience a successful journey free of unanticipated developments or "bumps in the road." You will find that consulting your detailed travel itinerary throughout your trip will result in a successful and enjoyable trip. You will likely also choose to maintain a travel journal to chronicle your journey for your own travel memories and to enable you to share your travel adventure with others.

Beginning the empirical research process is much like departing on your long awaited and anticipated trip. Once again, comprehensive pre-planning will equip you to depart on your journey and successfully navigate the many potential challenges inherent in thesis or dissertation travel. Following a well thought out travel plan that is fully endorsed by your travel partners will contribute to a meaningful journey that leads to your desired destination of a successful thesis or dissertation defense. As with other travels, you will find that maintaining a travel log or journal will prove beneficial for keeping track of your decisions along the way.

One important type of activity to document in your log are the methodological decisions you made. For example, as part of your research in human subjects training, you may first participate in training workshops or online modules which explain the details of how, why, and when certain protocol or copyright approvals are needed. Procuring approval for working with human subjects actually protects everyone involved, including you as researcher, your institution, your participants, and the faculty members supervising your project. When you document all of the actions you expect to take in order to conduct your empirical investigation, you are providing other researchers the opportunity to stop you from doing something inadvertently harmful, morally problematic, or procedurally unsound. Similarly, you will want to provide subjects, your research advisors, committee members and

© The Author(s), under exclusive license to Springer Nature Switzerland AG 2021   141
R. S. Fleming and M. Kowalsky, *Survival Skills for Thesis and Dissertation Candidates*, Springer Texts in Education,
https://doi.org/10.1007/978-3-030-80939-3_27

other observers the opportunity to identify issues with your study in advance, before they become problematic. Once you know that you have the legal, ethical, and philosophical approval to begin your study as described, you will feel not only relieved but also supported by others in your quest to bring new knowledge to light. In a way, this initial and ongoing documentation review by your faculty and university peers will have sanctioned your quest, and they will have formally encouraged you to carry on. Let the journey begin!

27.2 What You Need to Know

Recording the choices you've made and steps you've taken in your research activities will prove essential throughout the research process, especially in the interest of ensuring that you are actually addressing the desired research questions and following an appropriate and consistent methodology in answering those questions. While this approach is similar to chronicling any trip, as discussed earlier, the significance and magnitude of recording the details of your thesis or dissertation journey must be fully acknowledged. Keeping track of all of the decisions you made, including those options you rejected, will help you "defend" your choices later in your oral examination, and quite possibly to subsequent critics who are reading your final manuscript well after the project is over. Documenting your choices during the research process, thus reminding yourself of why you are carrying out certain tasks, is a survival skill which creates an essential backup, helping you recall many philosophical and procedural details later.

You will want to take notes about what you are doing right from the beginning, thus maintaining a running narrative of the steps you are taking to carry out the project. This will help you to add details later into your manuscript, or to explain anomalies in trying to follow your proposed protocol. Even seemingly small decisions about how to do particular tasks suggested in your methodology section should be recorded in a journal or log book, since these may later affect the results that you get even if you didn't anticipate an issue or experience any negative effects of those decisions. If you have notes about exactly what you did, this will enable other researchers to replicate your study, which is an important measure of research quality. It will also enable your committee members to see where potential problems began or later, where they can be mitigated.

If you need to deviate from anything in your research proposal or approved IRB protocol, speak up early and often. Many times, these changes can be incorporated into your application and approved quickly. Larger changes may necessitate time for the committee to review, discuss, and approve them. Changes are a natural part of improving a process, but if you change too much after you are approved to do a particular sequence, you may be unintentionally embarking on a different study entirely. Check with your research advisor or committee to determine if something is "too different" from what you originally proposed, or whether it is a cosmetic or substantive change. Think through the first several steps of each task before starting to do it. Try to anticipate problems along the way: Will you need extra time, supplies, appointments, etc.? When you record your data, do you need to set up an Excel spreadsheet in advance, or an input form, or a paper checklist? What happens when your participants are unavailable, or your initial outcomes are not at all of the quality or nature that you expected?

Anticipating issues by visualizing several actual steps in a research task can save time later. It may be easier if you "practice" with a nonparticipant or fake data first, so you can see how your procedures will work as you go along. A pilot study is often useful for this purpose, which can help you go through your steps and note adjustments in advance. You do not want to start collecting data and then find something wrong with one of your survey questions, independent variables, or categories. These will be difficult to change later, even after the first participant/sample is processed, so troubleshooting in advance can often help you avoid complicated problems entirely.

27.3   Student Experiences and Suggestions: *Time to Travel and Time to Recuperate*

Most students agreed that the most memorable point in their research journey was the day they completed it. However, it is not logical to work continuously every day, and perhaps for many years, without a brief stop along your travels to rest. Some students felt relieved upon completing their data collection, or after the long-awaited empirical research leg of their trip was complete once they wrote up their data analysis. Still others were most pleased when they did the final review of their manuscript to fix citation and formatting errors. Regardless of which points in your journey you identify as your benchmarks, it is important to take a mental break to recharge after completing one step and before embarking on the next. Several students mentioned that a brief respite from the stress of performing helped them to tackle each subsequent section with more motivation and energy.

Nearly all students find out about techniques for building breaks into their work flows from other students or other types of professionals. Graduate students often cannot recall any of their professors or advisors mentioning strategies for period-ically resting and recharging. Likely this was due to a fear that many students lose momentum in their project and either they take too long to return to it at the previous levels of attention, or they abandon it for years while resting. Still other students reluctantly recall that a significant break in their work patterns became so disruptive that they quit their graduate studies entirely. While some were successful in pleading to return despite poor progress, a few students regretted that they did not know their own goals or behaviors well enough to prevent a permanent break from academic life during the thesis or dissertation process. One student used the doc-umentation strategy mentioned earlier to write in their journal all of their reasons for staying or leaving their project or program, and committed to reading their written entries each month to see if they still felt the same way.

Several graduate students noted that they really wanted a rest, or a recreational outing with their families, or time to do sports or gather with friends who were not also students. Yet they knew for themselves that breaks which lasted too many days made them stray from their path. Some students felt that their time to concentrate on academics should be continual, so they designed schedules for themselves in such a way to ensure their self-imposed workload varied in intensity by day, by week or by season. Others used the times they waited for their advisors' feedback to take a mental break from their thesis or dissertation project, even if that meant working on other work-related things like their resume, cv, or job applications.

Still other students used particular tasks away from their computers or labs to become triggers for relaxation. Walking their dogs, meeting a relative, or eating certain favorite foods were signals for positive reinforcement for a job well done at any time good progress was made. Many practiced yoga, or spent time with a musical instrument or signing, or even surfed the Internet for fun topics as their recuperation strategies. However, if they became too accomplished in these other areas, or spent too much time using the relaxation tasks to avoid getting back to work, students confirmed that this was detrimental. Yet even those with the most self-discipline needed help along the way to judge how much time away was needed, or even how much leisure would suffice before reengaging with their project. With careful reflection and observation of your feelings and habits, you can determine the optimum ways to pause your travels for some rest and relaxation, which is always well deserved for such an advanced project!

27.4   Things to DO

- Recognize the importance of maintaining detailed notes as you complete each activity within the research process.
- Record all decisions you make, whether they seem insignificant or not.
- Aim for producing a research project that others will want to and be able to replicate successfully.
- Determine and utilize appropriate methods for recording data collection.
- "Test drive" your data collection processes prior to the collection of real data from study participants.

27.5   Things NOT to Do

- Avoid documenting your process because it seems like it might take too much time.
- Forget to consult with your research advisor regarding any proposed changes to your research plan, even if they seem small.
- Ignore the necessary IRB approvals for any changes to your research plan.

- Deviate from your approved research proposal or approved IRB protocol without waiting to receive appropriate approvals.
- Feel that your project is a failure because you have not produced significant relationships or society-changing outcomes.

Bibliography

Petre, Marian & Gordon Rugg. (2020). *The unwritten rules of the PhD research* (revised ed). London: McGraw Hill/Open University Press.

Single, Peg Boyle. (2011). *Demystifying dissertation writing: a streamlined process from choice of topic to final text.* London: Stylus.

Tom Clark, Tom, Liam Foster, & Alan Bryman. (2019). *How to do your social research project or dissertation.* London: Oxford University Press.

Collecting and Analyzing Data

28

28.1 Role in Survival and Success

Most travelers will want to collect various things while on a trip that they will later treasure as they reflect upon their travel journeys. While these treasured collectibles will obviously vary from one person to another, there are some typical ways that travelers chronicle their journeys, including capturing digital or video images. Some professionals bring more sophisticated photographic equipment. Many travelers will retain their travel itinerary, travel books and maps, or brochures that they picked up along the way to trigger their memories of their travel adventures. Others will capture visual images that have particular meaning to them. Sometimes, the best memories of a journey are the experiences remembered with the people one traveled with or met along the way.

Data collection and analysis within the research process has certain similarities to the above travel illustration. An essential difference is that collecting data as you complete your thesis or dissertation research must be done in a systematic manner, and often not as conveniently as most expect. In addition to providing the means to answer the research questions of your approved research proposal, your data collection process must be fully compliant with all applicable laws, regulations, policies, and procedures, and of course consistent with the approvals previously granted for your research project. The importance of systematically and properly collecting, securing, and protecting data cannot be overstated. Protecting the rights of study participants must also be fully ensured throughout the research process, and this begins even before the actual data collection. Since there are a multitude of ways to conduct data collection and analysis, most travelers will consult more experienced guides for directions.

Some disciplines will have preferred rules for handling data, or certain projects will not allow for deviation from imposed guidelines, whether those constraints are from the field itself, a project's funders or grantors, or even by a student's many tutors and advisors. Other subject areas allow for a wide range of methods for dealing with the data for your type of project. If you are required to propose data collection and data

© The Author(s), under exclusive license to Springer Nature Switzerland AG 2021   147
R. S. Fleming and M. Kowalsky, *Survival Skills for Thesis
and Dissertation Candidates*, Springer Texts in Education,
https://doi.org/10.1007/978-3-030-80939-3_28

analysis methods of your own choosing, you should simultaneously consider the goals of your project and your research question(s), and the analysis steps you will be expected to take, as well as your plans for increasing your skill and rigor in these areas. While these may be the most difficult parts of the journey for most thesis and dissertation travelers, they may prove to be the most satisfying. Learning the skills necessary for professionals in your field will only make you more valuable to it.

28.2 What You Need to Know

As you complete your research activities, you will be collecting information that is either quantitative, qualitative, or both, and your data activities should be designed to enable you to answer your research questions. The research questions stated and approved in your research proposal will largely dictate the nature of the required data, the sources of that data, and the appropriate methods you should employ in producing a quality project. There are standard ways to analyze data, both numeric and textual. You will need to take the time to learn these methods and to apply them skillfully. While many thesis and dissertation projects involve the collection of data from survey participants through surveys or interviews, others involve instrumentation or the use of data that has already been collected. Knowing which parameters and rules apply to you, and then setting aside time to research how to perform the operational and statistical processes required of you will be essential. However, recording unauthorized data that you did not have permission to gather, or including fabricated data or analysis in any part of your project could put you in a precarious legal and ethical position. Check the format and nature of your potential data to ensure that you are within guidelines provided by your advisor, institution or discipline.

You will want to learn best practices and tools for safely storing your data and accessing it as needed. It is essential that you try all of the available options for data procedures in advance before contacting your first participant or sample. In that way, your first attempt at using a procedure or practicing a method is not on your most important thesis or dissertation content, but on preliminary information on which you can practice. If you have not learned enough yet to make an informed and scholarly decision about your project, ask for direction from your research advisor and/or committee to procure initial information on what it is you should learn. Many faculty members consider independent learning of new techniques time well spent, since it applies specifically to your own project. Also consider a system to back up your data as you are collecting it, in case something goes wrong, and ensure that this backup method is within university policies and guidelines. Some sensitive data may not be safe to put into free online storage; investigate if your institution has particular rules or recommendations regarding which tools are most secure, encrypted, or protected.

The important survival skill here is developing a habit of keeping backups of the details of your project's trajectory, especially as you test out your new skills on your project's data or as you make revisions from advisors' suggestions. These will always help you in sharing your project details accurately with your committee and later, with experts in your discipline. And of course, extra copies will help you find your last known version when your computer crashes! Similarly, a simple running list of all of the actions you are taking with your data can help you step back in time as needed, to change direction at the suggestion of your advisor or to correct mistakes you may not have realized earlier. Although it may be tempting, don't try to analyze the data before it is all collected unless that is an explicit part of your approved method. Doing analysis too early might unduly influence your data collection process.

28.3   Student Experiences and Suggestions: *When the Journey Does Not Feel Like Your Own*

Late in their thesis or dissertation journey, some students report feeling like they are carrying out someone else's project. The steps they need to carry out in the methods section of their project seem like they were better suited for their professors, and the steps they need to take next may even seem like activities they would have never chosen if they could somehow start their project again. These feelings of alienation or uncertainty are actually quite expected when learning to do new types of thinking or figuring out how to deal with unfamiliar processes. Some students never really feel comfortable with their data or analysis methods, and that is fine. Most people do not become an expert at something on their first try, especially when learning sophisticated research processes.

It is imperative that you meticulously follow all of your institution's policies and procedures regarding the collection, storage, manipulation, and use of data. Conscientious compliance with these policies and procedures will ensure that you are taking the necessary precautions to protect the components of your research study. While most students easily comply with guidelines, of course there are some who do not determine in advance or practice trials of which tests they will run. Some encountered difficulties in dealing with missing or incomplete data, since they did not spend enough time reading about these issues or talking with others who have used similar methods. Others find out quickly where the likely trouble spots exist in their own level of understanding of data processes. Ideally they would have thought through many of these issues before data collection, but we all know that hindsight can be 20/20!

Many students learn how to use software programs or data tools by assisting senior students or faculty members with projects other than their own. Others learn by testing their intended procedures on sample data or by working through online tutorials. A few students have admitted that they just tried out a technique for the first time on their recently collected data, only to find out that they forgot several important steps and had to start over again, procuring new data because of a mistake that could not be corrected until it was too late. Practicing will probably build your confidence and help you learn about all of the options before you need to use them on the final project. Although most students felt like the momentum of their project stalled while they took a break from their travels, they later realized that it was fine to be a beginner again, at least for a while, as they learned some new skills in data analysis that were required for ultimately completing their projects.

A few students ended up with disastrous results because they rushed through particular stages or parts of their projects. These students became impatient and started analyzing their early data before it was all available. Doing so can inappropriately influence your data collection activities as well as waste your time, and naturally these students spent a lot of energy drawing conclusions that were ultimately incomplete and incorrect. Others were more successful in finding mentors or tutors, in taking new workshops or classes, in making appointments with their former professors, or in creating study groups among other students who were also at the data analysis stage or who were all using similar methods in their projects. In this way, graduate students can assemble a team of resources from whom to learn and with whom to consult. Often others can help troubleshoot in advance as well as figure out what went wrong, since they are viewing your own project with a fresh perspective. If you properly design and implement your data procedures and allow sufficient time for them to work, you will usually be pleased with the resulting data quality, which makes the rest of your manuscript that much easier to write.

28.4   Things to DO

- Determine the most appropriate data sources and collection methods in advance of any data collection activities.
- Meticulously follow your institution's policies and procedures for data collection, storage, manipulation, and the protection of human subjects.
- Be realistic in forecasting and allocating the necessary time to learn and then to complete data analysis activities.
- Review any proposed changes in your data plans with your research advisor.
- Allow realistic and sufficient time for seeking out and using best practices in your field.
- Run an analysis on sample data before analyzing the data that you collected.
- Ensure that your data is properly recorded and backed up throughout the collection and analysis stages of your project.

28.5   Things NOT to Do

- Fail to protect the rights of research subjects in all data collection and analysis activities.
- Inadvertently post online, in an unprotected digital location, or share accidentally any data for which participant identifiers have not been removed.
- Select a data analysis method because it is easy or simply because it is the only one you know.

- Attempt to use a data analysis software tool before taking the time to learn how to use it properly.
- Pretend that a data collection, storage, or analysis problem does not exist, or delay reporting it.
- Assume a member of your resource team will help you perform every step, or will do it for you because you do not know how.
- Misrepresent your data or provide inaccurate or incomplete data.

Bibliography

Glatthorn, A. A. (2005). *Writing the winning dissertation: a step-by-step guide.* Corwin Press.

Nicol, Adelheid A. M., and Penny M. Pexman. (2010). *Displaying your findings: a practical guide for creating figures, posters, and presentations.* Washington, DC: American Psychological Association.

Nicol, Adelheid A. M., and Penny M. Pexman. (2010). *Presenting your findings: a practical guide for creating tables.* Washington, DC: American Psychological Association.

Interpreting Research Findings

29

29.1 Role in Survival and Success

After returning from an extended trip for which you had high expectations, it is not unusual to compare your experiences to the expectations that you had prior to travel. Ideally, your travel experience not only met but exceeded your expectations, and was a worthwhile journey that you would recommend to others. This desirable outcome would clearly justify the time, costs, and sacrifices that you made to undertake the journey. The insights you gained through your travels would also enable you to provide valuable recommendations and guidance to future travelers.

The same is true when it comes to successful thesis and dissertation travel. After you have collected and analyzed your data using various statistical methods, coding schemes, or systematic methods, there comes a point in your research journey where you will want to interpret your research findings. Your results can be summarized into indicators of significance, strength of association, themes, or standard evaluative conclusions related to your method. Now is the time to interpret for others what those summaries, evaluations, and conclusions really mean.

It is true that multiple interpretations of a particular trip or destination can vary in nature and quality based on the traveler, the time spent on the journey or since arrival, and other factors. While some travelers loved a particular route or location or attraction, others may have hated it. However, more or less, authentic evaluations of the same item will often provide a baseline reaction that is shared by most. Your particular project, and the results that you will uncover, may share in this variation among other projects in your field or other approaches to the same topic as yours. However, there is probably less variability in the analysis of the data you have collected; the data actually just "say what they say," and it is your job to report this. In discussing your interpretation of the data, however, you are able to characterize and contextualize the data collected within the parameters of your research questions and purpose of the study. This last section of your manuscript, often

© The Author(s), under exclusive license to Springer Nature Switzerland AG 2021   153
R. S. Fleming and M. Kowalsky, *Survival Skills for Thesis*
and Dissertation Candidates, Springer Texts in Education,
https://doi.org/10.1007/978-3-030-80939-3_29

designated as discussion of the findings, will help you situate your project within the aims and purposes of your investigation, thus showing how and why undertaking this project was important, in the scholarly sense.

29.2   What You Need to Know

You likely had a particular goal in mind when originally proposing your research project. Review this overarching goal and your research topic, and explain how the results found in this particular project help you, others, or the field at large understand the topic. Revisit the research questions you drafted, and attempt to address them using the results, conclusions, and summaries from your findings. This is not the time to tell readers how much you personally have grown as a result of the thesis and dissertation process. Instead, focus your efforts on how your study can help others in your field to learn more about a particular phenomenon, group of people, pattern or outcome, or any other important scholarly information on your topic.

It is now the time to answer a number of important questions. Did your study attain its ultimate goal? Explain how it did, and then where it perhaps did not go far enough. One way to think of this is in terms of your project's nature, significance, and impact. Did you find anything new or unexpected? Did you confirm previous research? Explain what the data revealed. What is its significance in your context; in other words, why was this study important to do? What does it help us to know more about in this field, and why is that important?

Again, you can provide your answers to these questions in a scholarly context, not in a personal one. How would you do this study differently if you had to do it again? What is the potential impact of what you know now from the results? How can your study's results be used for other important purposes, decisions, or changes? Why is your study ultimately important to further work in your field? These types of questions may seem like future predictions, but they can indeed be based on the facts you have provided through the data you have collected. Try not to overstate your project's importance in the overall landscape of your discipline, but also do not diminish the role it has played in investigating something not yet studied.

Lastly you can provide information to others working in the same area as you. What recommendations would you make to future researchers? How might this line of inquiry be extended to include more or different projects? What related studies could be done by you or others which would inform a related aspect of your particular topic or field? Although you may feel that you are not qualified to make some of these recommendations, write them up as honestly and as detailed as possible, and your research advisor or committee members will help you to revise your tone or scope as part of the review process. Striving for a realistic and accurate interpretation of your research findings, when done in detail and based on your actual data, is a survival skill which can be valued by others for many years to come through the context and suggestions you provide in your manuscript.

29.3 Student Experiences and Suggestions: *Continual Lessons from Your Travels*

After completing your data analysis, the time has come to consider what you have learned that will enable you to answer the research questions that served as a basis for your travels. Many students felt that arriving at this stage of the journey took a long time. And most found it difficult to consider their research findings in light of their research goal and questions. Even graduate students may need help in determining whether their work was successful in fully answering the research questions that they identified early in their journey. But nearly all students said that their advisors encouraged them to attempt to make the interpretations connections for themselves, and in writing, before waiting for help from others. In fact, this would be the best time for the students to show the depth of their understanding and their ability to work at the graduate level. Your credibility as a thesis or dissertation traveler is at stake!

Some students struggled with trying to explain their data clearly, and others found it difficult to articulate what the data was actually revealing. Many learned in their research methods course that it was important to be totally honest in considering whether their research project fully accomplished its intended purpose. It is not unusual for someone receiving their masters or doctoral degree to have completed a project that did not show a successful treatment or a clear correlation of variables. However, accurate reporting of the data which was collected is imperative. Your research advisor and committee members will expect nothing less from you, as a candidate that they are mentoring to become a professional in their field. Several students discovered that they needed to discuss the ways in which their research project did not fully address the research questions that they had in mind when planning their journey.

In reporting their findings, some students felt embarrassed to discuss the challenges that they encountered during their research journey, especially when putting them in writing for all to see. One student felt overly confident that their project contained an amazing discovery, but they found out later after their committee's review that some calculations were incorrect. Another graduate student had the opposite issue, since they had misinterpreted a calculation which resulted in great significance for their project. This is why advisors are there to check your work. Some students exchanged manuscripts with their classmates, and others found writing groups, hoping they might notice large errors in advance of submitting work to their advisors and committees. Naturally, lessons learned from any research project which was well designed and rigorously carried out, even if those lessons were not the ones expected, can help researchers in the future by illuminating new aspects of the problem or identifying which paths were not as useful for travel.

A few students acknowledged that they certainly should have been more informed than their committee members regarding the specifics of their travels. Yet students who did not look to their committee members or other experts for guidance missed some opportunities for valuable feedback. One student still could not articulate the big picture of their research findings, even near the end of their journey. Thankfully, one committee member helped them prepare by providing detailed feedback for a specified time so that the student could acquire new skills to add parts of their discussion which were missing. Another found a writing tutor helpful to find weaknesses in their analysis, even if the tutor could not help interpret the data for them. And one student was determined to understand, express, and verify the significance of their work, so they revised their data analysis sections over and over again. By the time they were finished, their manuscript sounded so professional, like something you might see in a journal. Then again, that was essentially the goal in the first place!

29.4   Things to DO

- Examine your research findings in light of your research goal and questions.
- Determine the extent to which the study was successful in answering your project's research questions.
- Identify where your study did not fully address your research questions.
- Determine and discuss the significance and impact of your research study.
- Detail ways you would conduct the study differently if you had to do it again.
- Discuss the practical implications of your research findings.
- Identify recommendations that you would make to future researchers.

29.5   Things NOT to Do

- Forget to discuss the nature, significance, impact, and limitations of your research.
- Avoid discussing the design, collection, or analysis challenges of conducting your study accurately and honestly.
- Provide random or unrelated recommendations for future related research.
- Ignore direction from your committee and other professors about how to interpret both expected and unusual findings from your study.
- Fail to prepare your drafts according to the requirements and level of detail required by your department, institution, and discipline.

Bibliography

Allen, Jan E. (2019). *The productive graduate student writer: how to manage your time, process, and energy to write your research proposal, thesis, and dissertation and get published.* Sterling, VA: Stylus.

Garson, G. D. (2002). *Guide to writing empirical papers, theses, and dissertations.* Marcel Dekker.

Hale, S., & Napier, J. (2013). *Research methods in interpreting: a practical resource.* Bloomsbury Publishing.

Developing a First Full Draft Manuscript

30

30.1 Role in Survival and Success

Some travelers will decide to share their travels with others by documenting their journey in a written travel chronicle, or other published work. In doing so they have the opportunity to share their travel experience with others, including those who may have an interest in taking a similar trip in the future and desire to glean travel insights from their travel experiences. While such a writing exercise may be intended to produce nothing more than a letter to share with relatives or friends, some travelers will actually seek publication of their travel documentary in some written form, whether in a travel magazine or as a travel book. As you might expect we might say here, a typical outcome for your thesis or dissertation project is a journal article or possible monograph.

Preparation of your thesis or dissertation manuscript is similar to documentation of your travels is that in both activities, you are writing about your travel experience at the end of your journey, and relaying to others what has happened and what you thought of it. A difference is that the preparation of a thesis or dissertation manuscript is not an option at the pleasure of the thesis or dissertation traveler; rather it is a formidable requirement in completing the prescribed research process and earning your academic degree. And of course, another difference is in the scholarly tone you must take when recounting your background, steps, and outcomes on paper. Following the accepted format in your field and from your university's program will be an important part of the presentation of your work. Even the best projects will not arrive at their destination successfully if the presentation of their research processes is haphazard or incomplete.

Just as you would want to ensure that the first draft of a travel article or book "sold" itself and complied with the editorial guidelines of a prospective publication outlet, you will want to ensure that the first full draft that you share with your research committee is a stellar document that fully complies with all content and stylistic requirements. Submitting such a quality work product will save you much

R. S. Fleming and M. Kowalsky, *Survival Skills for Thesis and Dissertation Candidates*, Springer Texts in Education, https://doi.org/10.1007/978-3-030-80939-3_30

work later, as well as instill your committee's confidence in you as a proficient and professional researcher. For example, if your final manuscript submission must ultimately be written according to APA format (in other words, by the standard guidelines for academic papers from the American Psychological Association), then your first full draft must indeed exactly follow these guidelines. Your paper should look as close to a finished product as possible. It is unfair of you to ask committee members to read for content only and not for formatting. We recommend that both quality content and quality format must both be present in even the earliest versions of any scholarly paper at the graduate level.

30.2 What You Need to Know

Developing a first full draft manuscript is both an important activity and milestone in your thesis or dissertation journey. It should not be rushed, nor the task taken lightly. This draft should reflect your best work; if it does not, your journey of revisions will take all that much longer, and include back-tracks and detours which may seem to delay your travels more than is comfortable. By putting in work on the details before sharing, and offering a top quality draft of your entire manuscript, you display seriousness of intent and respect for the process. You should expect to receive feedback on your first full draft from your research committee that will likely trigger an iterative series of revisions to this draft. Many requests for changes are considered normal at this high level of performance and scholarly peer review. However, the more you can do to align this initial manuscript with the final expectations for your thesis or dissertation, the more subsequent work and frustration you will avoid for both yourself and your committee members.

When putting together the first part of your thesis or dissertation proposal and your results and analysis/discussion into one full paper, it is important to make sure that your final document sounds like it is indeed all about the same project. Sometimes you have made changes to your thinking, your protocol, or your research questions which now will require adjusting in order to reflect what you really did and what you really found. Many students have used a "fake it 'til you make it" process, in writing up parts of their study that they didn't really understand at the time those parts were composed. Now is the time to check your document for everything from weak arguments or thin connections with the literature to run-on sentences and mistakes of future tense (i.e., your paper still says you "will" take some steps, although that task has already been done for some time now).

In fact, many advisors will not even read a first full draft if it does not appear very close in formatting style to a finished thesis or dissertation. It is therefore important to develop a first full draft in the style of a final draft. The more you fix early in the process, the easier your revisions will be later. Following the successful formats of others, especially paper examples by graduates in your program who completed in the years immediately before you, is a survival skill which can save much time and energy.

30.3 Student Experiences and Suggestions: *Crafting a Complete Travel Story*

While the members of your research committee will have had opportunities to learn about various aspects of your travels during the earlier stages of your research journey, they will look forward to having the opportunity to review a completed draft. A full manuscript containing all of the appropriate parts makes your work seem more similar to the previously published works that you quoted in your literature review. Some students found the published literature to provide great examples of how to write up many aspects of their thesis or dissertation project. Others found that their skills were not quite good enough to provide their advisors with a journal-like manuscript. In either case, nearly all students came to recognize that any unpublished work is essentially a draft document, and that they should anticipate required revisions based on the feedback that they received from the members of their research committee.

A few students claimed that they were not interested in publishing as a professional once their degrees were awarded. Even so, they could not be lazy, since offering their best work in any shared manuscript still got them closer to being finished with that project. Most students explained that investing the time necessary to develop a high-quality draft manuscript the first time around had reduced the number and scope of later revisions they needed make. Others noticed that even when they submitted substandard work, and could list all of the flaws of their manuscript even though they were not sure how to fix them, being honest about what help was still needed worked best. Students in certain fields remembered being told that their first full draft manuscript should demonstrate to their faculty and academics in their discipline that they are capable of being a serious scholar within their field. Therefore, continuous effort on improvements is likely the best course of action for all graduate students.

Students may not always appreciate critical feedback on parts of the project on which they worked harder than they ever had in their school career. Some students report that even those faculty members who were enthusiastic about joining them on their journey became frustrated or angry at the quality of work they had submitted according to the directions given. These students later learned that they were expected to do even more than the minimum revisions advised by their committees, and to make noticeable improvements to the substance of the work before resubmitting. One student said their advisor felt that they disrespected their time by asking the advisor to review a version which contained only minimal changes. Other students could not get their advisors to specify the ways that their manuscript was lacking, yet still withheld formal approval. In these cases, it is important to find others knowledgeable in your field to help review your work and determine areas in which it is not yet acceptable. A few students thought that since their work was perpetually in draft form, that it did not require their best effort in proofreading either. However, this made their work seem unfinished and amateur to their committee members.

One student admitted that it took significant effort to regain the respect of the members of their research committee over an error-filled manuscript after an otherwise productive relationship on the project up to that point. Wondering what had gone wrong, the student asked his research supervisor why the project was suddenly not reviewed positively by their committee members. The student soon understood that the presentation of the work was not of professional writing quality, and it still had spelling and grammatical errors, formatting mistakes, and illegible data graphs which did not conform to any standard citation style of the university. Notably, even the best work can seem haphazard or rushed if it is not presented in the required formal style of your program, university, or discipline. Good quality work, even if not solving the world's most essential problems, can still garner praise for its substance, clarity, and completeness. Multiple students point out that feedback from their committee members will almost always trigger the need to make iterative revisions before the document is revealed to the world. Since most peer review processes work this was as well, catching mistakes or weaknesses in your work prior to publication can only enhance your project's reception in the field.

30.4 Things to DO

- Recognize that the time you invest in developing a high-quality first full draft manuscript will pay dividends later in the process in terms of reducing the things you will need to fix.
- Recognize that your first full draft will play an instrumental role in how your committee members will perceive you from this point forward.
- Realize the importance of not wasting the time of your committee members by sending them a manuscript draft that is deficient.
- Review other theses and dissertations that can provide insights as you prepare your first full draft.
- Recognize the importance of viewing everything as tentative until the final copy of your thesis or dissertation is accepted.

30.5 Things NOT to Do

- Fail to take the time to produce and submit a high-quality document that conforms to requirements and expectations.
- Spend too little time proofreading your document before submitting it.
- Dismiss the importance of not wasting the time of your committee members by sending them a manuscript draft that is deficient.
- Add random or extraneous information in order to make your paper longer.
- Be lazy and submit a document that does not represent your best work.

Bibliography

Casanae, Christine Pearson. (2020). *During the dissertation: a textual mentor for doctoral students in the process of writing.* Ann Arbor: University of Michigan Press.

Guerin, C., & Aitchison, C. (2014). *Writing groups for doctoral education and beyond innovations in practice and theory.* Taylor & Francis.

Van, Wagenen R. K. (1991). *Writing a thesis: substance and style.* Englewood Cliffs, NJ: Prentice Hall.

Receiving Feedback on Your Draft Manuscript

31

31.1 Role in Survival and Success

There are a great many instances in life where we do not get something right the first time, particularly if it is something in which we do not yet have much experience. An example of this would be submitting our first travel work to the editor of a desired publication outlet. While it will typically be rare not to receive feedback, including requested or recommended changes on any such submission, what one does with the feedback received will be instrumental in the successful publication of your travel story or book. Similarly, your travel editor might want different photos, with sharper focus on the details or visual images of a different aspect of the landscape. Instead of being angry about this, you would likely try to meet the magazine's expectations and produce the necessary items within a reasonable time frame.

Of course, the same is true with respect to the feedback that you should expect to receive regarding the first full draft manuscript that you submitted, as well as for one or many subsequent draft submissions. As discussed in the previous chapter, you will want to prepare your best effort and put your best foot forward with your first full draft manuscript. That being said, you must be prepared to receive informed, critical feedback from your research advisor and other committee members even if your submitted draft is the best writing you have ever done in your life. The expertise that your committee members apply regarding their knowledge of how good research is conducted, and any time they take to prepare insightful comments to assist you, should be appreciated in terms of their contribution to your resulting high-quality thesis or dissertation. While it can be difficult to receive and process their comments, emotional reactions should be secondary to academic ones. The comments are not about you as a person, but rather about the quality of the presentation you have provided. Heed these comments even if you may not agree with them at first; in fact, you may not know enough about academics in your field to see the value of these seemingly unusual adjustments yet.

R. S. Fleming and M. Kowalsky, *Survival Skills for Thesis and Dissertation Candidates*, Springer Texts in Education, https://doi.org/10.1007/978-3-030-80939-3_31

Effective time management will be an important component of your thesis or dissertation travel, and it is especially important when working with your research advisor. You will want to ensure that you allocate the necessary time to complete your revision work properly in advance of established deadlines. While you will certainly have various personal and professional responsibilities concurrent with this journey, you will want to do all within your power to prioritize and allocate your time so as to fulfill your academic responsibilities in a professional and timely manner. Do not let requests for revisions set you onto a journey of negative emotions; rather, respond to the academic improvements requested to the best of your ability and study more about particular areas if needed. Since you are expecting the same type of reliability in your advisor, offering your best and most timely work displays a measure of respect that you will likely receive in turn when feedback is provided.

31.2   What You Need to Know

Try not to conclude that you have submitted a perfect manuscript; there is always more to do, and revisions are a natural and important part of the process even for experts who have done this task many times before. You may feel that the initial feedback you received was too harsh, or too critical, or too detail-oriented, but in fact these are the hallmarks of useful feedback for a thesis or dissertation. You are entering a profession of people who can critique anything, and do so in the professional peer-reviewed literature for decades of their lives. In learning how to compose a quality manuscript, you too will realize that negative feedback is not necessarily a personal attack. Honest comments of the positive, negative, or neutral varieties are meant to improve your research project and make it more like the published literature which you have seen in library databases. You are nearly ready to join a group of well-established travelers with similar interests!

Reasonable expectations regarding the deadlines for your submissions and the quality of your submissions should be clearly understood. You will also want to be on the same page regarding the turn-around time you should expect. In other words, obtain an estimate from your research advisor about how much time will pass between the time you submit work to them and the time you will receive feedback. These types of inquiries, when made humbly and earnestly, will help manage expectations of all travelers. You should also discuss the type of feedback you can anticipate receiving from your research advisor, and the depth and speed of revisions required.

You will also want to always remember that your research advisor also has numerous demands on their time including teaching classes, conducting their own research, authoring journal articles or books, and supervising the work of other thesis or dissertation students. You should thus be patient as you await feedback on work that you have submitted, realizing that just as you were likely most productive when you found sufficient time to devote your undivided attention to your work, so too will your advisor need to carve out similar time to dedicate to reviewing your work and providing the feedback that you anxiously await.

Make corrections thoroughly and with enough detail so you can be proud of your explanations of the ways in which you fixed items properly. When in doubt, go back to your research advisor for more specific advice, and look for other readers to help unlock your thinking. Spend some time pondering your revisions before turning in the changes, since thesis or dissertation travel is not a race. Do what is asked of you and do it well, even if it takes longer than you would like. Accepting criticism gracefully and then acting on it conscientiously is indeed a high-level survival skill, and a sign of a true professional!

31.3 Student Experiences and Suggestions: *Waiting for News from the Road*

For most thesis or dissertation candidates, the ability to wait patiently to hear back from their research committee is something that does not come naturally. The anxiety, stress, or anticipation of criticism affects everyone, but in different ways. Most students can recall in vivid detail their experiences of waiting to hear back from their research advisor about work they had submitted for review. While some students managed not to become frustrated, others began to annoy their advisor or committee members with questions or changes before the professors had a chance to fully review the work. A few found out subsequently, through admonishments from their committee members, that impatience was not rewarded either. A graduate student said that their advisor explained that since their work was not created in a weekend, hence its review cannot likely be accomplished that quickly either. Yet all students admitted that work of better quality was returned more quickly to students, even if the number of comments received varied widely.

Many students recounted that they had trouble managing their anxiety or emotions as they waited for what seemed like an eternity to receive feedback from their committee members on the draft manuscripts that they had submitted. Some were quite excited to receive their reviews but then became upset at the amount of work that still had to be done in order for their project to meet the minimum requirements. Others assumed the worst with each passing day, but then were pleasantly surprised at the positive feedback they received. Moving your attention to a different topic or task, or even taking a well-deserved break while waiting for comments from your advisors is certainly helpful in alleviating any stress you may assign to this experience. For all students, recognizing the value of the feedback that they received and carefully considering and utilizing suggestions from readers were important learning experiences which enhanced their manuscript, even if those experiences were difficult ones at the time.

While patiently awaiting the feedback on their draft manuscripts, one student grew more and more angry with each passing day at not having heard from any member of their committee. Only later did the student learn that the usual approach in their program was to have their research committee set up a meeting to discuss the work among themselves after all had read the document, and then to have the chair meet with the student to go over the comments that were offered. It was important for that student to find out expectations from their chair and department in advance, instead of guessing about what might happen next. Other students report that they are encouraged to contact members of their committee freely and regularly as issues arise, thus solving problems before adding corrections to the full manuscript. Again, knowing which processes are required by your institution or preferred by your committee members will avoid many awkward interactions related to feedback.

Most students who subsequently publish their thesis or dissertation in a professional journal have shared that the feedback loop on articles or books was remarkably similar to that employed by their graduate programs. Since critical or negative feedback is expected in academic work, and specifically from those who do not know you via a blind peer review, this part of the process was not only seen by the students as necessary but also later viewed as helpful. Some students who were nervous at first when hearing of problems with their manuscript or project elements ended up being relieved that they now knew what to correct in order to prevent future negative critique. Even when other students found some official comments surprising or insulting, their advisors asked them to appreciate the time that each reviewer had offered to conscientiously consider their work and provide insightful comments to help them make the necessary revisions.

31.4   Things to DO

- Anticipate receiving constructive feedback from your advisor and committee members as you labor to transform your first full draft to a final manuscript.
- Recognize the importance and value of the feedback that you receive.
- Maintain your composure in reacting to feedback that you receive.
- Carefully review all feedback received, seeking clarification as necessary.
- Utilize the feedback received to make necessary revisions to your manuscript.

31.5   Things NOT to Do

- Conclude that you have submitted a perfect manuscript that will require few, if any, changes.
- Assume that your one correction for each suggestion will be accepted by your advisors without question.
- Become impatient when waiting for feedback from your committee members.
- Negatively react to feedback received on your work or become adversarial regarding requested changes to your draft.
- Try to talk your advisors out of some of the revisions they've requested, or try to create arguments among committee members in the process.

Bibliography

Barron, E. (2014). *The PhD experience: an insider's guide*. Palgrave Macmillan.

Calabrese, Raymond L, and Page A. Smith. (2010). *Faculty mentor's wisdom: conceptualizing, writing, and defending the dissertation*. Lanham, MD: Rowman & Littlefield Education.

Pretorius, Luke., Macaulay, Linette., & Cahusac de Caux, Basil. (2019). *Wellbeing in doctoral education: insights and guidance from the student experience*. Singapore: Springer Nature.

Making Appropriate Revisions to Your Manuscript

32

32.1 Role in Survival and Success

The editorial feedback received by a traveler who aspires to have their travel work published should be considered and responded to seriously. The extent to which the writer can understand, address, and incorporate solutions suggested by a well-intentioned reader will determine the likelihood of future acceptance and publication of their work. While you might not fully agree with all or part of what was asked to be changed, failure to respond to those changes properly will determine if you are just a traveler with a personal story to tell or a published author with a wealth of research information to share. The revision process for most writers is just as important as originating the manuscript in the first place. Revision is where rough patches get ironed out, errors or detours are fixed, and missing information is inserted. Just like travel, any portion of an itinerary traveled a second time will include adjustments to the route, and more detail in the scenery and attractions observed and described. These enhancements ensure accomplishment of the steps for each subsequent passage and with each new set of travelers who are following with you on your path.

Your research advisor and other committee members have taken the time to prepare and provide to you many types of feedback as a candidate under their supervision, often over a journey of multiple years. You will want to pause to understand fully and conscientiously any and all changes that they are recommending or requiring, and then commit to incorporating these changes as appropriate in your evolving manuscript. Rather than simply making each change in the simplest and quickest way possible, you should critically consider each one in terms of its contribution to enhancing your final thesis or dissertation manuscript. There must be some reason why these experienced researchers are "flagging" particular parts of your manuscript; strive to figure out the paper's underlying weaknesses and improve any other areas of the document which these changes might have affected.

171
R. S. Fleming and M. Kowalsky, *Survival Skills for Thesis and Dissertation Candidates*, Springer Texts in Education, https://doi.org/10.1007/978-3-030-80939-3_32

32.2   What You Need to Know

You may receive conflicting feedback from your committee members, and you may even receive contradictory suggestions from your main research advisor within a few weeks or months of each other. This often happens as a manuscript is in development, with smaller sections being reviewed more intensely than others. It may even occur as your readers have had more time to think about your project and discover additional ways to improve it. Navigating these recommendations successfully takes critical thinking skills on your part as well. What is the nature of the change they are seeking? What problem does it solve, or what weakness does it attempt to correct, in your writing or experiment?

Determining the reason for the critique may help you to improve your manuscript more than you may realize, but don't over-correct! Just like carefully planned travel steps, changing one item unnecessarily may impact a variety of other items which appear before or after, and whose correct explanations may be dependent on that newly-changed section. While you are making the suggested advisor revisions, be sure to ask in advance if you see for yourself another item which might benefit from a small revision. Your advisors will know if these changes are substantially different from what they have already approved. It is acceptable to adjust things in your paper "in the spirit of" the provided comments, as you try to learn from the comment about the weaker points of your document. Just making a cosmetic change in order to get the process over as soon as possible could lead to even more rounds of corrections later. Instead, research and prepare thoughtful corrections and note their locations in your paper so you can point to them easily.

You will likely receive many rounds of corrections, with some "wrong things" remaining in the manuscript until the very last minute, either because no one caught them, or they were overlooked in favor of other or larger corrections. Don't beat yourself up; even the best thesis and dissertations may have conceptual or grammatical mistakes in them that should have been noticed earlier. This is why your paper goes through multiple rounds of readers, each likely looking for something different, and each finding new items to fix easily in a project so large. Trust that multiple readers are not trying to stop you from achieving your goal, but rather they are seeking to help you produce a worthy scholarly product by the time it is presented and published.

Do the best you can, and improve every time. Don't just submit a few quick changes and expect it all to be done. Changes are usually many, and some substantial, in each round of feedback, no matter how good a writer you are. You should expect anywhere from two or three to ten rounds of feedback on your work. Make time to understand and learn more about the improvements suggested, as this is an overlooked survival skill. A conscientious effort that is not rushed will be rewarded with seamless transition to the next paperwork and approval stages. The best thesis or dissertation is a done one, so do what it takes to get to the finish line in style!

32.3   **Student Experiences and Suggestions: *Enhancing the Value of Your Travels for Others***

Some students are expected to show their full understanding of the feedback provided during formal reviews in various ways, and other students are asked to respond to all suggestions or concerns expressed by the members of their research committees. Whichever way your program requires this, it is up to you to discern your next steps and carry them out as requested. Some students were ready to quickly make the suggested revisions, while others needed help in understanding or interpreting what was required. Certain advisors encouraged students to proceed only after fully researching and appreciating the need for the particular revisions listed. Although many students report receiving recommendations that appear to be in direct conflict with each other, these issues were quickly settled by communicating with their research advisor. Most students concluded they were so relieved that they understood the feedback received, getting through this part of the process was cause for a celebration!

A few students, however, were ill-prepared to maintain their composure as they reviewed the comments from their advisors. Some students even initially refused to make the requested changes, and said they needed several weeks to decompress from what they viewed as a traumatic event. Professors would remind students at this point that the critique they have been given is about their project and their manuscript, and it is not meant to be taken as a personal attack, even if the comments sound harsh. Just as it is important to be patient as you await your committee's feedback, it is likewise essential to be gracious in receiving the suggestions that your committee members have taken the time to provide. One student made their dissatisfaction about their manuscript feedback known to their research advisor, committee members, and other faculty and students at their college. While it is certainly possible to debate the validity of any comments that were provided, publicly doing so is not likely to move any student's project forward. This student needed to practice maintaining their composure like a professional, in this and all other interactions they would subsequently have with the members of their research committee.

Some students sought to understand the underlying intent or reasons for recommended changes. They explained that if they themselves were going to be ultimately responsible for any changes made, they needed to figure out why their initial ideas were not appropriate and to learn why the new ways offered were deemed improvements. Most students did this with help from others on their committee, from senior students who had experienced similar issues before, or from contacts in their field who were familiar with the academic publishing process. Not all members of students' committees were on the same page with reactions to their draft manuscripts and the revisions to be recommended. One student described that certain committee members imposed several unrealistic demands regarding changes to the project that they thought were necessary. However, when the student's research advisor learned about this, they were able to mitigate several exaggerated demands and provide clarity for the student on how to proceed in satisfying all committee members by making particular changes.

A few students were surprised at the detail of feedback, and of the difficulty of what they were being asked to do, and were disappointed that they had to make more changes than they had anticipated. One student remembers their research methods professor who continually reminded their class that making revisions was a necessary and expected part of one's thesis or dissertation journey, and that any project without peer review would simply be someone's opinion. The guidance provided by your research advisor, your committee members, and even peer reviewers you may not know, will enable you to enhance the quality and value of your project and thus its credibility within your field and profession. In taking the readers' responses into account, students learned what areas might lead to further questioning and how they could reduce confusion about or misunderstanding of their work. Most students were ultimately relieved that theoretical mistakes, data errors, or flaws in their conclusions were noticed during the review process and not later on in their process, such as during their formal oral presentation, at a conference, or after publication in an academic journal. A conceptual crisis may have indeed been averted!

32.4 Things to DO

- Conscientiously consider and incorporate feedback received from your research advisor and committee members.
- Seek to understand the underlying intent of suggested changes, rather than just making them cosmetically, or as quickly as possible.
- Rely on your research advisor to assist in addressing conflicting or unrealistic demands for changes from other committee members.
- Realize that the time and effort you devote to making necessary revisions will enhance the quality and value of your study, as well as the respect that it receives within your field or profession.

32.5 Things NOT to Do

- Become frustrated with the numerous iterations of feedback you are likely to receive.
- Fail to seek clarification, when necessary, regarding feedback you receive.
- Panic when you receive continual feedback from your research advisor or committee members, even when you thought you might be done.
- Take corrections and suggestions to your manuscript, even if harsh, to mean they are an attack on you personally.
- Lose sight of your desired destination at the end of the journey.

Bibliography

Carter, Susan, & Laurs, Deborah. (2018). *Developing research writing: a handbook for supervisors and advisors*. New York: Routledge.

Murray, Rowena. (2017). *How to write a thesis* (4th ed). London: Open University Press.

Thomson, Pat, & Kamler, Barbara. (2016). *Detox your writing: strategies for doctoral researchers*. New York: Routlege.

Preparing for the Oral Defense

33

33.1 Role in Survival and Success

If you have ever taken a road trip that involved crossing the border and traveling into a different country, you are probably familiar with the reality that border crossings can present their own challenges. By understanding the process and preparing in advance you can be ready to pass muster with the customs agents and continue your journey. While it is not unusual for first-time travelers to be somewhat anxious as they drive up to the border check point, the more familiar you are with the border crossing guidelines, requirements, and process, the more quickly you will be able to cross over and continue on to the next leg of your trip. Specifically, learning about the customs and practices of the country to which you are traveling is likely to help you the most in understanding what to do and how to behave in a new land.

You will find that the same is true in your thesis or dissertation journey, in which most tasks are truly unfamiliar to everyone going through this experience for the first time. In many ways the oral examination or final defense event which you approach the end of your journey is similar to a border crossing experience. Just as taking the time to gain an understanding of what to expect before and during a border crossing from one country to another, you have been learning what is required by this unfamiliar nation and are now ready to seek permission to travel there. Preparing properly in advance to do so will enable you to continue your trip as designed, while avoiding various problems and delays. As you have heard before, taking the time to understand the process and prepare well before your thesis or dissertation defense event can ensure a pleasant, collegial experience.

Following the guidance provided by your research advisor, committee, and institution will enable you to prepare for a successful defense that will allow you to advance to the final steps of your journey and reach the destination that you have worked towards for a number of years. As with most things in life, preparation is the key to success. There is no more important stage of your research journey for which you will need to be fully prepared than your thesis or dissertation defense.

R. S. Fleming and M. Kowalsky, *Survival Skills for Thesis and Dissertation Candidates*, Springer Texts in Education,
https://doi.org/10.1007/978-3-030-80939-3_33

Thorough preparation of your work products, along with thorough preparation of your mind, is a survival skill that needs to be sharpened so that it produces your very best outcome.

33.2 What You Need to Know

Your preparation for your thesis or dissertation defense should begin long before the day of your oral examination. You will want to learn all you can about what to expect when you reach that anticipated, but often intimidating, milestone in your journey. You can do this in various ways, including participating in research courses and seminars and talking to other students after their oral examination experiences. Learning from the experiences of others who have completed their oral examinations and if permitted by your institution, observing the presentations or practice sessions of other candidates, can provide a range of many possible details which you can consider for your own preparation.

You should recognize that the best source of information regarding what to expect during your oral examination is without question your research advisor, especially since they will lead that session. You will want to become totally familiar with the policies and practices of your department, university, and discipline. It will also be essential that you have a "realistic preview" of the format that will be followed by your research advisor and committee in conducting your oral examination, as well as what you should be prepared to do during the examination itself. It is important that you realize that defenses can differ significantly from department to department, and from institution to institution, so follow the cues and style of your research advisor, suggested models, and field or discipline closely.

In the interest of having no surprises on the day of this major event in your journey, you will want to become familiar with a number of logistical matters, including where and when the session will be held, who will be invited or permitted to attend the session, and the anticipated length of the oral examination. You will want to know if other students and/or the public may be in attendance, and prepare accordingly. While it will obviously be your responsibility to review your manuscript and create visuals for the day of the oral examination, your research advisor will also have a role and interest in ensuring that you are fully prepared, since their reputation is also impacted by the success of advisees whose work they have supervised. Your advisor should review with you the purpose and objectives of the oral examination, the format that will be followed, what you will be expected to share in your presentation, the questions that you should anticipate being asked, and other suggestions designed to prepare you for your oral examination. Plan to deliver an awesome performance that will impress your committee members who essentially represent the wide range of critics in your intended discipline.

33.3   **Student Experiences and Suggestions: *Preparing to Share Your Travel Story***

As you progress through your research journey, you will reach a point where you realize that the time has come to share your travel experiences in a formal presentation. Some graduate students have had extensive experience in public talks before they present their work on their thesis or dissertation project. Others may be presenting in public for the first time. Either way, the members of the research committee who guided you throughout your journey, and others who are interested in learning about your research adventures, will be part of your knowledgeable audience. As with many trips that you will take, you cannot proceed without making the necessary travel arrangements; in this case, securing approval to schedule your defense and sharing preliminary examples of what you are likely to discuss at that event.

Many students reported that their research advisor and committee members ensured that they were ready before they agreed to approve their request to schedule this important event. In some ways, your public presentation of results reflects the research journey you are now completing, as well as the supervisory abilities of your faculty committee. Other students were more worried, since they did not feel that they had enough guidance and were expected to be quite independent in their preparation. Some spent unnecessary time worrying, although several others said they felt that they possibly over prepared. Most students explained that their research advisor provided them with a realistic preview of what to expect, and consequently offered advice on how to prepare in advance of this session. Other students were left to seek out their own examples of research talks, learning how others at their university or in their program shared their work and ultimately convinced the members of their committee that they had successfully completed the thesis or dissertation journey.

Most students agreed that their research advisor would not have scheduled their oral examination unless the other members of their committee were also convinced that they had reached a point in their travels where they could successfully share their completed work. Most students also felt they were preparing for what may have been the most serious presentation of their careers thus far. Some were unsure and felt that they were not as confident about the quality of their work and expected harsh critique as audience members examined the details of their research project. Whatever these graduate students were feeling at the time, they knew what was expected of them—that they must be prepared to defend the many decisions made during the course of their work.

In reviewing the posted announcements of upcoming oral examinations, some students were thrilled to see many names that they recognized from previous courses or that they first met when their journeys began. A number of students decided to conduct practice sessions, with their friends role playing the roles of research committee members, in order to calm their nerves by giving their presentation to a supportive audience in advance. Many students enjoyed presenting to their classmates who were familiar with the experiences of developing the project much earlier on, and they were pleased to impress their peers with the depth of work which had occurred since they last talked. Other students were quite entertaining as they asked and answered questions in the style of the examiners, providing essential experience along with humor and some stress relief, as they tried to predict what types of questions would likely be asked during their friends' oral examinations. These practice sessions forced students to not procrastinate in rehearsing their presentation, and also revealed timely analysis of the strengths and weaknesses of their preparation.

Understanding the process that will be followed during your oral examination is a must, according to nearly all graduate students. Many requested a session to review that process with their research advisor, in order to confirm that they properly understood what they would be expected to have prepared. In addition to gathering all of the components, many students found it helpful to try to share their travel story in an informative and persuasive manner, so that audience members had many of their questions answered as the presentation went along. While some students felt they were unprepared to respond to all of the questions that they were asked, many noticed that they felt quite knowledgeable about their project and found most questions to be relatively easy to answer. While it is always possible that you may be asked questions that you had not anticipated, the more you can do to anticipate questions and prepare your responses in advance, the better your presentation will be. As you move through this benchmark in your program and career, now is the time to put forth your most professional performance. If you know that you have done the absolute best that you could, then you will have no regrets!

33.4 Things to DO

- Learn as much as you can about the oral examination process of your department, college, or university.
- Review with your research advisor, and confirm your understanding of the process and format that will be followed during your oral examination.
- At least one day prior to the oral examination, pack all materials that you need to take with you.
- Get appropriate rest, relaxation, and nutrition the day and evening before your oral examination.
- Allow sufficient travel time to arrive early.

33.5 Things NOT to Do

- Fail to fully understand what to expect during the oral examination and prepare for all its details accordingly.
- Procrastinate in preparing to defend your thesis or dissertation.

- Be pessimistic about how things will go during the defense and its outcome.
- Forget that your research advisor would not have scheduled your oral examination unless they and other committee members believed that you were up to the challenge.
- Underestimate the importance of dressing and behaving professionally.

Bibliography

Karkukly, W. (2019). *The art and science of PhD research: a step-by-step guide to achieving a doctorate degree and conducting academic research*. Friesen Press.

Rudestam, Kjell E, and Rae R. Newton. (2015). *Surviving your dissertation: a comprehensive guide to content and process* (4th ed), Thousand Oaks, CA: Sage.

Swetnam, D. (1997). *Writing your dissertation: how to plan, prepare and present your work successfully*. How to Books.

Presenting Your Research During the Oral Defense

34

34.1 Role in Survival and Success

Just as the border agents have the important responsibility of ensuring that a traveler comply with all governmental requirements before passing through their checkpoint, likewise the members of your committee are expected to verify that your research and resulting thesis or dissertation fully meet procedural requirements of your institution as well as scholarly expectations of your discipline. You already understand the critical importance of becoming familiar with the specific process and requirements of your department, college, or university, as well as the expectations of your research advisor and committee regarding this important culminating event in your thesis or dissertation journey. In addition, you must master the content of your own manuscript as well as the literature, methods, and goals of your subject area. Without this understanding, travel through the last portions of your journey will be quite difficult. Therefore, knowing your destination well and following its directions, customs, and traditions is an important survival skill.

You must be prepared to present your research project in an effective manner, covering various essential aspects of your work including the research questions that you sought to answer, what you did to discern the answers to these questions, and an explanation of the findings of your study. Your research advisor will provide you with an understanding of how research is presented in accordance with institutional and department norms. You may already know much about the standards in your field via what you have learned from your literature review, and you may have also investigated academic and professional organizations, attended conferences or read their proceedings, and followed the careers or publications of new or experienced faculty members. This information can help guide you toward the appropriate scholarly levels of performance for your oral examination.

© The Author(s), under exclusive license to Springer Nature Switzerland AG 2021   183
R. S. Fleming and M. Kowalsky, *Survival Skills for Thesis
and Dissertation Candidates*, Springer Texts in Education,
https://doi.org/10.1007/978-3-030-80939-3_34

34.2 What You Need to Know

If you have properly prepared in accordance with the guidance received from your research advisor and other members of your committee, the day you defend your thesis or dissertation will become perhaps the most memorable day of your pilgrimage. It is the day that you finally have the opportunity to formally share your work with your committee and perhaps others before it is made available to the larger academic and professional communities. After your advisor reviews the process to be followed you will be asked to introduce your research and why you selected this topic. Likely your answer should be less personal and emotional and more academic. You will be expected to share your research questions and the methodology you utilized in conducting your research. Your answers should be provided in enough detail so that experts in these methods can judge your rigor and knowledge in enacting the steps of your project. And it will be important that you summarize your findings and the study's limitations, as well as the contribution that your research makes to the existing body of knowledge. Your recommendations for future research along this path of inquiry are also expected.

You should tailor your presentation to take into account your audience, which may be comprised of senior researchers in your field, of faculty members in related fields, and of new thesis or dissertation students. You will need to address the aspects of your work in which you know the audience will be interested, based on the guidance you received from your advisor and other committee members. You will want to remember that you should be the most knowledgeable person in the room regarding your work, and thus present your work with confidence. You will want to deliver your overall presentation, as well as its component parts, in accordance with the time limitations within which you have been asked to work, so as to leave sufficient time for committee members to raise questions, and for you to address each question properly.

While anticipating likely questions in advance is a prudent strategy, you will want to make sure that you always answer the actual question being asked, rather than trying to repeat a related but memorized answer that you have scripted out in advance. You should answer questions in a concise manner, affording committee members the opportunity to ask for further elaboration or clarification as they deem appropriate. Together, your presentation and your responses to committee questions should be informative and persuasive. They should validate your committee's decision that you are prepared to advance to the rank of "researcher" or "scholar," rather than perpetually remain at the level of "student." You should remember that an affirmative decision by your committee attests to not only your work to date, but also the confidence that committee members have in you to continue to conduct academic research without the benefit and oversight of a faculty committee.

34.3 Student Experiences and Suggestions: *Sharing Your Travel Adventures*

As unbelievable as it might seem, there will be a point in your research journey where the time has come to formally share your travel adventures with important and interested individuals. One student remembered that as they entered the room where their oral examination was scheduled, they summoned as much confidence and enthusiasm as they could, knowing that they had already completed a marvelous journey, regardless of any comments provided on that day. Their presentation would simply be the opportunity to officially reveal what they had learned in the years prior, and to share both their good and their bad travel experiences with others. One of the most satisfying aspects of the oral presentation for some students was advising others who may be planning similar journeys.

Another student wanted others to remember that, while there may be other faculty members and perhaps some graduate students in attendance at a dissertation defense presentation, the primary audience that you must be prepared to impress are the members of your research committee. Although many students recall being intimidated during the oral examination process, they were calmed by the fact that they knew what kinds of things the members of their research committee had asked about in the past. If you have followed the guidance of these travel guides throughout your research journey and properly prepared in advance, there should not be any surprises as they fulfill their roles in examining your work. Naturally, even those students with the most thorough plans were surprised when new questions came up; however, these were not critiques but suggestions for future research or interesting observations and wonderings by those who seemed genuinely interested in the project.

A few students were urged by their research methods professor to always begin by taking the time to thank your research advisor and committee members for their willingness to travel with you and provide sound advice throughout your journey. While gratitude usually helps in many ways, it must be sincere. Other students were upset with their committee members or advisor on the day of their oral presentation, and their sarcasm and bitterness was clearly felt by the audience. It is important to remember that while you might not welcome this opportunity to talk for hours about your project and its flaws, there will be time limits that you must respect as you prepare and deliver your presentation. For some students who remained unable to see this as a learning experience, this time limit could not arrive too soon! Most students who were comfortable in presenting their project with all of its complexities felt that the time passed quickly, and they could have talked even longer. Some students did not realize that they would not have time to share all of the details of their research, and subsequently spent too much time explaining different pieces instead of the main points. Another student had prepared to discuss the key aspects of their research and alert the audience to points where they could request more details later in the talk. Most students were asked to focus on the significance of their project, and any limitations of its design, including what they would do differently if they had to start again.

As a seasoned traveler who has now completed a successful research journey you will be expected to answer a number of difficult questions regarding your travels. Some students were reminded by their research advisor to be respectful of all questioners, and to professionally respond to every question that they are asked, even if that meant saying they did not know the answer. While some students viewed the presentation part of their oral examination as the most intimidating aspect, others thought the question and answer period was more stressful. To reduce their anxiety, students remembered that this step has been an essential prerequisite through which every faculty member traveled themselves. Others had heard advice saying it was simply a requirement, noting that the main task was to demonstrate the skills that can support future research journeys. At graduation, one student shared that while they initially viewed their dissertation defense presentation as the end of their journey, they changed their mind after reflecting on the many emotions and activities that day. The student decided that it was also the beginning of many new travel adventures, and their interest in several new ideas had grown out of questions that they were asked during their presentation. Now that's great evidence of learning!

34.4 Things to DO

- Begin by thanking your research advisor and committee members for their willingness to assist you throughout the research process.
- Make sure you cover all key aspects of your research activities in your presentation.
- Realize that you will not have time to deliver a comprehensive presentation of your work.
- Be prepared to discuss any limitations of your study and what you would do differently if you were doing this study again.
- Maintain patience in hearing the details in audience questions and in providing your answers.

34.5 Things NOT to Do

- Fail to allow your research advisor to facilitate the oral examination in the manner that they deem appropriate.
- Show frustration with the process or committee members at any point during the oral examination.
- Avoid actually answering the specific questions asked.
- Allow yourself to become confrontational with committee members.
- Forget to remain professional, confident, and composed throughout the oral examination.

Bibliography

Flamez, Brandé, A. Stephen Lenz, Richard S. Balkin, & Robert L. Smith. (2017). *A counselor's guide to the dissertation process: where to start and how to finish.* New York: Wiley.

Murray, R. (2009). *How to survive your viva: defending a thesis in an oral examination.* Open University Press.

Sterne, N. (2015). *Challenges in writing your dissertation: coping with the emotional, interpersonal, and spiritual struggles.* Rowman & Littlefield.

Potential Oral Defense Outcomes

35

35.1 Role in Survival and Success

While most travelers usually embark on their journey with great expectations, including thinking that every aspect of their travel will be flawless, even an individual with limited travel experience will recognize that will not always be the case. Most seasoned travelers have a story or two regarding travel issues involving such challenges as traffic delays, road closures and detours, and weather-related issues. As a thesis or dissertation traveler, you likewise desire that your travels will go as planned and that you will not experience any significant difficulties along the way. Ideally, your research committee will be impressed with the work that you have done, your command of the subject matter, the value of your research contribution, and your professionalism and skill in presenting your research, resulting in them giving you a "thumbs up" to continue the process and complete your work. The reality is that they may also recommend or require that you make revisions to your thesis or dissertation. You should also recognize that some candidates do not successfully complete their oral examination. Knowing about these potential outcomes in advance will help motivate you to give your very best in these final stages of the process.

In enacting their roles and responsibilities, the research advisor and committee members are expected to evaluate whether the candidate has successfully completed their research in accordance with the research topic and scope that the committee had approved earlier. They will be interested in how the finished thesis or dissertation aligns with the research plan articulated in the research proposal, as well as with the published literature on similar topics. In addition to the responsibility that they have to their institution and profession, they have the responsibility of not only affirming a candidate's present research, but also confirming their ability to engage in future scholarly work without the guidance and supervision such as that provided throughout this current journey.

© The Author(s), under exclusive license to Springer Nature Switzerland AG 2021   189
R. S. Fleming and M. Kowalsky, *Survival Skills for Thesis
and Dissertation Candidates*, Springer Texts in Education,
https://doi.org/10.1007/978-3-030-80939-3_35

In conducting the oral examination reviewers will utilize certain criteria that your research advisor should share with you in advance of your defense. You will want to understand thoroughly the criteria and be prepared to measure up fully to these evaluation standards. The use of established criteria will enable your committee members to professionally enact their responsibilities in an objective, rather than subjective, manner. This represents an extremely important aspect of maintaining the integrity of the overall research process.

35.2 What You Need to Know

After presenting your research and answering any and all questions in accordance with the guidance that you have received from your research advisor, you should expect to be excused from the room while your committee deliberates and votes to determine the outcome of your efforts. You will then be brought back into the room at which time your research advisor and, perhaps, other committee members will share feedback from their deliberations, along with supporting rationale for the decision that they have rendered. They will also explain what that decision means, and what you will be expected to do next. Most likely, some revisions are still in order. Now is the time to embrace the suggestions provided to you as your "exit requirements," and to prepare them with gusto! Increase your motivation for a strong finish, since these adjustments are a good sign that your work is close to the expected and desired final product. Revising your work with renewed energy and enthusiasm is a survival skill as you enter this last major stage of the thesis or dissertation process.

There are typically four possible outcomes available to most research committees. The first represents the best outcome that you could hope for in that the committee is so impressed with your work and presentation that they approve your thesis or dissertation as submitted, and require you to make no changes. While this would be a true cause for celebration on your part as well as your committee, it is important not to get your hopes up and to remember that while this outcome would be ideal, it rarely happens. The second outcome is fortunately rare, in that it involves the committee failing the candidate and thus denying them the opportunity to continue the journey as planned. You can avoid such a tragic "derailment" by conscientiously working with your advisor and committee members throughout the research process and preparing appropriately for your oral examination.

The remaining two possible outcomes fall on a continuum between these two extreme end points. Both require the candidate to do additional work in making requested revisions to the thesis or dissertation. In the case of the committee determining that minor revisions are in order, the researcher will be expected to make these revisions and then resubmit the document for review by the research advisor. This is a fairly typical outcome of an oral examination. In most cases, the other committee members may entrust the research advisor, as chair of the committee, to review the revisions to see if they comply with what the committee requested and, as appropriate, to approve the revised submission on its behalf.

The last possible outcome of an oral examination is for the committee to require major revisions to the thesis or dissertation. While general comments and direction will often be given by the research advisor and other committee members at this time, the candidate will usually be directed to meet with their research advisor to discuss many major and minor changes that will be required before resubmission. While this outcome requires much more work, as a professional you will want to accept the reality of your situation and readjust your travel plans and activities as appropriate. We would suggest that you make sure that you fully understand the tasks ahead of you and take a short break before proceeding. It will be imperative that you fully address any concerns identified during your oral examination in accordance with the guidance that you receive from your research advisor. Completing work and meeting deadlines are no less important at this stage than at any earlier time in your journey.

Once you have completed your work to the satisfaction of your committee members, they will sign an approval form that will need to be submitted to the appropriate office in a timely manner. You will also be expected to complete any other procedural formalities that your institution requires in advance of awarding your degree at the end of this journey. Since the remaining work at this point is likely divided between easier tasks and harder ones, and may include both formatting and writing issues of various types, remember to leave time in your schedule and provide consistent intellectual effort to work on the necessary revisions.

35.3 Student Experiences and Suggestions: *What Will the Travel Critics Say?*

Graduate students often learn about the traditions, practices, and stories of students in their universities as they progress through their programs. One student was continually confused upon learning that at their institution there were various potential outcomes of one's oral examination, instead of just pass or fail. The good news was that all of their classmates had their work examined initially by one or more advisors, who helped note areas of concern or strength in advance of the official evaluation. Other students remembered watching senior students who subsequently passed questionable presentations, but who received lists of necessary adjustments to make before approvals were forwarded and signature pages offered to the graduate school office. Although it may seem that the levels or standards for passing the oral defense vary across projects, most students realize that trying to compare their performance to others is difficult and perhaps unnecessary. Different project designs will generate different questions, and one student's speaking or writing skills may not be exactly the same as another's. Therefore, most students were advised by their peers and their professors to just relax and inform everyone about what they researched, since they were actually now the experts in the room!

Many students plan or hope for the desired outcome of having their manuscript approved exactly as submitted, with the committee not suggesting or requiring any changes. However, most students' work required at least some revisions, and usually further explanations of particular points in their arguments or explanations. While some graduate students were surprised at the amount of changes requested of them, many agreed that the feedback they received had improved the way their project was viewed. While one student's manuscript had been marked to note numerous errors on each page, but did not generate much discussion during the presentation, another's session included much discussion among attendees but resulted in few adjustments to the paper itself. No two projects are the same, and faculty advisors have the final say in whether a thesis or dissertation is in its final form. Regardless of skill level, language fluency, or discipline, most students report that they found a few minor revisions that needed to be made even after their faculty approved their work. Although all students seemed to tire of yet another round of feedback, most realized that their committee members were just trying to enable their growth and help to further enhance the valuable contribution of their research project.

One student received conditional approval of their dissertation, with the understanding that they would meet with their research advisor to review a number of revisions that were in order. While obviously a little disappointed with the outcome of their dissertation defense, the student regained their composure quickly and kept up their momentum in finishing the requested items in a timely manner. This pleased their advisor, who they said was also relieved and happy that the project had been completed. Another student avoided making corrections quickly, and instead became upset, angry and confused at receiving mixed reactions from the committee and audience. The student became frustrated and talked about quitting the program, and really needed someone to help talk through their difficulties. The student talked to many classmates who encouraged them to keep working. Although their research advisor tried to help too, those conversations did not go well. So the other members of the student's committee made regular appointments with the candidate to discuss smaller aspects of the problems and helped the student develop ways to address them. Several weeks later, the advisor verified that the student has made all of the requested revisions, and the committee approved the student's revised manuscript after the student made a brief presentation to them on the revised work.

Many graduate students would agree that if you work hard and pay attention to the guidance of your research advisor and committee members throughout your journey, you will be confident that you will survive the oral presentation requirements of your program. It is, however, important to realize that it is possible to avoid other less optimal outcomes, including being requested to make major changes to your manuscript and being prevented from advancing toward graduation and completion of your degree. Most students avoid such tragic travel experiences by seeking, listening to, and acting on the guidance they receive, even if that guidance is not easy to understand at that moment. Often, engaging with friends you know very well, or even brainstorming with other academic acquaintances who may see your project from a fresh perspective, may help you identify the final tasks that you must complete. Then as you finish each revision, you can check them off your list and know that you have responded to all that has been asked of you.

35.4 Things to DO

- Develop an understanding of the possible outcomes of the oral examination.
- Be appreciative of the willingness of your research advisor and other committee members to serve as your travel guides.
- Be prepared to accept the decision of your committee gracefully and professionally.
- Seek interpretation and guidance regarding what the decision rendered by the committee means and what you will be expected to do from that point forward.
- Stay the course and continue to apply quality time and mental energy to the remaining tasks at hand.

35.5 Things NOT to Do

- Engage in behavior uncharacteristic of a professional.
- Challenge the decision rendered by your committee.
- Debate the basis on which the committee reached the decision.
- Forget to fully address all issues requiring revision in a timely manner.
- Create ill will on the part of the committee members that you will still need to rely on to complete your project.
- Let your frustration diminish your interest in or ability to forge ahead in your journey.

Bibliography

Goldsmith, John A, John Komlos, and Penny S. Gold. (2001). *The Chicago guide to your academic career: a portable mentor for scholars from graduate school through tenure.* Chicago: University of Chicago Press.

Kirchherr, Juian. (2018). *The lean PhD: radically improve the efficiency, quality and impact of your research.* Red Globe Press.

Sundström, Mikael. (2020). *How not to write a thesis or dissertation: a guide to success through failure.* Edward Elgar.

Publishing Your Work

36

36.1 Role in Survival and Success

If you are like most travelers, you will want to share your wonderful travel experiences with others, both during your trip and after returning home. You will perhaps chronicle your adventure by capturing a massive array of photographs or digital images with the intent of sharing the marvelous things you did and saw during your travels with family and friends. Through technology you are able to let significant people in your life actually share these marvelous experiences with you as they happen through viewing digital images that you send them. Giving small notes of thanks to those who have helped you accomplish this journey, or "paying it forward" by providing advice to others who may travel, is a rewarding part of these experiences long after they are concluded.

As enjoyable as your travels hopefully were, sharing the treasured moments of your trip with others can be equally rewarding. Sharing with those you know, as well as those you do not yet know, can be a powerful experience, and the same is true regarding your thesis or dissertation. While at the end of this often exhausting journey it is not unusual to take the time to breathe and regain control of your life, it would be tragic if you were to miss the opportunities that you have to share your work with others. Just as you would typically not share your travel experiences with a limited few people, so too you should seek the opportunities and avenues available to you to share your research with others.

While there are various ways for you to do so, including presenting at academic conferences and professional meetings, we urge you to take advantage of opportunities to publish your work in academic or professional journals or through a book or book chapter. These are excellent ways that a thesis or dissertation traveler can share their experience and research with peers, and there are likely other outlets which can be recommended by your advisor or other faculty members. Your effort to get your work accepted into a quality publication represents a strong finish to a long and difficult journey, and this particular survival skill can help lead you toward a fulfilling and successful career in the future.

© The Author(s), under exclusive license to Springer Nature Switzerland AG 2021   195
R. S. Fleming and M. Kowalsky, *Survival Skills for Thesis
and Dissertation Candidates*, Springer Texts in Education,
https://doi.org/10.1007/978-3-030-80939-3_36

36.2   What You Need to Know

The unfortunate reality for all too many thesis or dissertation travelers is that their journey ends at the point they submit their completed manuscript and required paperwork to their college or university, thus meeting the institution's final requirements to complete their thesis or dissertation and be awarded their degree. In contrast to their desire to share what they learned in their real world travels with many others, they are satisfied to share it with their research committee and limited others within their institution rather than affording those of common spirit who might have an interest in their work the opportunity to learn from it. Naturally, you should respect your own instincts here, and consider your future career path and goals, when determining why, how, and where to share details of your work.

Publishing your work in academic and professional journals will afford you the opportunity to leverage what you have learned in order to grow along with others within your field's academic and professional communities. Ideally, your work will challenge peers and veterans in the academy to conduct further research enhancing the body of knowledge related to your research area and interests. Likewise, sharing your work may enable practitioners to gain insights which they can operationalize in the real world. After surviving your thesis or dissertation, consider whether you owe it to yourself and others to share what you have learned. Your research may remain "alive" simply by placing it into the streams of academic discussion, rather than merely shelving a copy of your bound thesis or dissertation on your bookshelf, with all that hard work quickly forgotten by all.

It is important to point out and discuss post-journey publication opportunities in addition to the obvious options to publish your entire work or a major section of it. You may also be able to author additional articles quickly, based on aspects of your thesis or dissertation. These should be written and targeted at the particular audience of a given academic or professional journal, and can point toward your full manuscript for additional details and discussion. Selecting an appropriate journal to which you may contribute your work is important. You will want to seek publication opportunities that align with the nature of your work, and with potential readers who will find what you have to say useful. Your research advisor, committee members, and even journal editors can often provide valuable guidance as you target potential publication outlets and conceptualize and author articles which provide value added explanations for your intended audience.

We encourage you to pursue each and every opportunity that presents itself to share your work with others. Doing so is a key professional responsibility of every academic, and as such of every successful thesis or dissertation traveler. While there is a bit of variation in the nature of the many options which you may pursue, submitting refined work such as your thesis or dissertation (which has been read and revised multiple times) may make the process easier to begin. In addition to pursuing publication opportunities, you will want to consider where your future travels will take you career-wise, and how you can continue to share your travel experiences and partner on new experiences with others.

36.3   Student Experiences and Suggestions: *Sharing Your Travel Story with the World*

Many students acknowledge an unfortunate reality at the end of many research journeys of their peers, when their graduate degree is framed and placed on their wall, yet the expense and energy of that effort does not lead to any improvements in their lives. It is true that some weary travelers settle in to recover from their long journey and never get around to seeking the opportunities that are available after their thesis or dissertation project has been completed. Most students report that their advisors encouraged them to share their work with a larger audience within their field or profession through publishing it. Yet many admit they believed their final manuscript was the ending of its usefulness, and everyone knows those students who, from the start, viewed their completion of their research project as the ultimate closure of their educational pursuits. Once they completed their degree requirements, some graduate students lacked the desire to further share their travel experiences and discoveries, especially if doing so involves more writing and revising.

As instrumental as published journal articles were in their research, these students may not have felt the need as newly degreed professionals in their fields to actually pursue any opportunities to add to the existing body of knowledge. Other students were interested in further publishing and presenting, but did not know where to start. Yet most students had colleagues or friends who had already published multiple articles, chapters, or conference papers before finishing their thesis or dissertation manuscript and certainly before they were awarded their degrees. Students who were successful in pursuit of more widely sharing their work usually had a motivator or mentor who explained the process to them or helped the student determine what options were available to participate further in their discipline. As with many other things in life, asking good questions and seeking out those who may have the answers will yield much good information!

Some graduates simply did not realize that there were many outlets through which they could publish their work, even while still a student. Most had completed projects which would be particularly interesting to many professionals, and a great number of projects at any university will have immediate practical applications that would interest and appeal to the readers of a variety of publications. A few students made it known among their research group that they wanted to continue both their research and writing after completing their degree requirements. Other students found that their committee members and other university faculty, based on their thorough understanding of their students' research or on their own work in similar areas, were uniquely qualified to suggest target academic and professional journals where graduate work would be a good fit. As a result of casual questioning around campus and at professional meetings, many students learned how to publish in their field and even became collaborators and coauthors with contacts they met along their journey.

Some students' professors had told them stories of previous graduates who over a number of years had continued their research travels. In following the alumni through their publications, a network of students, professionals, and academics had then developed as the group kept in contact over time. Several students said that their professors were so grateful that they had shared the privilege of having so many great future scholars on their research teams, and multiple students mentioned that those they had asked about publishing and ideas for sharing ended up leading them to new job openings or grant opportunities as well. It became easier for other students to learn how their university's faculty members assembled extensive publication records, and to discern how training graduate students helped them as well to become respected researchers and prolific speakers. A few students found it quite natural to explore, identify, and pursue related publication opportunities as part of their existing positions or as a complement to their existing job descriptions, now that they possessed the skills to enact impressive initiatives and create new value for their organizations.

36.4   Things to DO

- Recognize your professional responsibilities and the benefits of sharing your work with others.
- Ask for and review suggestions of publication outlets from your research advisor, committee, and other faculty.
- Identify journals that would be receptive to your article, and revise or develop your submission with the journal's target audience in mind.
- Review and meticulously follow submission guidelines or requirements.
- If you receive a rejection or request to revise and resubmit, stay the course as you likely learned to do at some point during your thesis or dissertation journey.

36.5   Things NOT to Do

- Abandon your interest in your research topic after completion of your thesis or dissertation.
- Fail to pursue publishing opportunities related to your research.
- Submit articles to journals that are not a good fit for your contribution.
- Fail to fully comply with journal submission guidelines or requirements.
- Become frustrated if it takes a while to hear back regarding submissions or you receive a rejection or a request to revise and resubmit your article.

Bibliography

Germano, W. (2014). *From Dissertation to Book*, 2nd edn. Chicago: University of Chicago Press.

Luey, B. (2007). *Revising your dissertation: Advice from leading editors* (updated edition). Los Angeles: University of California Press.

Rocco, T. S., & Hatcher, T. G. (2011). *The handbook of scholarly writing and publishing*. New York: Wiley.

Planning Your Future Research Activities

37

37.1 Role in Survival and Success

While many travelers decide to travel forever at some point during their journeys, and they look forward to planning another trip again as soon as they can, others for whatever reason settle on reflecting on their earlier travels rather than embarking on new adventures. While there are certainly a number of valid reasons that they choose not to travel or are unable to travel, they may realize they may miss many great experiences that would unfold as a result. Experience in traveling soothes many potential difficulties, and even removes some challenges that novices might encounter on their initial journeys in the same or similar directions. While we recognize that some students may want to stop traveling for a while (or forever!), most take a short breather and then start planning the next journey.

The same is true with scholars who reach the end of their graduate school experience. For some, their travel continues as they undertake additional research and pursue many exciting professional opportunities. Others adopt a different view, and for the most part curtail their research adventures after completion of their initial (albeit long) journey. Many new experiences will be open to you now that you have been vetted as a competent researcher and only once you have completed your graduate training. Explore even more, as time and resources allow! Even if you sometimes feel too tired to do more, spend some time planning your next steps, even if they are not academic or scholarly ones. This planning for "what's next" is an essential skill which will continue the momentum of your success. Your motivation, new organizational skills, or other experiences may actually propel you toward your other goals and dreams in ways you had not previously imagined.

© The Author(s), under exclusive license to Springer Nature Switzerland AG 2021   201
R. S. Fleming and M. Kowalsky, *Survival Skills for Thesis and Dissertation Candidates*, Springer Texts in Education,
https://doi.org/10.1007/978-3-030-80939-3_37

37.2   What You Need to Know

In charting your future career aspirations and direction, and the supporting activities that will be necessary if you are to achieve your goals, you will soon realize the importance of determining the next destination to which you desire to travel. Of course, you will then consider the various things you will need to do along the way to reach that destination. Developing an appropriate "research stream" following completion of your thesis or dissertation journey will prove instrumental in guiding many future professional decisions, including those related to the research that you undertake and the ways in which you contribute to the body of existing knowledge by sharing your work with others.

Selecting a research stream, or in other words a sequence of potential topics to explore which define your intended area of expertise, is similar in some ways to selecting the topic that you researched for your thesis or dissertation. Once again, this decision will often take into account the counsel and guidance of others, but it is a decision that only you can and should make. This decision will have career implications since it will influence the future direction of your research activities. It should be made only after conscientious consideration of your scholarly and professional interests. While you may have pursued a research topic for your thesis or dissertation that you discovered was not ideal, you now have the opportunity to refine your area of interest or select a new one if appropriate. Taking specific and deliberate actions in planning your next steps is a true survival skill for your career and life.

In the world of organizations and strategic planning we refer to "mission-driven" organizations. All that an organization does should be related to fulfilling its stated mission, which is formulated only after extensive reflection and deliberation. Just as an organization's mission statement will play an essential role in determining whether it achieves its full potential, so too the research stream you pursue will play a significant role in your own personal mission, and will be closely related to areas of your future professional activities, accomplishments, and success. The more clearly you identify your mission, the easier it is to drive your future activities towards its fulfillment!

You might be thinking about the earlier difficulty you may have experienced in determining your research interests and identifying and refining your thesis or dissertation topic. However, realize that as you make equally important decisions, you have the benefit of the lessons that you learned in your earlier journey regarding your research interests and skills. Initially, many scholars will continue along the travel path that they initially explored in completing their thesis or dissertation. Should you desire to take that route of travel, the limitations and areas for future research identified in your own thesis or dissertation will often serve as an important starting point in articulating your planned "research stream." Alternately, you may want to define your research area more broadly, or even refine or possibly expand your initial research interests. While this is quite natural, you will always have the opportunity to "reinvent" yourself in the future by further defining your favorite areas of research and pursuing a path toward them.

As we near the end of this book, we trust that this chapter will inspire and empower you to be proactive and aggressive in charting your future research activities. You may have noticed that we introduced the word "scholar" in this chapter to describe you. Once you have successfully completed your thesis or dissertation, you have demonstrated that you are in fact a true scholar, able to conduct academic research professionally and rigorously, and to provide results which help to improve the world in which we live. As authors we challenge you, as a new scholar, to continue on the road of those senior scholars whose work has served to enlighten you and prepare you for future success.

37.3 Student Experiences and Suggestions: *Charting Your Future Research Journeys*

Students from a variety of disciplines remarked that their institutions hosted periodic career events and scholarly social activities during the course of their graduate programs. Some students kept in touch with their research advisors after graduation and they celebrated students' successful journeys with them each year. While several graduates suspected that the faculty's motives were to get them to return for another degree or to help work on a postdoctoral project, most were appreciative that their professors remembered them at all! Late in their program, many students reported meeting professors at their own university whom they had not yet met or spent time with, yet each of them was interested in learning about their future research plans. One student said his research advisor was particularly pleased to hear that they and several members of their class had planned to develop a series of several articles based on their dissertation projects. And of course, most students noticed that they received much positive reinforcement for continuing to use the analytical skills that they had developed under the guidance of various research experts. Building on one's thesis or dissertation research is the route that many graduates pursue, at least initially, for beginning their careers as professional researchers, authors, and faculty members themselves.

Some students knew that they did not want to become academics, and so they started their own businesses or marketed their newfound skills to major corporations. At some point, most students determined one or more research streams and career paths to follow based on their professional aspirations and plans. Others needed more time and additional research travels before they would be in a position to discern if their ideas for the future were on the right track or not. While many graduates decide to stay the course with their initial research interest and discipline for part or all of their careers, others discover areas that better align with their qualifications and future goals. You are the only person who can determine the most appropriate path for you. But you can always ask others for feedback on your ideas!

One student took several years away from academia before realizing that they had potential to become a respected researcher in their field. At the time, the student just thought they would have to reinvent themselves, but the continuous feedback they received from others helped them narrow down where their natural areas of knowledge and abilities could help improve the world. The student's decision to choose a slightly modified path was made only after extensive conversations with professionals in a variety of fields, as well as conscientious and informed contemplation. It appears that this was a wise decision for that student since, after a break of a few years beyond awarding of their degree, they went on to become a recognized and respected professional within a new, evolving area within their original field. Many other students were delighted to hear about all of the exciting ways that their classmates were utilizing strategies gained during their graduate programs. After the initial shock of understanding that a huge project which took most of their daily time and energy had finally come to an end, most students were able to reflect on the value of what they had experienced, both personally and professionally. Most students realized that while each is making unique contributions to their organizations, professions, and society, they have all discovered the right destinations and routes of travel for themselves, which is an excellent outcome by any measure.

Nearly all students felt appreciation for the professors and mentors who were responsible for developing their talents in order for them to become better thinkers, communicators, and contributors to the world in which we all live. A particular student research team faithfully repeated their supervisors' encouragement to have the courage to keep moving forward, and to be open to reinventing themselves when necessary or appropriate. In this way, the lessons learned by candidates for a thesis or dissertation are indeed lessons for life. As we as authors come to an end of our travels with you, we both thank you for the opportunity to join you as your travel guides. We look forward to hearing that you have successfully completed your journey and that you continue to travel, specifically in order to find new paths that you can share with others. Congratulations on your successful travels to date, and best wishes for all of the travel that your future will hold!

37.4 Things to DO

- Reflect on the lessons learned in completing your thesis or dissertation.
- Evaluate the new knowledge and skills that you have acquired during this journey which can be utilized in the future.
- Give serious consideration to continuing research in the area you investigated in completing your thesis or dissertation.

- Ponder an appropriate line of research which aligns with your future professional pursuits.
- Sketch out some ideas of "what's next" even if you cannot enact new plans immediately.

37.5 Things NOT to Do

- Give up on research, or on using all of the advanced skills you have acquired, soon after completing your thesis or dissertation.
- Select a research area that does not correspond with your qualifications, interest, or future goals.
- Fail to take the time to develop a realistic "research stream" that is customized to your interests.
- Lack the courage to recognize when changing the direction of your research is appropriate.
- Forget to "reinvent" yourself at times and in ways that are meaningful to you and your career goals.

Bibliography

Brubaker, M. D., & Brubaker, D. (2011). *Advancing your career: Getting and making the most of your doctorate.* Lanham, MD: Rowman & Littlefield.

Epstein, D., Kenway, J., & Boden, R. (2007). *Writing for publication.* Sage.

Urbano, D. (2020). *How to make your doctoral research relevant: Insights and strategies for the modern research environment.* Edward Elgar.

Final Thoughts

38

Throughout this book we have referred to your journey or pilgrimage in the successful completion of your academic program's thesis or dissertation requirement. In navigating this monumental and potentially life-changing journey, you have gained knowledge and experience that only result from taking this very unique and difficult trip. Others may not have had the exact same experiences as you, especially those who have never attempted or completed these academic and personal milestones. You may have encountered more than one "bump in the road," from which you will continue to learn, as you share your thoughts with other travelers who may look to you for guidance as they take a similar trip of their own. Learning more about your field, and learning more about yourself in the process, has hopefully made this part of your lifelong journey most rewarding.

Once you complete each new task of any future project, you will want to remember to allow time to celebrate, regenerate, and prepare for the next phase of your journey. Before embarking on another expedition, hopefully you have thoughtfully considered the various motivators that can inspire you to get work done, as well as the distractions that are capable of taking you away from your work. While engaging in activities you find relaxing are important at appropriate times throughout any journey, spending extended periods of time on your usual bad habits could seriously derail your progress, as they have for previous travelers. As you completed each phase of your journey, we hope you have taken the time to consider your success in managing your own behavior, and made any adjustments in your approach as needed. This may be the real type of growth which happens during graduate school.

Yes, there may be a time in the future that you will be afforded the opportunity to give back to your profession and its aspiring future scholars through serving as their research advisor or as a member of their committee. You may have an invitation to contribute to a project in your community or among colleagues in your profession. Or, you may learn of new ways to continue to work on yourself as a project in moving forward! We trust that the guidance you have gleaned from this book has

© The Author(s), under exclusive license to Springer Nature Switzerland AG 2021   207
R. S. Fleming and M. Kowalsky, *Survival Skills for Thesis and Dissertation Candidates*, Springer Texts in Education, https://doi.org/10.1007/978-3-030-80939-3_38

made your travels easier and potentially more rewarding. Your new understandings, together with the insights that you have gained as a seasoned traveler, will help you persevere and overcome many trials and tribulations inherent in thesis or dissertation travel and in life in general. We know your experiences will serve you and provide needed assistance to those who need your help, however, that time may come which requires your expertise in organizing future professional adventures. Surprisingly, you may discover that even in a smaller or supporting role in the learning process, you will once again embark on a shared journey of discovery, and will remember the ultimate joy of travel.

We have learned from the experiences of students from around the globe. Their travels are not unlike those of famous individuals, whose relationship to the journey was not unlike your own. Reflection on the sage words of wisdom from travelers past will surely prepare you for a success on whatever paths you choose. You have likely heard the famous quote, "A journey of a thousand miles begins with a single step," which is attributed to the Chinese philosopher Laozi. While your own voyages will not likely involve literal travel over this distance, at times it will seem that they do. Taking one day and one step at a time, and approaching each new challenge with a spirit of wonder and gratitude, are true survival skills for this project and for a lifetime. You probably have also heard the words of American astronaut Neil Armstrong, which build on a similar sentiment. "That's one small step for man and one giant leap for mankind," are words that served to inspire the nations of the world, indicating that the seemingly unattainable can be realized through hard work and perseverance. The same is true as you embark on your chosen journey. While your achievement may not compare to that of the Apollo 11 Moon landing, it will propel your professional career into new future "orbits."

We close with the common sentiment which explains that anything worth doing is worth doing right. While the initial utterance of this wise sentiment is hard to trace, its words clearly provide valuable advice for any personal or professional undertaking, including your thesis or dissertation project. While many travelers desire to see as much as they can in the shortest period of time, a cursory approach to travel in the "fast lane" can deny you the opportunity to make a real, lasting contribution to your profession and the world. As they say, take the time to "stop and smell the roses" in order to experience all the sites along your wonderful travelling adventure. Our journey as your authors has likewise involved a wonderful shared voyage as we sought to provide you with the insights and travel experiences that will contribute to a successful, enjoyable journey. We anticipate that reaching your destination will help you to recognize that the trip was worth taking.

We look forward to someday hearing about the great accomplishments of your future journeys. Perhaps someday our orbits will cross.

Survival Skills List

Chapter 1. Pledge Perseverance

Chapter 2. Enhance Awareness

Chapter 3. Check on Your Time Management

Chapter 4. Be Realistic

Chapter 5. Consider Resource Allocation

Chapter 6. Offer Compliance

Chapter 7. Demonstrate Punctuality

Chapter 8. Nurture Resiliency

Chapter 9. Find Focus

Chapter 10. Monitor Decision Making

Chapter 11. Understand Responsibilities

Chapter 12. Reveal Honesty

Chapter 13. Show Flexibility

Chapter 14. Encourage Collegiality

Chapter 15. Increase Patience & Tactfulness

Chapter 16. Strive for Clarity

Chapter 17. Maintain Endurance

Chapter 18. Keep an Open Mind

Chapter 19. Employ your Best Critical Thinking

Chapter 20. Respect the Process

© The Editor(s) (if applicable) and The Author(s), under exclusive license
to Springer Nature Switzerland AG 2021
R. S. Fleming and M. Kowalsky, *Survival Skills for Thesis
and Dissertation Candidates*, Springer Texts in Education,
https://doi.org/10.1007/978-3-030-80939-3

Appendix: Even More Specialized Resources

In addition to the resources at the end of each chapter, here is a list of additional books which may help you construct, enact, and reflect on your journey—before, during, and after!

Allison, B., & Race, P. (2004). *The student's guide to preparing dissertations and theses*. London: Routledge Falmer.

Angelle, P., Agnello, M. F., Amlund, J. T., Caffarella, R. S., Chance, P. L., Edmonson, S., Fulmer, C., Gonzalez, M. L., Calabrese, R. L., & Smith, P. A. (2010). *The doctoral student's advisor and mentor: sage advice from the experts*. Lanham, MD: Rowman & Littlefield.

Axelrod, B., & Windell, J. (2012). *Dissertation solutions: a concise guide to planning, implementing, and surviving the dissertation process*. Lanham, MD: Rowman & Littlefield.

Bitchener, J. (2018). *A guide to supervising non-native english writers of theses and dissertations*. New York: Routledge.

Bloomberg, L. D., & Volpe, M. (2018). *Completing your qualitative dissertation: A road map from beginning to end*. Sage Publications.

Boyle, J., & Ramsay, S. (2020). *Writing a science PhD*. London: Macmillan International.

Brabazon, T., Lyndall-Knight, T., & Hills, N. (2020). *The creative PhD: Challenges, opportunities, reflection*. New York: Emerald.

Bryman, A. (2016). *Scoial research methods* (5th ed.). London: Oxford University Press.

Bui, Y. N. (2013). *How to write a master's thesis*. Sage Publications.

Carter, C. (Ed.). (2018). *Successful dissertations: The complete guide for education, childhood and early childhood studies students*. London: Bloomsbury Publishing.

Casanave, C. P., & Li, X. M. (2008). *Learning the literacy practices of graduate school: Insiders' reflections on academic enculturation.* Ann Arbor: University of Michigan Press.

Durkin, D. B. (2020). *Writing strategies for the education dissertation.* New York: Routledge.

Evans, D., Gruba, P., & Zobel, J. (2014). *How to write a better thesis.* New York: Springer.

Fisher, E., Thompson, R., & Holtom, D. (2014). *Enjoy writing your science thesis or dissertation! A step-by-step guide to planning and writing a thesis or dissertation for undergraduate and graduate science students* (2nd ed.). London: Imperial College Press.

Fitzpatrick, J., Wright, D. J., & Secrist, J. (1998). *Secrets for a successful dissertation.* Thousand Oaks, CA: Sage.

Fulton, J., Kuit, J., Sanders, G., & Smith, P. (2013). *The professional doctorate: A practical guide.* London: Palgrave Macmillan.

Golde, C. M., & Walker, G. E. (2006). *Envisioning the future of doctoral education: Preparing stewards of the discipline.* San Francisco, CA: Jossey-Bass.

Grix, J. (2018). *The Foundations of Research* (3rd ed.). London: Palgrave Macmillan.

Gustavii, B. (2012). How to prepare a scientific doctoral dissertation based on research articles. Cambridge: Cambridge University Press.

Harman, E., Montagnes, I., McMenemy, S., & Bucci, C. (2003). *The thesis and the book: A guide for first-time academic authors.* Toronto: University of Toronto Press.

Harrison, E. (2021). *Your psychology dissertation.* Thousand Oaks, CA: Sage.

Herr, K. (2015). *The Action Research Dissertation.* Thousand Oaks, CA: Sage.

Lee, A., Kamler, B., & Aitchison, C. (2010). *Publishing pedagogies for the doctorate and beyond.* New York: Taylor & Francis.

Lomas, R. (2011). Mastering your business dissertation: how to conceive, research, and write a good business dissertation. London: Routledge.

Luey, B. (2010). *Handbook for academic authors.* New York: Cambridge University Press.

Lunenburg, F. C., & Irby, B. J. (2008). *Writing a successful thesis or dissertation: Experiences and strategies for students in the social and behavioral sciences.* Thousand Oaks, CA: Corwin.

Murray, R. (2009). *How to survive your viva: Defending a thesis in an oral examination.* Maidenhead, England: Open University Press.

Nygaard, L. P., & Solli, K. (20020). *Strategies for writing a thesis by publication in the social sciences and humanities.* New York: Taylor & Francis.

Oliver, P. (2008). *Writing your thesis.* Los Angeles: Sage.

Paltridge, Brian & Sue Starfield. Thesis and Dissertation Writing in a Second Language: A Handbook for Supervisors. New York: Taylor & Francis, 2007.

Piantanida, M., & Garman, N. B. (2009). *The qualitative dissertation: A guide for students and faculty.* Thousand Oaks, CA: Corwin.

Pyrczak, F. (2000). *Completing your thesis or dissertation: Professors share their techniques and strategies.* Los Angeles: Pyrczak.

Rocco, T. S., & Hatcher, T. (2011). *The handbook of scholarly writing and publishing.* San Francisco: Jossey-Bass.

Roush, K. (2020). *A nurse's step by step guide to publishing a dissertation or DNP project.* Indianapolis, IN: Sigma Theta Tau International Honor Society of Nursing.

Wallace, M., & Wray, A. (2011). *Critical reading and writing for postgraduates.* London: Sage.

Made in United States
North Haven, CT
03 April 2022

17872562R00130

THE ULTIMATE COPYCAT RECIPES FOR BEGINNERS

How to Make the Most Delicious Italian Restaurant Dishes at Home

consent, and the publication of the trademark is without permission or backing by the trademark owner. All trademarks and brands within this book are for clarifying purposes only and are the owned by the owners themselves, not affiliated with this document.

Table of Contents

CHAPTER 4 CALIFORNIA PIZZA KITCHEN™

Sicilian Cheese Bread

Pasta
Mizithra Pasta
OSF's Manager's Special

Sauces and Salads
White Clam Sauce
Chicken Caesar Salad

Specials
Spaghetti Vesuvius
Shrimp Fettuccine

Desserts
New York Cheesecake
Chocolate Mousse Cake

CHAPTER 7 ROMANO'S MACARONI GRILL™

Antipasti
Calamari Fritti
Stuffed Mushrooms

Beef, Chicken and Seafood
Chicken Scaloppine
Parmesan Crusted Sole
Chianti Pork Chop

Pasta
Lobster Ravioli
Pasta Milano

Desserts

Introduction

Italian cuisine has become quite popular for its rich, spicy and exotic taste, but you might probably think all there is to it is pasta, pizza, and lasagna, but that is barely even scratching the surface. Italian cuisine encompasses a variety of tasty, saucy, cheesy, and spicy dishes that will have you smacking your lips in delight. Ones that you won't be able to stop thinking about after just one taste.

Surprisingly, what you might consider as popular Italian food in America is barely a taste of true Italian cuisine. Thankfully, local Italian restaurants have thought to bring that taste of diversity close to you and each time you let your senses get bombarded by that rich goodness, what happens? You want more because once is never enough! I mean, who doesn't love a little bit of Italian goodness? But you can't possibly eat out forever when there is a more pocket-friendly option. Don't worry, I'll tell you all about it later.

Now, where was I?

Yes! There is this little rumor I hear going around about Italian food and I'd like to deal with that before we move forward. Some people argue that Italian foods are unhealthy because they tend to be high in carbs and fats, but that is not quite true. It is true that Italian cuisine tends to be very healthy because they often include salads, legumes, fresh fish, and olive oil, but of course that can change when cured meats, cheeses and creamy sauces are used. So, I'll put it down to choice, but just to reassure you, I'll share a couple of reasons why Italian foods are good for your health.

Healthy Ingredients

I said that before, but I think it needs saying again. If you are worried about the health implications, just bear in mind that you do not have to go for meals that are too high in carbs and unhealthy fats. Although, most Italian foods contain olive oil and seafood, which are rich in unsaturated fats and omega-3 fatty acids, which promote cardiac health.

Fiber Rich Ingredients

Porcini mushrooms, beans and lentils are great sources of fiber and are used frequently in Italian cuisine. You would find most of these ingredients in their seafood dishes, pasta and soups. These are certainly good for your digestive system and would help you maintain a balanced diet.

Fresh Ingredients

Most of your favorite Italian foods often have fresh onions, tomatoes, garlic, pepper and seafood. So, you'll be taking in a lot of minerals, vitamins and healthy fats. These nutrients will definitely even the scale on your diet; after all, fresh ingredients are the best.

Now that we know something about Italian cuisine, let's delve a little into copycat recipes and how we can work with that to make tasty Italian food at home without breaking the bank. So, what are copycat recipes?

Copycat recipes are a recreation of signature meals from popular restaurants. Yes, it's true! You can now make meals from your favorite restaurants at home. Amazing, right? Yours might not taste exactly like theirs, but I promise that if you follow the instructions I will share in the recipes below to the letter, you'll come very close to it.

Contrary to what you might have thought, there is definitely no secret ingredient to these delicious meals. They do not add a pinch of fairy dust or say abracadabra while cooking. They use regular ingredients but it's all about using the right ones and following the right steps. Don't worry, I'll show you how.

So you might be wondering, why go through the stress of making these meals at home in the first place, especially if you have no skill in the kitchen? First of all, let me tell you that you need not be a celebrity chef or have any culinary expertise to recreate these meals, and secondly, you'll be saving yourself some extra cash. Think about it, why spend so much on what you can eat in one seating when you can make so much more at home?

In just a few short steps, you'll be able to recreate recipes from your favorite Italian restaurants. You no longer have to worry about satisfying your craving for the Lasagna from your local Italian restaurant; I am bringing it straight to your kitchen! No hassle and no catch!

Just think about the many possibilities! You'll be able to recreate meals from popular Italian restaurants like Buca Di Beppo, Olive Garden, Magianno's Little Italy and more! I am sure your friends and family won't believe it until they get a taste of your masterpiece. So, what do you say? Shall we surprise them?

Chapter 1
Buca Di Beppo™

I know you can't wait to get started but did you know that the first Buca Di Beppo was opened in 1993 in Minneapolis? It also currently has 76 locations in the United States alone and is considered one of the top Italian restaurants in America.

Appetizers
Fried Mozzarella

- Prep Time: 10 Minutes
- Cook Time: 10 Minutes
- Serves: 4

Ingredients
- 1 medium sized egg
- ½ cup of flour
- Extra virgin olive oil (to fry)
- ½ of Italian bread crumbs
- Pepper and salt to taste
- ½ pound of mozzarella (fresh ball)

Steps

1. Cut the ball of mozzarella into eight slices.
2. Put the flour and a pinch of pepper and salt into a medium sized bowl and mix until well combined.
3. Crack the egg into a small bowl, add a teaspoon of water and beat lightly.
4. Put the crumbs into a dry bowl and set aside.
5. Gently roll the mozzarella slices in the flour mix until well coated, then dip them in the egg wash before rolling them in the bowl of bread crumbs until well covered.
6. Put a large non-stick pan over medium heat and add a few tablespoons of oil and leave to heat up for 2-3 minutes.
7. Add the coated mozzarella slices and allow to cook on each side for a minute or two until evenly browned.
8. Serve with marinara sauce and enjoy!

Bruschetta

- Prep Time: 5 Minutes
- Cook Time: 5 Minutes
- Serves: 2

Ingredients

Bread
- 3 ounces of garlic olive oil
- Half a loaf of round bread

Bruschetta
- A quarter tablespoon of salt
- Half a cup of red onions (diced)

- A pound of Roma tomatoes
- 4 tablespoons of olive oil
- A quarter tablespoon of ground black pepper
- 4 cloves of garlic (peeled and diced)
- 2 tablespoons of chopped basil

Steps

Bruschetta
1. Wash the Roma tomatoes and pat them dry.
2. Cut the ends off each tomato and remove the seeds. Dice the tomatoes and leave at room temperature.
3. Put the diced tomatoes, onions, garlic, olive oil, chopped basil, pepper and salt. Mix well and set aside.

Bread
1. Cut the bread crosswise until you have two equal halves. Place each piece on a baking tin and brush with a thin layer of garlic olive oil.
2. Put in the oven and allow to bake at 350°F for 2-5 minutes or until golden and crispy.
3. Remove from the oven and serve topped with bruschetta.

Note: You can also use a grill for the bread if you would prefer. Just allow each piece to cook for a minute or two on each side until golden.

Mozzarella Caprese

- ◆ Prep Time: 10 Minutes
- ◆ Cook Time: 0 Minutes
- ◆ Serves: 4

Ingredients

- ◆ 10 fresh basil leaves
- ◆ 1 yellow bell pepper (roasted and chopped)
- ◆ Salt and pepper to taste
- ◆ 1 red bell pepper (roasted and chopped)
- ◆ 1 teaspoon of oregano
- ◆ 1 tablespoon of olive oil
- ◆ 1 tablespoon of cracked black peppercorns
- ◆ 2 large Roma tomatoes (cut into wedges)

- 1 teaspoon of chopped garlic
- 5-10 fresh basil leaves
- 2 tablespoons of fresh basil (chopped)
- 5 ounces of fresh mozzarella ball (sliced)

Steps

1. Place the mozzarella slices on one side of a large platter, making sure they are evenly spaced.
2. Put the tomato slices on the other side, alternating with red and yellow roasted pepper slices.
3. Put the chopped garlic, olive oil and oregano into a small bowl, stir until well mixed, then drizzle over the entire platter. Sprinkle with a dash of pepper and salt, then serve garnished with chopped basil and fresh basil leaves.

Soups and Salads

Chopped Antipasti

- ◆ Prep Time: 12 Minutes
- ◆ Cook Time: 0 Minutes
- ◆ Serves: 4

Ingredients
- ◆ 2 green olives
- ◆ 3 pepperoncini peppers
- ◆ 1 medium cucumber (sliced and halved)
- ◆ 28 grams of pepperoni (thinly sliced)

- 2 black olives
- ½ cup of Italian vinaigrette
- 220 grams of Roma tomatoes (cut into wedges)
- ½ cup of roasted bell peppers
- ½ cup of red onions (julienned)
- ½ cup of crumbled feta cheese
- ½ cup of provolone cheese (diced)
- One medium head of lettuce
- 42 grams of mortadella (thinly sliced)

Steps

1. Put the onions, greens, tomatoes and cucumber in a large mixing bowl, add the dressing and mix well, then transfer onto a platter.
2. Arrange the pepperoni and mortadella slices on either side of the platter.
3. Top with crumbled feta, provolone cheese, roasted peppers, and pepperoncini.
4. Put the olives on the side and serve.

Apple Gorgonzola

- Prep Time: 15 Minutes
- Cook Time: 0 Minutes
- Serves: 8

Ingredients

Mustard Vinaigrette
- Salt and pepper to taste
- 1 teaspoon of oregano
- 1 clove of garlic
- ½ cup of olive oil
- ½ piece of red onion (julienned)
- ½ cup of apple cider vinegar

- 2 tablespoons of Dijon mustard

Candied Pecans
- ¼ teaspoon of salt
- ¼ cup of sugar
- A pinch of ground red pepper
- ½ teaspoon of salt
- ½ ground ginger
- 2 tablespoons of butter
- ½ black pepper
- 1 ½ cups whole pecans

Salad
- 1 cup of dried cranberries
- 1 green apple (sliced)
- 1 cup crumbled gorgonzola cheese
- 1 green apple (diced)
- 2 Romaine lettuce hearts (chopped)

Steps
1. Put all the vinaigrette ingredients into a blender and blend until smooth, then pour into a zip-lock bag until ready to use.
2. Put the cheese, lettuce, walnuts, diced apples, and cranberries into a large bowl and toss with one cup of mustard vinaigrette, then put in a serving bowl and top with sliced apples.
3. Put all the ingredients for the candied pecans into a frying pan. Put over medium heat and allow to cook until the nuts are toasted and the sugar is caramelized.
4. Grease a strip of tin foil and transfer the candied pecans there to cool.
5. When cool, add the candied pecans into the bowl of salad then pour the vinaigrette over it and serve.

Italian Wedding Soup

- Prep Time: 15 Minutes
- Cook Time: 30 Minutes
- Serves: 4

Ingredients

- 1 pound of pastina
- 4 cups of chicken broth
- Salt to taste
- ½ teaspoon of oregano
- ¼ cup of escarole (chopped)
- 4 ounces of boneless chicken breast
- ½ a teaspoon of freshly ground black pepper
- 5 ounces of sausage meat

- 2 cups of grated Romano cheese to garnish
- 2 cups of diced red pepper
- ½ cup of Romano cheese
- 2 eggs
- Olive oil cooking spray

Steps

1. Preheat your oven to 350°F.
2. Roll the sausage into small balls, then place on a greased cookie sheet and bake for 5 minutes. Remove and set aside to cool.
3. Bring a medium pot of water to a boil, add half a teaspoon of salt, then add pastina. Allow to cook until al dente and drain.
4. Slice the chicken breast into strips and set aside.
5. Coat a baking sheet with olive oil cooking spray and place the chicken strips on it. Sprinkle with oregano, pepper and salt, then bake in the preheated oven for 5 minutes. Remove and set aside once done.
6. Heat the chicken broth and bring to a boil. Add sausage meatballs, pastina, chopped escarole and cooked chicken.
7. Crack the eggs into a small bowl, add half a cup of Romano cheese, stir and add to the boiling pot of soup, stirring gently until egg mixture becomes firm.
8. Pour into bowls and serve garnished with red pepper and Romano cheese.

Entrees
Salmon Sorrento

- Prep Time: 15 Minutes
- Cook Time: 27 Minutes
- Serves: 4

Ingredients
- 1 tablespoon of capers
- 6 small Italian plum tomatoes (diced)
- 1 pound of salmon fillet
- 3 tablespoons of lemon juice
- 6 green olives (chopped)
- 6 black olives (chopped)

- 2 tablespoons of finely chopped cilantro
- 3 cloves of garlic (minced)
- Salt and pepper to taste
- 3 tablespoons of extra virgin olive oil

Steps

1. Set a large skillet over medium-high heat and allow it to heat for about a minute, add olive oil and swirl until the bottom of the skillet is completely coated.
2. Add green and black olives, tomatoes, capers salt and pepper, parsley, garlic and lemon juice. Stir until well mixed.
3. Allow to cook for 2-3 minutes, stirring occasionally so that the mixture doesn't stick to the bottom of the skillet.
4. Set to medium and allow to cook until the mixture loses one-third of its moisture, stirring occasionally, about 5 minutes.
5. While the mixture cooks, rinse the salmon and pat dry with a piece of paper towel.
6. Push the sauce to one side of the skillet and put the salmon in.
7. Scoop the sauce over the salmon and cook covered for 17 minutes or until the salmon is fork tender.

Chicken Saltimbocca

- ◆ Prep Time: 25 Minutes
- ◆ Cook Time: 20 Minutes
- ◆ Serves: 6

Ingredients

- ◆ 2 tablespoons of capers
- ◆ 4 large boneless, skinless chicken breasts
- ◆ 1 tablespoon of butter
- ◆ 1 tablespoon of finely chopped sage
- ◆ w̄ cup of white wine
- ◆ Flour for dusting
- ◆ 2 tablespoons of lemon juice
- ◆ 6 slices of prosciutto

- A can of water canned artichoke hearts (drained and halved)
- 2 tablespoons of olive oil
- w̄ cup of heavy cream
- Salt to taste
- 2 slices of lemon

Steps

1. Put the chicken between two pieces of wax paper and pound flat with a wooden ladle (not too thin), then cut each piece into four.
2. Season each piece with salt and sage, then sprinkle some flour on one side.
3. Put the prosciutto on the unfloured side of each piece of chicken and pound until it sticks and each piece is at least half an inch thick.
4. Pour the oil into a pan and set over medium heat. Put the chicken (prosciutto side down) and allow to cook until browned, then flip and cook the floured side until golden. Once cooked, put the chicken into a sealable plate to keep warm.
5. Drain out excess oil, add oil and cook until reduced by half.
6. Add lemon juice, butter, artichokes, and cream, stir and cook until the sauce thickens.
7. Put the chicken on a serving platter, drizzle generous amounts of sauce over it and top with capers.
8. Serve garnished with lemon wedges (optional).

Chicken Limone

- Prep Time: 20 Minutes
- Cook Time: 25 Minutes
- Serves: 2

Ingredients

Chicken
- 1 tablespoon of capers
- 2 boneless, skinless chicken breasts
- ¼ cup of extra virgin olive oil
- Salt and pepper to taste
- w̄ cup all-purpose flour
- Sliced lemons (to garnish)

Lemon Butter Sauce

- ½ cup of white wine
- ¼ teaspoon of salt
- ½ cup of heavy cream
- ½ cup of butter
- 2 teaspoons minced garlic
- 1 lemon

Steps

1. Put the chicken between two pieces of wax paper and pound until they are a quarter inch thick, then cut each piece into two.
2. Put the wine and garlic into a small saucepan, stir and set over medium heat. Once boiled, reduce to a simmer until the wine is reduced by half, about 3-4 minutes.
3. Strain into a bowl to remove garlic, then set aside.
4. Rinse out the pan, then add butter and place over medium heat again.
5. When the butter is fully melted, add the wine, cream and salt, then stir to combine.
6. Squeeze the juice of half a lemon into the mixture, bring to a boil, then allow to simmer for 10-12 minutes. Once done, cover and remove from heat.
7. Put the olive oil in a large skillet, set over medium-high heat.
8. Powder each piece of chicken lightly with flour and season with pepper and salt to taste.
9. Place in the skillet and sauté for 4 minutes on each side until golden.
10. Put the chicken on a platter, top with capers and drizzle a generous amount of sauce on top.
11. Serve garnished with lemons (optional).

Chicken Marsala

- Prep Time: 15 Minutes
- Cook Time: 25 Minutes
- Serves: 3

Ingredients

- Salt and pepper to taste
- 3 boneless, skinless chicken breasts
- ¼ cup of all-purpose flour
- ¾ cup of Marsala wine
- 1 cup of sliced mushrooms
- 6 tablespoons of olive oil
- 1 teaspoon of chopped parsley
- 2 tablespoons of butter

Steps

1. Place the chicken breasts (skin side down) between two pieces of plastic wrap, lightly pound until half-inch thick, then set aside.
2. Put two tablespoons of olive oil with pepper and salt into a large bowl, mix until well combined.
3. Add pounded chicken breasts and toss to coat.
4. Pour the remaining oil into a large skillet, then allow to heat at medium for about a minute.
5. Sprinkle the chicken breasts with flour, then dust until lightly coated.
6. Place in the heated skillet, skin side down. Sauté for 2-3 minutes or until golden. Flip and repeat for the other side.
7. Preheat your oven to 400°F.
8. Put the golden chicken breasts into a 13x9 inch pan and allow to cook for 12-15 minutes (do not discard the oil in the skillet).
9. Sauté the mushrooms in the skillet until lightly browned, add wine and allow to simmer until it reduces by half.
10. Remove the skillet from heat, add butter to the mixture and stir until it melts.
11. Remove chicken from the oven and put into the mushroom mix, toss and allow to cook for 2 more minutes over medium-high heat.
12. Put the chicken on a platter, drizzle sauce over it and serve topped with parsley.

Pasta

Chicken Carbonara

- Prep Time: 20 Minutes
- Cook Time: 20 Minutes
- Serves: 4

Ingredients

- 2 tablespoons of minced garlic
- 4 boneless, skinless chicken breasts
- 18 ounces of cooked spaghetti
- 4 ounces of thinly sliced prosciutto (chopped)
- ¼ teaspoon of ground black pepper
- 5 tablespoons of olive oil

- ¾ cup of heavy whipping cream
- w̄ cup of frozen peas
- ¾ cup of Alfredo sauce

Steps

1. Put two tablespoons of oil into a large skillet pan, set over medium heat and sauté the chicken for 3-5 minutes or until cooked through. Once cool enough to handle, cut into strips and put in a sealable plate to keep warm.
2. Put the remaining oil into a large sauté pan and set over medium heat. Once hot, add prosciutto and sauté until lightly brown. Add minced garlic and sauté until fragrant.
3. Add the chicken strips, alfredo sauce and whipping cream. Mix and allow to simmer for 3-5 minutes, stirring occasionally. Add frozen peas and black pepper, then stir again.
4. Pour very hot water over cooked pasta, stir and allow to heat for 1-2 minutes, then drain.
5. Toss pasta with sauce in a large pot until well incorporated.
6. Serve garnished with fresh minced parsley.

Cheese Manicotti

- Prep Time: 20 Minutes
- Cook Time: 40 Minutes
- Serves: 2

Ingredients

Béchamel sauce
- 2 tablespoons of flour
- 2 cups of milk
- 2 tablespoons of butter
- ½ teaspoon of salt
- A dash of nutmeg
- A pinch of white pepper

- Marinara sauce

Pasta

- 4 manicotti shells
- ½ cup of Romano cheese

For The Filling

- ¼ cup of Italian parsley (chopped)
- 12 ounces of ricotta cheese
- 1 teaspoon of salt
- ½ cup of provolone cheese
- ½ cup of mozzarella cheese
- ¼ Romano cheese
- 2 medium sized eggs

Steps

Béchamel Sauce

1. Melt two tablespoons of butter in a small sauté pan over medium heat, add flour and stir until well combined, then allow to cook for 5 minutes.
2. Pour the milk into a small saucepan and bring to a simmer, add salt, nutmeg and white pepper, stir and add to the butter mixture.
3. Allow to simmer for 10 more minutes, then set aside.

Shells

1. Fill the manicotti shells with the filling ingredients using a pastry bag.
2. Pour the marinara sauce at the bottom of a casserole dish.
3. Carefully put in the stuffed shells, then pour the rest of the béchamel sauce and add Romano cheese.
4. Preheat your oven at 425°F for 2 minutes.
5. Put the casserole dish in the oven and cook uncovered for 25 minutes.

6. Serve topped with minced fresh basil leaves.

Penne Alla Vodka

- Prep Time: 20 Minutes
- Cook Time: 15 Minutes
- Serves: 3

Ingredients
- ¼ cup of vodka
- 4 tablespoons of butter
- 3 cups of marinara sauce
- 2 tablespoons of minced garlic
- 1 cup of grated Romano cheese
- ½ onion (thinly sliced)
- 12 fresh basil leaves (chopped)
- ½ cup of heavy cream

- ½ teaspoon of kosher salt
- ½ teaspoon of freshly ground black pepper
- ½ teaspoon of hot red pepper flakes
- 1 pound of penne
- 3 tablespoon of flat leaf parsley (chopped)

Steps

1. Put the butter into a large sauté pan, set over medium heat and allow to melt. Add onion and stir fry until fragrant and translucent.
2. Add minced garlic and allow to cook for 2-3 minutes, stirring occasionally.
3. Put in the fresh basil leaves, red pepper flakes and parsley. Cook for another minute, stirring frequently.
4. Remove from heat and add vodka, then stir until well mixed.
5. Put the pan over medium-high heat and cook for 2-3 minutes. Add marinara and allow to simmer for 3-5 minutes.
6. Add the heavy cream, stir and allow to boil for 3-5 minutes or until it thickens, stirring frequently.
7. While the sauce cooks, bring a pot of water to a boil, add half a teaspoon and put in the penne.
8. When the penne is al dente, drain and set aside until ready to use.
9. Once boiled, add Romano cheese to sauce and season with salt and pepper to taste.
10. Transfer the cooked penne to a pot, pour in sauce and toss until well combined.
11. Serve topped with some Romano cheese.

Desserts

Colossal Brownie Sundae

- Prep Time: 60 Minutes
- Cook Time: 0 Minutes
- Serves: 6

Ingredients

Chocolate and Vanilla Custard
- 10 egg yolks
- 4 cups of milk
- ¼ cup of flour
- 1 teaspoon of vanilla
- 1 cup of sugar

Layered Dessert

- 2 cups of chocolate custard
- ½ cup of Grand Marnier
- 2 cups of whipping cream
- 2 loaves of pound cake
- 8 ounces of nougat with nuts (chopped)
- 1 cup of maraschino cherries (chopped)
- 2 cups of vanilla custard
- ½ pound of semi-sweet chocolate (chopped)

Steps

For Custard

1. Put the milk and sugar into a small saucepan, stir to combine and set over medium heat, then bring to a boil.
2. Put vanilla, egg yolks and flour into a medium sized mixing bowl and whisk until it thickens.
3. Mix a small amount of the hot milk in the egg mixture, then pour the mixture into the rest of the hot milk and whip into a smooth custard.
4. Pour the custard back into the saucepan and cook over medium heat, stirring continuously until thick.
5. Share the custard into two bowls, add the chopped semi-sweet chocolate into one of them and stir until well incorporated, then refrigerate both bowls of custard.

For Dessert

1. Slice the pound cake into 4×4 quarter inch pieces and place them at the bottom of a crystal bowl.
2. Top with Grand Marnier and drizzle with an even layer of vanilla custard.
3. Sprinkle with cherries, chocolate and nougat. Add more pound cake, more Grand Marnier, then drizzle an even layer of chocolate custard.

4. Sprinkle with cherries and chopped chocolate. Repeat until you have a few more layers, then refrigerate.
5. Pour whipping cream over the layered dessert and refrigerate until stiff.
6. Serve topped with whipped cream.

Tiramisu

- Prep Time: 40 Minutes
- Cook Time: 12 Minutes
- Serves: 4

Ingredients

Espresso Marinade
- 2 tablespoons of dark rum
- 1 cup of espresso

Lady Fingers
- 1 cup of all-purpose flour
- ¾ cup of sugar

- 6 large eggs

Mascarpone Cheese Mixture
- ¾ cup of powdered sugar
- 1 pound of mascarpone cheese
- 3 tablespoons of dark rum

For Serving
- w̄ cup of biscotti chocolate (crumbled)
- 1 tablespoon of cocoa powder

Steps

For The Lady Fingers
1. Preheat your oven to 350°F.
2. Grease a large cookie tray with butter and set aside.
3. Sift the flour and sugar and set those aside too.
4. Crack the eggs into a large mixing bowl, add sugar and whip with a mixer on high speed until frothy and thick.
5. Reduce the speed and slowly incorporate the flour and whip until well combined.
6. Scoop some batter onto the tray, forming three 6-inch-wide circles (you may have some batter left over).
7. Bake in the preheated oven for 12 minutes or until golden brown.
8. Remove from the oven and place on a cooling rack to cool at room temperature (best done a day before), then store in a sealed container at room temperature.

To Assemble Tiramisu (Done a day before)
1. Make the espresso and allow to cool completely, then add the rum and mix.
2. Mix the sugar, rum and mascarpone, then stir until well combined.
3. Soak the lady fingers in the espresso marinade for a few seconds and place at the bottom of a round 6-inch bowl.

4. Spread a thin layer of the mascarpone cheese mixture over the lady fingers. Repeat this process until you have two more layers (top lap layer should be cheese).
5. Seal with plastic wrap and refrigerate overnight.
6. Serve topped with chocolate biscotti and cocoa powder.

Kids

Spaghetti and Meatballs

- Prep Time: 15 Minutes
- Cook Time: 55 Minutes
- Serves: 6

Ingredients

Meatball Sauce
- ¼ cup of olive oil
- 6 cloves of garlic (minced)
- 2 tablespoons of olive oil
- 1 large Spanish onion (diced)

- ¼ cup of fresh Italian parsley (chopped)
- Salt and pepper to taste
- A can of plum tomatoes with juice
- 1 celery (chopped)

Meatballs

- 4 large eggs
- 2 ½ pound of ground beef
- 2 teaspoons of salt
- ½ cup of Romano cheese (grated)
- ¼ cup of fresh garlic (chopped)
- ¾ cup Italian seasoned breadcrumbs

Steps

Meatballs

1. Put all the ingredients into a bowl and mix by hand, then shape into small, round balls (golf ball size), and let rest for an hour.
2. Put the olive oil into a large pan and set over medium heat, add onion, garlic, and celery, stir and cook until fragrant.
3. Break the tomatoes and add them into the pan with juice, stir and add parsley.
4. Season with salt and pepper to taste.
5. Allow to boil for 5-10 minutes, then reduce heat and add the meatballs.
6. Allow to simmer for 45 minutes, then serve meatball sauce over pasta.

Fettuccine Alfredo

- Prep Time: 10 Minutes
- Cook Time: 10 Minutes
- Serves: 4

Ingredients
- Juice and zest of one lemon
- A pack of fettuccine egg pasta
- 2 cups of freshly grated Parmesan cheese
- Freshly chopped parsley (optional)
- 1 cup of heavy cream
- ¼ teaspoon of kosher salt
- Pepper to taste
- A pinch of powdered nutmeg

- 1 cup of half and half
- 8 tablespoons of salted butter

Steps

1. Put a large pot of water over high heat, add half a tablespoon of salt and bring to a boil.
2. Add pasta and cook until al dente, then drain and set aside.
3. Melt the butter in a large saucepan over medium heat, add cream and the half and half. Allow to heat for 1-2 minutes, then turn off heat and add lemon zest and juice.
4. Add a cup and a half of cheese and stir until smooth, then put in the nutmeg and mix well.
5. Season with salt and pepper to taste.
6. Add the cooked fettuccine pasta and toss until well combined and sauce begins to thicken.
7. Serve immediately.

Note: The sauce can be made a day before to save time. All you have to do is store it in an airtight jar or container and refrigerate until you are ready to use. When ready to use, heat over a low heat, stirring frequently until well heated.

Chapter 2
Olive Garden™

Olive Garden is one of the fastest growing chains of Italian restaurants. They first opened their doors in 1982 in Orlando and opened 145 more locations only seven years after. In fact, many Americans would say they had their first true taste of Italian food at a local Olive Garden restaurant. They have been on the fast rise ever since and now own over 800 locations globally.

Appetizers
Shrimp Scampi Fritta

- Prep Time: 10 Minutes
- Cook Time: 15 Minutes
- Serves: 4

Ingredients
- ½ teaspoon of fresh parsley
- ½ cup of dry white wine
- ¼ teaspoon of salt
- 5 lemon slices (to garnish)
- 2 tablespoons of white onion (finely chopped)
- 2 cups of cornstarch

- 1 tablespoon of freshly squeezed lemon juice
- w̄ cup of heavy cream
- 1 cup of unsalted butter (cut into cubes)
- Vegetable oil for frying
- ⅛ teaspoon of ground white pepper
- 1 pound of shrimp (shelled and defined)
- ½ cup of white vinegar

Steps

Fried Shrimp

1. Put a half cup of vegetable oil onto a large pan, set over medium heat and allow to heat for a few minutes.
2. Roll the shrimp in the cornstarch until properly coated, then add to hot oil.
3. Fry the shrimp for 2-3 minutes or until golden (fry in batches if your pan isn't large enough).
4. Remove from oil and place on a piece of paper towel to soak up the excess oil.

Shrimp Scampi Sauce

1. Put a heavy-bottomed pan on medium heat. Add vinegar, wine and onion, stir and allow to cook until the liquid reduces by half.
2. Add the butter and stir until it melts completely, then put in the white pepper, salt, parsley, lemon slices, lemon juice, and heavy cream. Stir to combine, then allow to cook for 3 more minutes.
3. Put the shrimp on a serving platter and drizzle with a generous amount of white wine sauce.
4. Serve and enjoy!

Lasagna Fritta

- Prep Time: 1 Hour 30 Minutes
- Cook Time: 25 Minutes
- Serves: 8

Ingredients
- 2 eggs at room temperature
- Vegetable oil for frying
- 1 teaspoon of Italian seasoning
- 2 cups of shredded mozzarella
- 1 ½ cups of marinara sauce
- 1 ½ cup of Alfredo sauce
- 1 box of lasagna noodles
- 1 tablespoon of Italian seasoning
- 4 cups of whole milk ricotta

- 2 eggs
- 1 cup of Pablo crumbs
- 2 small containers of shredded three-cheese blend (Romano, Asiago and Parmesan)

Steps

1. Put one container of the three-cheese blend in a large mixing bowl, add ricotta, a teaspoon of Italian seasoning and two eggs (at room temperature). Stir until well combined, then set aside.
2. Follow the instructions on the package to boil the noodles, drain and rinse with cold water, then cut off the ribboned edges with a pizza cutter.
3. Spread even amounts of the cheese mixture over each noodle, then fold one end two inches in and overlap with the other, pressing down lightly to seal it. Repeat this process for the rest of the noodles (gives about 16 pieces).
4. Place the noodles (sealed side down) and freeze for an hour.
5. Remove the noodles from the freezer 15 minutes before frying.
6. Crack two eggs into a shallow bowl and beat lightly.
7. Put half the second container of the three-cheese blend into another bowl, add Panko crumbs and 1 tablespoon of Italian seasoning, then stir to combine.
8. Put one cup of vegetable oil into a large skillet, set over medium-high heat and leave for 2-3 minutes until hot.
9. Put the lasagna bundles in the egg wash, then dredge in the crumb mixture until properly coated. Repeat this process for all the lasagna bundles and drop them on the baking tray.
10. Put 3 bundles of the lasagna bundles in the hot oil and allow to cook until 2-3 minutes on each side or until golden, then remove and place on paper towels to drain the excess oil. Continue to fry the lasagna bundles in batches of three until they are done.
11. Heat the marinara and Alfredo sauce separately.
12. Place the lasagna bundles on a serving platter, ladle some marinara sauce over them and repeat with Alfredo sauce, then sprinkle the rest of the three-cheese blend over them.

13. Serve and enjoy.

Soups, Salads and Breadsticks

Zuppa Toscana

- Prep Time: 5 Minutes
- Cook Time: 40 Minutes
- Serves: 8

Ingredients
- 8 slices of bacon
- 3 cups of water
- 4 cups of chopped kale
- 3 cloves of minced garlic
- Salt and pepper to taste
- 1 teaspoon of crushed red pepper flakes

- ½ a piece of red onion (diced)
- 450 grams of Italian sausage
- 3 ½ cups of low-sodium chicken broth
- 1 cup of heavy whipping cream
- 5 russet potatoes (thinly sliced)
- Parmesan cheese (to garnish)

Steps

1. Put the sausage in a large pot and allow it to brown over medium heat for 3-5 minutes, flipping it frequently so it doesn't burn, then remove from heat and set aside.
2. Cut the bacon into bite-sized pieces, then put into a pot and cook over medium heat for 2-3 minutes or until crispy.
3. Add onion and cook until translucent, stirring occasionally.
4. Add minced garlic and cook until fragrant, stirring frequently.
5. Pour in the water and chicken broth, stir, then season with pepper and salt to taste.
6. Add cooked sausage, potatoes and red pepper flakes, then cook covered for 10 minutes or until the potatoes are fork tender.
7. Add the kale and bring to a simmer, about 5-10 minutes.
8. Add the heavy cream, Stir and bring to a boil, stirring occasionally.
9. Ladle into soup bowls and serve topped with Parmesan cheese.

Italian Salad

- Prep Time: 15 Minutes
- Cook Time: 0 Minutes
- Serves: 4

Ingredients

Dressing
- ¼ teaspoon of black pepper
- ¼ cup of olive oil
- 1 teaspoon of Italian seasoning
- 2 tablespoons of white vinegar
- ¼ teaspoon of sea salt
- ½ teaspoon of garlic powder

- 2 tablespoons of mayonnaise

Salad
- 4-6 pepperoncini peppers
- 1 box of chopped Romaine hearts
- 20 garlic-flavored croutons
- ½ cup of whole black olive
- w̄ red onion (thinly sliced)
- w̄ cup of shredded Parmesan cheese
- 2 Roma tomatoes (sliced)
- ½ cup of green olives

Steps

Italian Dressing
1. Add mayonnaise, olive oil, salt, white vinegar, Italian seasoning, garlic powder and black powder into a small bowl and mix well with a whisk.

Salad
2. Tear the lettuce into large pieces by hand and put them into a large bowl. Add pepperoncini, black olives, croutons, onions, tomatoes and green olives.
3. Add your desired amount of dressing and toss until the salad is well coated.
4. Serve sprinkled with shredded Parmesan.

Breadsticks

- Prep Time: 25 Minutes
- Cook Time: 11 Minutes
- Serves: 12

Ingredients

Topping
- ½ teaspoon of sea salt
- 3 tablespoons of melted butter
- ¼ teaspoon of garlic powder

Dough
- 2 tablespoons of sugar

- 1 ½ cup of warm water
- 2 tablespoons of softened butter
- 4 cups of all-purpose flour
- 1 tablespoon of salt
- 1 tablespoon of instant yeast

Steps

Dough

1. Pour the warm water into a bowl, add sugar and yeast, mix with an immersion blender until the yeast dissolves completely, then allow to sit and froth for 5-10 minutes.
2. Add two cups of flour, butter and salt to the mixture and mix until well combined. Add the rest of the flour and mix (preferably by hand) until it's soft and doesn't stick to your hands.
3. Sprinkle some flour on a clean, dry surface and place the dough there. Roll it into a long log and cut into 12 pieces, then roll those pieces into six-inch-long logs too.
4. Spray a thin layer of olive oil cooking spray on two cookie sheets, then gently lay the rolls on the tray, leaving at least an inch between each piece.
5. Set the temperature of your oven to 170 degrees and put the rolls in, then allow them to rise for 20 minutes.
6. Once risen, remove from the oven and brush with half of the melted butter, then sprinkle with salt.
7. Preheat your oven to 400°F and bake them for 12-15 minutes.
8. Put the rest of the butter, sea salt and garlic powder into a bowl, mix well and brush over breadsticks once done.

Minestrone Soup

- Prep Time: 15 Minutes
- Cook Time: 25 Minutes
- Serves: 4

Ingredients

- ¼ cup of tomato paste
- 1 zucchini (sliced)
- 2 tablespoons of olive oil
- 1 bay leaf
- Fresh chopped parsley (to garnish)
- 2 ribs of celery (sliced)
- 2 teaspoons of Italian seasoning
- 1 small onion (diced)
- ½ cup of frozen cut green beans

- 1 can of white beans (drained and rinsed)
- 2 medium carrots (peeled and sliced)
- 2 cups of baby spinach
- 1 can of diced tomatoes
- ½ cup of small shell pasta
- 1 can of kidney beans
- 4 cups of vegetable broth
- 3 cloves of garlic (minced)
- ½ teaspoon of freshly ground pepper
- 2 cups of baby spinach leaves

Steps

1. Put the olive oil into a large pot and set over medium heat.
2. Once hot, add carrots, onion, zucchini and celery and cook for 3-5 minutes or until tender, then add garlic and cook until fragrant, stirring frequently.
3. Stir in the broth, tomatoes paste, Italian seasoning, tomatoes and bay leaf, then bring to a simmer.
4. Add kidney beans, white beans, pasta and green beans and allow to simmer over medium heat for 10-12 minutes.
5. Season with pepper and salt to taste, then add spinach leaves and cook covered until wilted.
6. Serve garnished with fresh parsley and enjoy!

Chicken E Fagioli

- Prep Time: 10 Minutes
- Cook Time: 20 Minutes
- Serves: 8

Ingredients

- 1 teaspoon of dried basil
- 1 cup of ditalini pasta
- ¾ teaspoon of dried thyme
- 2 tablespoons of olive oil (divided)
- 1 can of Great Northern beans (drained and rinsed)
- 1 can of diced tomatoes
- 1 onion (diced)
- 3 cloves of garlic (minced)
- 1 can of red kidney beans

- 3 cups of chicken broth
- 1 teaspoon of dried oregano
- 1 pound of spicy Italian sausage (casing removed)
- 2 stalks of celery
- 1 can of tomato sauce
- 3 carrots (peeled and diced)
- Freshly ground black pepper to taste
- ½ teaspoon of kosher salt

Steps

1. Bring a large pot of salted water to boil and cook pasta until al dente (or according to package instructions), then drain and set aside.
2. Put one tablespoon of olive oil into a large stock pot and set over medium heat. Add Italian sausage and cook for 3-5 minutes or until browned, crumbling the sausage as it cooks. Once done, remove from heat and drain excess fat.
3. Pour the remaining olive oil onto another stockpot, add onion, garlic, celery and carrots and allow to cook for 3-5 minutes or until tender, stirring occasionally.
4. Add the tomato sauce, chicken broth, Italian sausage, diced tomato, thyme, oregano, basil and one cup of water, stir and season with kosher salt and pepper to taste, then cook covered.
5. Bring to a boil, reduce heat and allow to simmer for 10-15 minutes or until the vegetables are fork tender.
6. Stir in the beans and pasta and cook until heated through.
7. Ladle into soup bowls and serve immediately.

Chicken and Seafood

Shrimp Alfredo

- Prep Time: 10 Minutes
- Cook Time: 30 Minutes
- Serves: 4

Ingredients

Shrimp
- 1 teaspoon of chopped garlic
- 12 ounces of shrimp (peeled and deveined)

- ¼ teaspoon of ground black pepper
- ½ teaspoon of salt
- 1 tablespoon of butter

Alfredo Sauce
- ¾ cup of grated Parmesan cheese
- 2 cups of heavy cream
- ½ teaspoon of garlic powder
- 4 ounces of butter

Pasta
- 12 ounces of fettuccine pasta

Steps

1. Bring a large pot of salted water to a boil, add pasta and allow to cook until al dente, then drain and set aside.
2. Season the shrimp with black pepper and salt.
3. Put a pan over medium heat, add butter and allow to melt, then add chopped garlic and cook until fragrant, stirring occasionally.
4. Add shrimp and cook on each side for 2-3 minutes or until it turns pink (do not overcook).
5. Combine the butter and cream in a small saucepan and cook only until small bubbles begin to form.
6. Add the grated Parmesan cheese and stir quickly until it melts, then add the garlic powder and stir again.
7. Put the pasta into a large bowl and serve topped with shrimp and Alfredo sauce.

8. **Note:** You can add a couple of spoons of cream cheese if your Alfredo sauce appears too thin.

Seafood Portofino

- Prep Time: 20 Minutes
- Cook Time: 25 Minutes
- Serves: 10

Ingredients

Portofino Sauce
- 10 cloves of garlic (minced)
- 2 ounces of butter
- 1 cup of heavy cream
- 1 cup of white wine
- ½ piece of yellow onion (diced)
- ¼ cup of shrimp stock

- ¼ cup of roux
- 1 teaspoon Old Bay seasoning
- 1 cup of milk

Seafood Portofino
- 1 pound of scallops
- 2 pounds of shrimp
- 3 tablespoons of olive oil
- 1 pound of precooked linguine (hot)
- 1 pound of crawfish
- 60 mussels

Steps

Portofino Sauce
1. Melt the butter in a large pan over medium heat. Add onion and garlic, stir and allow to cook until translucent.
2. Pour in the white wine, set the heat on high and bring to a boil, then turn down the heat to medium-low. Cook covered for 5 minutes, stirring occasionally.
3. Stir in the shrimp stock, roux and Old Bay seasoning, then allow to cook for 3 minutes.
4. Turn the heat to high, add heavy cream and milk, stir and bring to a boil. Turn the heat to medium and allow to simmer for 5 minutes, stirring occasionally.

Seafood Portofino
1. Pour the oil into a sauté pan and allow to heat over medium flame for a few minutes, then add shrimp, scallops, mussels (should be open) and crawfish, then cook until heated through, stirring occasionally.
2. Pour in the Portofino sauce and allow to cook for 2-5 minutes.
3. Move seafood to one side of the pan and add the linguine to the other side.

4. Toss until the linguine is properly coated, then allow to cook for 2-3 minutes. Once done, serve topped with fresh chopped parsley.

Chicken Alfredo

- Prep Time: 20 Minutes
- Cook Time: 30 Minutes
- Serves: 4

Ingredients
- 2 boneless, chicken breasts
- 12 ounces of fettuccine pasta
- 2 tablespoons of chopped parsley (to garnish)
- 2 tablespoons of olive oil
- 1 ½ tablespoons of flour
- 2 cups of heavy cream
- 1 ½ teaspoon of fresh ground pepper
- ½ cup + 2 tablespoons of butter

- ¾ cup of grated Parmesan cheese
- 3 cloves of garlic (minced)
- 1 ½ teaspoon of salt

Steps

1. Cook the pasta according to the instructions on the package, then drain and set aside.
2. Put a cast-iron grill pan over high heat, then add olive oil. Once hot, add two tablespoons of butter, then put in the chicken breasts and season with pepper and salt to taste.
3. Cook chicken breasts for 3-5 minutes on each side until golden and cooked through. Put into a sealed container and set aside until cool enough to handle.
4. Melt the remaining butter in a large skillet over medium heat. Add garlic and cook until fragrant. Reduce heat to low and season with remaining salt and pepper.
5. Slowly stir in the butter, then add the cream, stirring until well combined.
6. Cook for 5-10 minutes or until the sauce starts to thicken. Add half a cup of Parmesan cheese, stir and cook until smooth. Remove from heat and keep warm until ready to serve.
7. Put the cooked pasta in a serving bowl, top with grilled chicken and drizzle a generous amount of sauce over it.
8. Serve garnished with parsley and enjoy.

Pasta

Chicken Scampi Pasta

- Prep Time: 20 Minutes
- Cook Time: 25 Minutes
- Serves: 6

Ingredients
- ½ teaspoon of dried basil
- 4 tablespoons of unsalted butter (divided)
- ½ yellow bell pepper (thinly sliced)
- 4 tablespoons of flour (divided)

- 1 pound of angel hair pasta
- 1 cup of grated Parmesan cheese (divided)
- 2 tablespoons of garlic (minced)
- 1 teaspoon of kosher salt
- 1 pound of boneless, skinless chicken breast
- ½ red bell pepper (thinly sliced)
- ½ teaspoon of red pepper flakes
- ½ cup of heavy cream
- 1 teaspoon of dried oregano
- 2 tablespoons of olive oil
- 1 cup of chicken broth
- 1 cup of white wine
- 2 tablespoons of minced garlic
- ½ green bell pepper
- ½ teaspoon of ground black pepper
- 1 tablespoon of lemon juice

Steps

1. Put a cast iron skillet over medium-high heat, add 2 tablespoons of butter. Once melted, add onions and bell peppers, stir and allow to cook for 2-3 minutes. Transfer the vegetables to a bowl and set aside until ready to use.
2. Put the remaining butter in the skillet and allow melt over medium heat, add half of the flour and the garlic. Stir and allow to cook for just a few seconds.
3. Add oregano, red pepper flakes, chicken broth, wine and basil, then allow to cook for 18- 20 minutes or until the liquid in the mixture reduces by half.
4. Cook the pasta in a large pot of boiling water over medium heat until al dente, drain (do not rinse) and set aside.
5. Add two tablespoons of olive oil to a second pan and put over medium heat.
6. Season the chicken breasts with pepper and salt, then dredge in the rest of the flour.

7. Put the flour-coated chicken in the pan of hot oil and cook for 3-5 minutes on each side or until golden and cooked through. Remove and set aside.
8. When the sauce is ready, add the heavy cream and mix until the sauce is thick and creamy.
9. Add half of the Parmesan cheese and lemon juice, then mix until well combined.
10. Add the pasta and bell pepper mixture, then toss until well mixed.
11. Serve topped with chicken and Parmesan.

Oven Baked Tortellini Alfredo

- Prep Time: 5 Minutes
- Cook Time: 30 Minutes
- Serves: 4

Ingredients

- 1 tablespoon of garlic (minced)
- 2 chicken breasts
- ½ cup of shredded mozzarella
- 1 bottle of herb and garlic marinade
- ½ cup of grated Romano cheese
- ¼ cup of Panko crumbs
- 6 tablespoons of butter

- 1 bag of dried cheese tortellini (cooked according to instructions on the package and drained)
- Salt and pepper to taste
- ½ cup of grated Parmesan cheese
- 1 ½ cup of heavy cream
- 1 ½ cup of milk
- 2 tablespoons of all-purpose flour

Steps

1. Preheat your oven to 350°F.
2. Place the chicken breasts between two pieces of plastic wrap and pound until they are at least half an inch thick.
3. Pour the marinade over chicken and toss to coat, then put into the oven and allow to bake for 25 minutes.
4. Melt the butter in a saucepan over medium heat, add garlic and sauté until fragrant.
5. Add the rest of the ingredients (except Panko crumbs and mozzarella) into the saucepan and stir until well combined, then bring to a simmer. Once done, remove from heat and set aside.
6. Remove half a cup of Alfredo sauce to set aside and pour the rest into a large bowl. Add the cooked pasta and toss until well coated.
7. Remove chicken from the oven and slice into bits, then set aside.
8. Change the settings on your oven to broil-high.
9. Grease a casserole dish with olive oil cooking spray, then pour in pasta and top with the rest of the Alfredo sauce.
10. Add chicken, Panko crumbs and mozzarella, then broil for 3-5 minutes or until cheese starts to crust and brown.
11. Remove from the oven and serve.

Note: You should boil the pasta 4-5 minutes shy of the time written on the package because the pasta will still cook in the oven.

Desserts

Lemon Cream Cake

- Prep Time: 30 Minutes
- Cook Time: 45 Minutes
- Serves: 12

Ingredients

- ½ teaspoon of vanilla
- 3 egg whites
- ½ cup of flour
- 1 box of white cake mix

- 1 teaspoon of fresh lemon juice
- 1 ½ cups of heavy whipping cream
- w̄ cup of oil
- 1 ½ cups of cream cheese
- 1 tablespoon of lemon zest
- ½ cup of powdered sugar
- ¼ cup of cold butter
- 1 ¼ cups of water
- 2 teaspoons of fresh lemon juice
- 3 cups of powdered sugar
- 1 ½ tablespoons of fresh lemon juice

Steps

1. Put the cake mix, egg whites, water, two teaspoons of fresh lemon juice, oil and lemon zest into a large bowl, stir with a wooden spoon or electronic mixer until well combined.
2. Grease and flour a spring-form pan, then pour in the batter and bake for 40-45 minutes at 350°F. Place on a wire rack once done and allow to cool.
3. Put the softened cream cheese, half a tablespoon of fresh lemon juice, half of the powdered sugar into a bowl, stir until smooth, then set aside.
4. Put the heavy whipping cream into a medium bowl and whisk until stiff peaks form, then combine with cream cheese mixture, preferably by hand.
5. To make the crumb topping, combine the butter, flour, remaining sugar, one teaspoon of lemon juice and vanilla in a food processor until smooth.
6. Cut the cooled cake in half, crosswise. Drizzle the remaining lemon juice on each side, then spread half of the mixture on the bottom end of the cake and place the top half on top, then spread the remaining cream on the top and sides of the cake.
7. Sprinkle the crumb topping over the cake and pat some the sides too.

8. For better results, refrigerate for 20-30 minutes, then cut into slices and serve.

White Chocolate Raspberry Cheesecake

- Prep Time: 35 Minutes
- Cook Time: 1 Hour 25 Minutes
- Serves: 8

Ingredients

- 2 cups of whipped cream
- 1 chocolate cookie crust
- ⅔ cup of raspberry sauce
- ½ cup of white chocolate
- 4 cups of cream cheese
- 4 large egg yolks
- ¾ pure cane sugar

- ½ teaspoon of salmon extract
- 2 teaspoons of vanilla extract

Steps

1. Spray a nine-inch spring-form pan with cooking spray and line the outside of the pan with aluminum foil to stop moisture from seeping into the cake, then put in the chocolate cookie crust.
2. Preheat your oven to 325°F.
3. Combine the cream cheese, vanilla extract, almond extract and cane sugar with a mixer, add egg and mix until creamy and smooth, then pour over cookie crust.
4. Drizzle the raspberry sauce over the batter, making sure to spread it out evenly, then make swirls with the sauce using a fork or table knife. Add more sauce and repeat the process.
5. Place the spring-form pan in a roasting pan with at least half a cup of water at the bottom.
6. Place the pan into the oven and bake for 80-90 minutes at 325°F or until the cake is cooked through.
7. Leave the cake to cool in the oven with the oven door open for 30-40 minutes or until cool enough to handle, then remove from the oven and allow to cool completely.
8. Once cool, cover and refrigerate overnight.
9. Decorate your cheesecake with whipped cream and white chocolate the next day.
10. Use a vegetable peeler to shave off bits of the white chocolate and sprinkle over the cake.
11. Make small swirls of whipped cream around the cake. Then slice up and serve.

Kids

Meat Sauce Pasta

- Prep Time: 10 Minutes
- Cook Time: 35 Minutes
- Serves: 10

Ingredients
- ½ cup of finely chopped pepperoni
- 6 cups of marinara sauce
- 1 pound of ground beef
- 1 teaspoon of Italian seasoning
- 1 can of crushed tomatoes
- 2 tablespoons of olive oil

- 1 cup of chopped onions
- 1 pound of Italian sausage (casing removed)
- 20 ounces of cooked pasta (hot)

Steps

1. Put the olive oil into a large pot, add onions and sauté over medium heat until translucent.
2. Add crushed tomatoes and marinara sauce and bring to a simmer over low heat.
3. Cook the Italian sausage and ground beef in a large skillet over medium heat until browned and cooked through, drain excess fat and add the meat to the sauce.
4. Add chopped pepperoni and Italian seasoning, then bring to a simmer for 15-20 minutes. Season with salt and pepper to taste.
5. Serve over cooked pasta and enjoy!

Chapter 3
Bertucci's™

The first Bertucci's pizza and bocce opened its doors in 1981 in Massachusetts. They currently have 58 locations and although they now operate under a new owner, their meals haven't lost the true Italian essence.

Appetizers
Maryland-Style Crab Cakes

- Prep Time: 10 Minutes
- Cook Time: 15 Minutes
- Serves: 6

Ingredients
- ½ teaspoon of salt
- 1 pound of crab meat (well-drained)
- 2 eggs
- 1 ½ cups of Panko crumbs
- 3 tablespoons of mayonnaise
- 2 tablespoons of sweet onion (finely chopped)

- 2 teaspoons of Old Bay seasoning
- 3 dashes of Tabasco sauce
- 2 teaspoons of Dijon-style mustard
- 2 tablespoons of fresh parsley
- ½ teaspoon of Worcestershire sauce
- ½ teaspoon of freshly ground black pepper
- 1 tablespoon of freshly squeezed lemon juice
- Vegetable oil for frying

Cocktail Sauce
- 2 tablespoons of lemon juice
- ½ cup of ketchup
- ½ teaspoon of Worcestershire sauce
- 1 tablespoon of prepared horseradish

Tartar Sauce
- 1 tablespoon of sweet onion (chopped)
- ½ cup of mayonnaise
- 1 teaspoon of Dijon-style mustard
- Salt and pepper to taste
- 1 tablespoon of freshly squeezed lemon juice
- 1 tablespoon of sweet pickle relish (drained)

Steps
1. Crack the eggs into a large mixing bowl, add the mayonnaise and whisk until smooth.
2. Add the Worcestershire sauce, Old Bay seasoning, lemon juice, Tabasco, pepper and salt, and whisk until well combined.
3. Add the crab, onion and parsley, stir until well mixed.
4. Add the Panko crumbs and mix properly until the mixture is able to hold when molded (add ¼ cup more if it breaks apart easily).
5. Grease the inside of a w̄ measure cup with non-stick cooking spray, scoop in the crab mixture and flatten the top with the broad side of a spoon until smooth.

6. Turn the cup upside down on a large, flat plate. Tap gently on the bottom of the cup to free the crab cake, then gently press it down. Repeat this process until all the mixture has been molded and pressed down.
7. Cover with a plastic wrap and refrigerate for 1-2 hours, then prepare the sauces while it cools.

For The Cocktail Sauce

1. Put the horseradish and ketchup in a small bowl and stir until well combined.
2. Add lemon juice, Worcestershire sauce and stir until well combined, then refrigerate until ready to use.

For The Tartar Sauce

1. Put all the ingredients for the sauce into a medium mixing bowl, whisk until well combined and smooth.
2. Season with pepper and sauce to taste and refrigerate until ready to use.

To Fry Crab Cakes

1. Add about 1 ½ cup of vegetable oil to a large frying pan and heat over medium-high heat for 2-3 minutes.
2. Fry the crab cakes in batches and allow to cook on each side for 2-3 minutes or until golden.
3. Place a piece of parchment paper on a flat plate and place the fried crab cakes on it to drain the excess oil.
4. Serve the crab cakes hot with some tartar and cocktail sauce.

Roasted Tuscan Vegetables

- Prep Time: 5 Minutes
- Cook Time: 12 Minutes
- Serves: 4

Ingredients

- 2 tablespoons of balsamic vinegar
- 1 zucchini (cut lengthways)
- ⅛ teaspoon of basil
- 1 yellow squash (cut lengthways)
- ½ cup of olive oil
- Freshly ground black pepper to taste
- ½ teaspoon of dried Italian herbs
- 1 teaspoon of chopped fresh garlic

- ¼ cup of freshly grated Parmesan cheese
- 1 red onion (quartered)
- 1 tablespoon of seasoned vegetable base
- 1 red bell pepper (cut in half and seeds removed)

Steps

1. Preheat your oven to 400°F.
2. Place the vegetables on a baking sheet, drizzle with half of the olive oil and grill for 2-3 minutes on each side, then remove and set aside.
3. Pour the rest of the oil into a large mixing bowl, add garlic, Italian herbs, vinegar, Parmesan cheese, black pepper and seasoned vegetable base. Stir until well combined and smooth, then set aside.
4. Cut the vegetables into 1-2-inch bits and throw them into the seasoned mix. Toss until properly coated then put into an aluminum grilling pan.
5. Put the pan on a grill and cook the vegetables for 5 minutes, flipping them every once in a while so that they don't burn and that the cheese melts completely.
6. Put on a serving platter and serve garnished with basil.

Soups and Salads

Baby Arugula and Grilled Chicken

- Prep Time: 20 Minutes
- Cook Time: 20 Minutes
- Serves: 4

Ingredients

Marinade
- ½ cup of honey
- ½ cup of olive oil

- ½ teaspoon of pepper
- ½ cup of balsamic vinegar
- 1 teaspoon of Salt
- ¼ cup of dijon mustard

Salad

- 4 chicken breasts
- 1 tablespoon of olive oil
- A pack of bocconcini cheese (Cut each ball in half)
- 3 Roma tomatoes (diced)
- 2 red onions (sliced)
- 1 pack of baby arugula
- 2 sweet potatoes (chopped)
- 1 cup of chopped carrots

Steps

1. Preheat your oven to 450°F.
2. Season the potatoes with pepper and salt to taste, toss with olive oil, then put into the oven and allow to roast for 20 minutes.
3. Put all the ingredients for the marinade in a bowl and whisk until well combined.
4. Cut the chicken into large slices and put into a ziploc bag, pour the marinade all over the chicken and shake to coat, then seal and let sit for 10 minutes.
5. Set your grill to medium-high and allow it to heat for a minute or two.
6. Remove the chicken from the ziploc bag and grill for 15 minutes, flipping regularly until evenly browned.
7. Rinse the arugula, then place in a colander to drain.
8. Once the chicken is cooked, remove from heat and allow to cool, then cut into thin slices.
9. Share the roasted potatoes and vegetables between four bowls, top with sliced chicken and cheese, then serve.

Italian Sausage Soup

- Prep Time: 20 Minutes
- Cook Time: 1 hour
- Serves: 3

Ingredients

- 2 cloves of garlic (minced)
- 4 cups of chopped kale
- Kosher salt to taste
- 1 pound of hot Italian sausage (case removed)
- 1 cup of shredded mozzarella cheese
- 1 yellow onion (sliced)
- w̄ cup of white rice

- ¼ teaspoon of red chili flakes
- 2 tablespoons of extra virgin olive oil
- 2 cans of whole plum tomatoes
- 4 cups of low-sodium beef broth
- 1 teaspoon of fennel seeds

Steps

1. Put the olive oil in a large Dutch oven and allow it to heat over medium-high heat.
2. Add the sausage and allow to cook for 3-5 minutes or until well browned, using a wooden spoon to break them apart.
3. Add the garlic, onions, and fennel seeds, and cook for 1-2 minutes or until fragrant.
4. Add the tomatoes (with juice), chili flakes and broth.
5. Cook covered until it starts to boil, then reduce the heat to medium and allow to simmer for 40 minutes, stirring occasionally and mashing up the tomatoes with the broad side of a spoon.
6. Add rice and allow to cook for 15 more minutes or until the rice is properly cooked.
7. Remove the soup from the heat and stir in the kale, then allow to sit until the leaves are wilted.
8. Season with kosher salt and pepper to taste, then pour into bowls and serve topped with shredded cheese.

Pasta

Rigatoni Abruzzi

- Prep Time: 20 Minutes
- Cook Time: 1 hour
- Serves: 4

Ingredients

- 2 cloves of garlic (minced)
- A can of garlic and onion spaghetti sauce
- A can of roasted bell pepper (chopped)
- 1 onion (diced)

- 4 Italian sausages
- ½ teaspoon of dried oregano
- ½ tablespoon of crushed red pepper
- 1 box of penne pasta
- 1 teaspoon of sugar
- ½ teaspoon of fresh basil (chopped)
- 2 tablespoons of olive oil
- ½ teaspoon of fresh parsley

Steps

1. Put a non-stick pan over low heat, add olive oil and allow to heat for a few minutes.
2. Once hot, add onions and allow to cook until translucent and soft.
3. Put the sausages into another pan and sauté for 5-6 minutes on each side or until browned, then add two tablespoons and allow to cook for 3-5 more minutes.
4. Put the tomato sauce into a saucepan, add fried onions, sugar, parsley, garlic, oregano, red pepper flakes and basil. Stir until well mixed, then turn down the heat and allow to simmer for 5-10 minutes.
5. Add sausage and red bell peppers and allow to cook for 15-20 minutes.
6. Follow the directions on the box to cook the pasta with a dash of oil and salt, then drain.
7. Serve pasta topped with sauce and garnish with shredded Parmesan cheese and fresh basil, if desired.

Chicken Domani

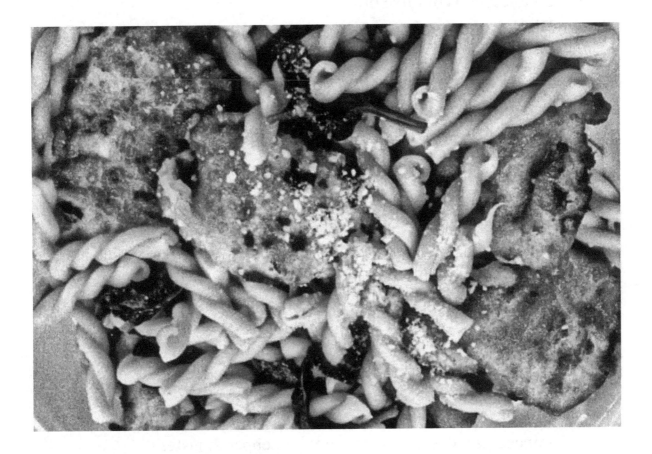

- Prep Time: 15 Minutes
- Cook Time: 30 Minutes
- Serves: 4

Ingredients

- 1 box of gemelli pasta
- 3 boneless, skinless chicken breasts
- 2 eggs
- ½ cup of Panko crumbs
- 4 cloves of garlic (minced)
- 1 bottle of chardonnay white wine
- ½ block of Asiago cheese (grated)

- ½ teaspoon of Sriracha hot sauce
- 1 bag of spinach
- 2 tablespoons of olive oil
- Black pepper to taste

Steps

1. Crack the eggs into a small bowl and beat lightly, then set aside.
2. Cut each chicken breast crosswise, then cut each of the pieces in half.
3. Dip each of the pieces of chicken in the egg. Shake off the excess, then dredge them in the crumbs until they are all properly coated, then set aside.
4. Heat the oil in a large pan over medium heat, then add the chicken, and cook on each side for 2-3 minutes on each side or until golden, then transfer to a plate lined with a piece of paper towel to soak up the excess oil. Repeat this process for the rest of the chicken, then set aside.
5. Bring a large pot of salted water to a boil and cook the pasta following the directions on the box, then drain.
6. Pour the white wine into a wide saucepan, add grated cheese and minced garlic, stir and season with pepper to taste.
7. Add Sriracha sauce (or more if you want it spicy) and cook for 5 minutes or until bubbles start to form, then turn down the heat and allow to simmer.
8. Add the spinach and chicken and allow to simmer for 10-15 minutes.
9. Put the pasta in a large mixing bowl, scoop some of the sauce over it and toss well. Repeat the process until the pasta is well soaked.
10. Serve and enjoy!

Entrees

Sautéed Chicken Piccata

- Prep Time: 20 Minutes
- Cook Time: 45 Minutes
- Serves: 4

Ingredients

- ½ cup of chicken broth
- 4 boneless, skinless chicken breasts
- 3 tablespoons of lemon juice
- 2 tablespoons of grated Parmesan cheese
- ¼ cup of brined capers

- Salt and pepper to taste
- w̄ cup of flour
- ¼ cup of fresh chopped parsley
- 4 tablespoons of olive oil
- 4 tablespoons of butter

Steps

1. Make a shallow cut crosswise on each piece of chicken breast, then spread them out before placing them between two pieces of plastic wrap. Pound them until they are at least a quarter inch thick.
2. Put the flour, pepper, grated Parmesan and salt into a medium bowl and mix until well combined.
3. Rinse the pieces of chicken and shake to get off excess water, then dredge into the flour mixture until properly coated.
4. Heat the oil and half the butter over medium heat in a large frying pan. Add chicken and allow to cook on each side for 3-5 minutes on each side until golden.
5. Remove the chicken and place on a serving platter, then cover with a plastic wrap or aluminum foil to keep warm.
6. Pour the broth into a saucepan, add lemon juice and capers, stir and allow to cook until the sauce reduces by half.
7. Add the remaining butter and mix until fully melted.
8. Drizzle the sauce over the chicken and serve with pasta, then garnish with lemon wedges and parsley.

Four Cheese Ravioli

- Prep Time: 15 Minutes
- Cook Time: 30 Minutes
- Serves: 4

Ingredients

- ½ teaspoon of salt
- 2 tablespoons of olive oil
- ½ cup of chopped fresh parsley
- ¼ cup of unsalted butter
- 1 pack of frozen four cheese ravioli
- 2 medium shallots (thinly sliced)
- ¼ cup of black pepper

- 3 Roma tomatoes (sliced)
- ½ cup of dry white wine

Ingredients

1. Heat oil and half the butter in a large skillet over medium-high heat until the butter is completely melted.
2. Add the shallots and sauté for 2-3 minutes or until golden.
3. Add tomatoes and sauté on high for 3-5 minutes or until they lose moisture completely.
4. Pour in the wine and allow to cook until the liquid evaporates and the tomatoes are soft.
5. Season with pepper and salt, then add the remaining butter and parsley, stir and allow to cook until the butter melts completely.
6. Bring a large pot of salted water to a boil, add the ravioli and allow to cook until al dente, then drain.
7. Transfer the drained ravioli to a large pot, add tomato mixture and toss until well combined.
8. Serve and enjoy!

Pizzas

Silano Pizza

- Prep Time: 10 Minutes
- Cook Time: 30 Minutes
- Serves: 4

Ingredients

- Half a pound of chicken (cooked and diced)
- 1 refrigerated pizza dough
- ½ cup of whipping cream
- 1 medium head of broccoli

- 8 ounces of mozzarella cheese (cut into half-inch slices)
- ¼ teaspoon of pepper
- 5 tablespoons of Parmesan cheese
- 2 tablespoons of lemon juice
- Half a teaspoon of olive oil

Steps

1. Preheat your oven at 400°F.
2. Grease a cookie sheet with olive oil cooking spray, then place the pizza dough on it and spread it until it is at least an inch shy of touching the edge of the tray.
3. Put the whipping cream into a medium bowl, add pepper, lemon juice and Parmesan cheese to make the sauce.
4. Top the pizza with half of the white sauce, making sure that it is evenly spread.
5. Put the broccoli and chicken on the pizza and top with the other half of the white sauce.
6. Bake the pizza for 15 minutes or until the crust is golden and crispy.

Nolio Pizza

- Prep Time: 20 Minutes
- Cook Time: 40 Minutes
- Serves: 4

Ingredients
- 1 tablespoon of olive oil
- 1 cup of heavy whipping cream
- 1 ball of pizza dough (home-made or store bought)
- 1 cup of shredded prosciutto
- 1 teaspoon of ground white pepper
- 1 medium onion (thinly sliced)
- 1 ½ cup of shredded mozzarella

- 1 medium lemon juice

Steps

1. Preheat your oven to 400°F.
2. Put the heavy cream into a small saucepan and cook over medium heat until it thickens.
3. Add lemon juice and white pepper, stir and remove from heat.
4. Sauté the onions in the olive oil over medium heat until they are lightly browned, then drain and set aside.
5. Roll out the dough and place on a greased pizza pan.
6. Sprinkle the cheese all over the dough and top with shredded prosciutto.
7. Drizzle the cream mixture over the prosciutto and top with browned onions.
8. Bake for 10- 12 minutes, then remove from the oven and cut into equal slices.

Desserts

Limoncello Mascarpone Cake

- Prep Time: 10 Minutes
- Cook Time: 35 Minutes
- Serves: 12

Ingredients

- 3 eggs
- 2 ½ cups of flour
- ½ cup of limoncello
- 1 teaspoon of baking soda

- Zest and juice of one lemon
- 1 ½ cups of sugar
- ½ cup of softened butter
- ½ cup of buttermilk
- ½ teaspoon of salt

Frosting
- 2 cups of heavy cream
- 2 cups of mascarpone cheese
- ⅔ of powdered sugar
- 1 ¼ cup of lemon curd

Steps

For The Cake
1. Preheat your oven to 350°F.
2. Grease two nine-inch round cake pans with butter or olive oil, then line them with a piece of parchment paper.
3. Lightly grease and flour the papers, then set aside.
4. Put the lemon juice, limoncello and lemon zest into a small bowl and stir until well combined.
5. Put dry ingredients into another bowl and mix well, then set aside too.
6. Put the cream, butter and sugar into a large bowl, mix well, then add one egg at a time and stir until well combined.
7. Add small amounts of the flour, limoncello and buttermilk, alternating until fully incorporated.
8. Pour the batter into the pans and bake for 20-25 minutes, then remove from the oven and set aside to cool in the pans. Once completely cooled, remove the cake from the pans.

To Make Frosting

1. Put the mascarpone cheese and lemon curd into a medium bowl and whip until they start to form soft peaks.
2. Slowly stir in the sugar until well combined, then fold the mixture into the whipped cream until well incorporated.
3. To frost, place one round cake on a platter, top with $\bar{w}$ of the frosting, then put the second cake over the frosting.
4. Cover both cakes with the rest of the frosting and decorate with white chocolate shavings if desired before cutting into slices.

Flourless Chocolate Cake

- Prep Time: 15 Minutes
- Cook Time: 45 Minutes
- Serves: 12

Ingredients

- 1 teaspoon of pure vanilla extract
- ½ cup of water
- 1 cup of salted butter
- ¼ teaspoon of salt
- 6 medium eggs (at room temp.)
- 2 ¼ cups of bittersweet chocolate chips
- ¾ cup of granulated sugar

Steps

1. Preheat your oven to 300°F.
2. Grease a nine-inch round glass pie plate with some butter and set aside.
3. Put a small saucepan over medium heat, add water, sugar and salt, stir and heat until completely dissolved.
4. Put the chocolate chips in a microwave-friendly bowl and microwave on high for 1-2 minutes, stirring in between until fully melted.
5. Cut the butter into bits, add them in the chocolate and stir until melted.
6. Pour in the sugar mix and stir until well combined, then beat in the eggs, one at a time.
7. Add the vanilla extract and mix until smooth.
8. Pour the batter into the pan, then fill a larger pan with boiling water until it is almost halfway full.
9. Carefully place the cake into the large pan of boiled water until it is halfway up the side.
10. Leave the cake pan in the water bath for 45 minutes. Once done, remove and allow to cool on a wire rack (the center will still appear wet).
11. Refrigerate the cake overnight in the pan for the best results, then cut into slices and serve topped with ice cream, whipped cream or fresh berries.

Kids

Chicken Rigatoni

- Prep Time: 20 Minutes
- Cook Time: 22 Minutes
- Serves: 1

Ingredients

- 1 cup of rigatoni pasta (cooked without salt)
- 1 tablespoon of green peas
- ¼ teaspoon of minced garlic
- 1 tablespoon of extra virgin olive oil

- ¼ cup of shredded mascarpone cheese
- 1 teaspoon of white onion (finely chopped)
- ¼ cup of pasta sauce
- 1 boneless, skinless chicken breast (cut into bite-sized pieces)
- Salt to taste

Steps

- Heat the oil in a medium non-stick pan over medium heat. Add chicken and cook for 5-7 minutes or until browned, stirring frequently.
- Add the onions and cook until soft and fragrant, then add garlic and cook for 1-2 minutes.
- Add pasta sauce and allow to simmer on low for 5-10 minutes, then season with salt to taste.
- Add mascarpone, stir and allow to cook for 2-3 minutes or until well combined, then remove from heat.
- Add the pasta to the sauce and toss until well combined, then serve.

Chapter 4
California Pizza Kitchen™

California Pizza Kitchen was opened in 1985 by Larry Flax and Rick Rosenfield in Beverly Hills. They combined their passion for food and have continued to do so to date, with over 250 locations across the United States and 11 other countries. They have made it easy for students, travelers and sports fans to access their meals by diversifying their services, but why wait until you have to travel or go for a football match at the local stadium?

Appetizers

Lettuce Wraps

- Prep Time: 15 Minutes
- Cook Time: 25 Minutes
- Serves: 4

Ingredients

Sauce
- 2 teaspoons of minced garlic
- 2 teaspoons of minced ginger
- ½ teaspoon of cornstarch

- ¼ cup of soy sauce
- 1 ½ teaspoons of water
- 1 ½ tablespoons of sugar
- 2 ½ teaspoons of seasoned rice vinegar
- 3 tablespoons of rice wine
- 2 ¼ teaspoon of Asian sesame oil

Crispy Rice Sticks
- 1 pack of wonton wraps
- 4 cups of canola oil
- ¼ cup of rice sticks

Lettuce Wraps
- 2 cups of crisp rice sticks
- 1 ½ tablespoons of canola oil
- 2 scallions (chopped)
- 4 shiitake mushrooms (stemmed and chopped)
- 8 leaves of iceberg lettuce (washed)
- 1 pound of ground chicken
- ½ teaspoon of chili oil
- 1 cup of lettuce wrap sauce
- 1 can of water cup chestnuts (drained and chopped)

Steps

To Make Sauce
1. Put the water into a small bowl, add the cornstarch, stir and set aside.
2. Put the rice wine, vinegar, and soy sauce into a small saucepan and slowly stir in the cornstarch until well combined, then add sugar and sesame oil. Cook over low heat for 2-3 minutes or until it starts to simmer.

3. Add ginger and garlic, stir and allow to cook for five more minutes, stirring occasionally.
4. Remove from heat and set aside until ready to use.

Crispy Rice Sticks

1. Pour the oil into a large pot and set over medium heat for 1-2 minutes.
2. While the oil heats, unfold the wonton wraps gently and cut them into quarter inch strips, then gently toss to separate them.
3. When the oil is hot, add the wonton strips, pressing down with a wire skimmer as soon as they start to puff up. Fry for 30 seconds or until slightly golden, then remove from heat.
4. Place the fried sticks on pieces of parchment paper to drain off excess oil and allow to cool completely.

To Make Lettuce Wraps

1. Put a pot on high heat, drizzle half the oil at the bottom and add the minced chicken, crumbling it with the spoon as you stir. Cook for 6-7 minutes until browned, then put on pieces of parchment paper to drain the excess oil.
2. Put the pot back on the heat and add the rest of the oil, allowing it to heat up before putting in the mushroom and chestnuts, then stir fry for 1-2 minutes.
3. Add the minced chicken, then add half of the cooked sauce. Allow to cook for 1-2 minutes or until the chicken darkens in color and the sauce is completely absorbed.
4. Add the chili oil and scallions, stir fry for about 30 seconds, then turn off the heat.
5. To assemble, put small portions of the rice stick on each lettuce leaf, top with the chicken mixture and serve with the remaining sauce on the side.

Tuscan Hummus

- Prep Time: 20 Minutes
- Cook Time: 0 Minutes
- Serves: 3

Ingredients

- ¼ cup of freshly squeezed lemon
- 10 cloves of garlic
- 2 tablespoons of fresh Italian parsley (minced)
- 1 ½ teaspoon of salt
- ¼ cup of cold water
- 2 cans of cannellini (drained)
- ½ cup of tahini

- ⅛ teaspoon of ground coriander
- 1 ½ tablespoon of soy sauce
- 1 ½ teaspoon of cumin
- ½ teaspoon of cayenne pepper

Checca

- ½ cup of extra virgin olive oil
- 2 large Roma tomatoes (sliced)
- 2 teaspoons of salt
- 1 tablespoon of minced fresh basil
- 1 tablespoon of minced garlic

Steps

1. Mince the garlic cloves using the steel blade of a food processor, stopping occasionally to scrape down the sides.
2. Put in the beans and process until they are just coarsely chopped.
3. While the machine runs, puree the beans while slowly pouring the tahini through the feed tube.
4. With the food processor still running, add soy sauce, lemon juice and olive oil through the feed tube, stopping it occasionally to scrape down the sides.
5. Stop the processor, remove the lid and add the cayenne pepper, salt, coriander and cumin, then process until well combined.
6. Add the cold water if the mixture seems too thick; if not, you can skip this step.
7. Pour the hummus into a bowl, cover with plastic wrap and refrigerate for an hour or two before serving.
8. Put all the checca ingredients into a mixing bowl, toss to combine and refrigerate until ready to serve.
9. Serve the hummus chilled with some tomato checca on top and some toasted pita bread on the side.

Soups and Salads

Sedona Tortilla Soup

- Prep Time: 10 Minutes
- Cook Time: 10 Minutes
- Serves: 8

Ingredients
- 4 cups of chicken broth
- 3 tablespoons of olive oil
- ⅛ teaspoon of ground white pepper
- ½ cup of cilantro (chopped)

- 4 cups of white corn kernels
- 7 corn tortilla squares
- 2 cups of shredded Cheddar cheese
- 2 tablespoons of minced white onion
- ½ teaspoon of chili powder
- 1 ½ cup of water
- 1 tablespoon of kosher salt
- 2 ½ teaspoons of cumin
- w̄ cup of tomato paste
- 6 cups of chopped tomatoes
- 1 ½ teaspoon of minced jalapeno pepper
- 1 ½ tablespoons of minced garlic

Steps

1. Fry the tortilla in the olive oil over medium-high heat until golden and crisp.
2. Add the onions, garlic and jalapeño, allow to cool for 1-2 minutes or until the onion becomes soft and translucent.
3. Add half the corn kernels, then bring soup to a boil and allow to cook for 3-5 minutes. Remove from heat and set aside.
4. Puree the soup with an immersion blender until smooth, add the rest of the kernels and put the soup back on heat and allow to cook for 5-10 minutes, stirring frequently to avoid burning it.
5. Serve garnished with sharp Cheddar and fresh cilantro.

Italian Chopped Salad

- Prep Time: 10 Minutes
- Cook Time: 0 Minutes
- Serves: 6

Ingredients

Salad

- ½ cup of chopped ham
- 1 can of chickpeas (drained and rinsed)
- 10 large fresh basil leaves (chiffonade)
- 1 large head of Romaine lettuce
- 1 cup of fresh mozzarella pearls (halved)

- 1 cup of chopped salami
- 2 cups of Roma tomatoes (cut into quarters)
- ½ cup thinly sliced red onion
- w̄ cup of thinly sliced pepperoncini

Dressing

- w̄ cup of olive oil
- 2 tablespoons of Dijon mustard
- ½ teaspoon of minced garlic
- Salt and pepper to taste
- 2 tablespoons of freshly squeezed lemon juice
- 3 teaspoons of white sugar
- 3 tablespoons of red wine vinegar
- 1 teaspoon of dried parsley
- 1 teaspoon of dried oregano

Steps

1. Put all the dressing ingredients into a sealable jar, season with pepper and salt to taste, then shake vigorously to combine. Refrigerate until ready to use.
2. Wash the lettuce, then dry with a salad spinner. Roll the pieces up and slice them thinly into ribbons, then set aside.
3. Add the tomatoes, chickpeas, ham, mozzarella pearls, red onion, basil leaves, pepperoncini and salami. Toss well, then set aside.
4. Take the dressing out of the fridge, shake well, then add to the amount of salad you are ready to eat immediately as both don't sit well together for a long time.

Pizzas

BBQ Chicken Pizza

- Prep Time: 35 Minutes
- Cook Time: 20 Minutes
- Serves: 8

Ingredients

- 2 tablespoons of chopped fresh cilantro
- 1 ¼ cup of diced chicken
- 2 cups of shredded mozzarella cheese
- ½ cup of barbecue sauce

- 1 tablespoon of olive oil
- 2 tablespoons of shredded smoked Gouda cheese
- Semolina for handling
- 2 small balls of homemade or store-bought pizza dough
- ¼ piece of red onion (sliced)

Steps

1. Cook the chicken in a large frying pan over medium-high heat for 5-6 minutes, then remove and refrigerate until chilled.
2. Once chilled, drizzle two tablespoons of barbecue sauce over it, toss until properly coated, then refrigerate until ready to use.
3. Place a pizza stone in the middle level of your oven, then preheat for 1 hour at 500°F.
4. Spread each ball of dough until they are 8-9-inch-wide, using the semolina to facilitate the handling, then spread out a quarter of barbecue sauce on one of the pizzas, making sure to spread it out evenly.
5. Sprinkle with a tablespoon of Gouda cheese, then top with ¾ cup of shredded mozzarella.
6. Top with half the amount of chicken and onion slices, then place on the pizza stone and allow to bake for 8-10 minutes or until the pizza crust is golden and crispy.
7. When completely cooked through, remove from the oven and top with fresh cilantro before cutting into slices.
8. Repeat steps 4-7 for the other ball of dough.
9. Serve and enjoy!

Thai Chicken Pizza

- Prep Time: 30 Minutes
- Cook Time: 20 Minutes
- Serves: 2

Ingredients

- 2 teaspoons of active dry yeast
- 1 tablespoon of honey
- 3 cups of all-purpose flour
- 1 cup of warm water
- 1 teaspoon of salt

Toppings

- ¼ cup of cilantro (chopped)
- 2 teaspoons of chili oil
- 3 ½ tablespoons of peanut butter
- 1 carrot (shredded)
- ½ pound of chicken breast (shredded)
- 3 tablespoons of brewed tea
- 2 tablespoons of toasted sesame seeds
- 2 teaspoons of honey
- 3 tablespoons of rice vinegar
- 1 ½ tablespoons of green onions
- ½ teaspoon of red pepper
- ½ teaspoon of sesame oil
- 2 tablespoons of olive oil
- ½ cup of shredded mozzarella cheese
- 1 tablespoon of minced fresh ginger
- 2 tablespoons of soy sauce

Steps

1. Place a pizza stone in the middle tier of your oven and allow it to preheat for 1 ½ hour at 450°F.
2. To make the dough, pour the water into a large bowl, add honey and stir until it dissolves, then sprinkle the yeast over the water and stir and allow to stand for 5 minutes or until the yeast starts to foam on the top of the water.
3. Mix the salt and flour in another bowl, make a well in the center and pour in yeast mixture and olive oil.
4. Mix the flour into the wet ingredients until well combined. If it breaks apart, add one tablespoon of water and mix by hand again (add more if necessary each time you mix).
5. Move the dough onto a lightly-floured surface and knead until it's smooth and stretchy, about 15 minutes.
6. Mold the dough into a bowl and cut into a greased bowl, then cover with a moist towel and let it rise for 1 hour or until it

doubles in size.

7. Season the chicken strips with salt and pepper, then sauté in olive oil for 5-7 minutes or until cooked through.
8. Put the rest of the topping ingredients (except cheese) into a blender and process until smooth.
9. Drizzle two tablespoons of the sauce mixture into the chicken and toss to coat, then refrigerate until to use.
10. Punch down the dough, then cut into two equal parts, then roll out each piece until it is 8-9 inch wide.
11. Spread a quarter cup of the peanut sauce over each stretched-out dough part.
12. Share the cheese equally between each pizza and spread over the sauce.
13. Bake for 8-10 minutes or until the crust is crispy and gold.
14. Remove from the oven and sprinkle with cilantro and carrot.

Tacos and Sandwiches

Fish Tacos

- Prep Time: 15 Minutes
- Cook Time: 30 Minutes
- Serves: 5

Ingredients
- 2 cups of all-purpose flour
- 1 cup of white rice
- ¼ head of cabbage (shredded)

- 2 cups of mahi-mahi (skinned, boned and cleaned, then cut into strips)
- 10 small corn tortillas
- 2 large eggs (lightly beaten)
- Vegetable oil for frying
- 3 green onions (finely chopped)
- 4 tablespoons of water
- 2 cups of Panko crumbs
- ¼ teaspoon of freshly ground black pepper
- ¼ teaspoon of kosher salt
- ¼ head of radicchio

For The Dressing

- 8 tablespoons of Sriracha sauce
- 1 cup of ranch dressing
- ¼ teaspoon of kosher salt
- Freshly ground black pepper to taste

Steps

1. Put four tablespoons of water into the egg mixture and set aside, then put the bread crumbs into another bowl and set aside too.
2. Season the fish strips with pepper and salt to taste, toss in the bread crumbs before dipping in the egg wash, then dredge the crumbs again until well coated.
3. Once all the fish strips are properly coated, add one cup of vegetable oil into a Dutch oven and allow to heat for 3-4 minutes.
4. While it heats, cook your rice according to the instructions on the packet.
5. To make the dressing, mix the Sriracha and ranch sauce together. Note that it will be really spicy, so you can cut back on the Sriracha if you do not want it to be too hot, then season with kosher salt and black pepper.
6. Once the oil is hot enough, add the fish and fry in batches for 3-5 minutes each time or until the breading is golden.

7. Remove from the oil and put in a colander or on a few pieces of paper towels to drain.
8. To assemble, put a small serving of rice, green onion, mahi-mahi, radicchio, and cabbage on each tortilla, then serve with the sauce on the side.

Grilled Veggie Sandwich

- Prep Time: 5 Minutes
- Cook Time: 8 Minutes
- Serves: 4

Ingredients

- 1 red onion (sliced)
- ¼ cup of mayonnaise
- 1 zucchini (sliced)
- 3 cloves of garlic (minced)
- Olive oil cooking spray
- 1 small yellow squash (sliced)
- ½ cup of crumbled feta cheese

- Focaccia bread (cut horizontally)
- 1 cup of sliced red bell pepper
- 1 tablespoon of lemon juice

Steps

1. Combine the minced garlic, mayonnaise and lemon juice in a small bowl, then refrigerate until ready to use.
2. Preheat your grill on high for 1-2 minutes.
3. Spray a thin layer of olive oil over the vegetables and the garlic.
4. Place the zucchini and bell peppers close to the middle of the grill, then place the squash and onions around them and allow the peppers to cook for 4-5 minutes on each side while the rest cook for 3 minutes.
5. Once done, remove from the grill and set aside.
6. Spread a thin layer of the mayonnaise mix on the cut side of the focaccia bread, then top with some feta cheese.
7. Place the bread with the cheese side facing up, then flip the lid closed and grill for 2-3 minutes (make sure the bottom doesn't burn).
8. Once the cheese is slightly melted, remove from the grill and serve topped with grilled veggies and another piece of bread.

Chapter 5
Carrabba's™

The first Carrabba's was opened in Houston, Texas in 1986, serving only the best of Italian cuisine, and have rapidly progressed since then and now have over 200 locations. So, roll up your sleeves and let's get to work!

Appetizers

Zucchini Fritte

- Prep Time: 30 Minutes
- Cook Time: 1 hour
- Serves: 6

Ingredients

- ¼ teaspoon of pepper
- 2 medium zucchini
- Olive oil cooking spray
- 1 teaspoon garlic powder
- 2 egg whites
- ½ cup Parmesan cheese

- ½ cup flour
- ½ teaspoon of salt
- 1 ½ cups of Panko crumbs

Roasted Garlic Aioli
- 1 head of garlic (roasted)
- 1 egg yolk
- 1 cup olive oil
- 1 teaspoon of white wine vinegar
- ¼ teaspoon of kosher salt
- Ground black pepper to taste
- 1 teaspoon of Dijon mustard

Steps

1. Preheat your oven to 400°F.
2. Put the Panko crumbs into a food processor and blend until fine and smooth.
3. Add garlic powder, pepper, Parmesan, and salt, then pulse again just until the ingredients are properly mixed, then transfer into a bowl.
4. Crack the eggs into a bowl, add a tablespoon of water and beat until frothy.
5. Cut the zucchini into thin three-inch-long pieces, then dip each piece into the powdered crumbs, dust lightly, then dip in the egg wash before dredging in the flour again until properly coated.
6. Line a baking sheet with aluminum foil and coat with a thin layer of olive oil cooking spray.
7. Spray a thin layer of cooking spray over the zucchini and bake for 10-15 minutes until golden and crispy.
8. To roast the garlic, cut the head off the bunch, drizzle with a small amount of olive oil, then season with just a pinch of salt. Wrap in foil and put into the oven and bake for 45 minutes at 400°F. Allow to cool, then squeeze the garlic cloves out of their skin.
9. For the aioli, combine the vinegar, yolk and mustard in a small bowl. Stir in the oil (a bit at a time) until you have a thick paste.

10. Squeeze the garlic out of their skins and add them to the mixture. Whisk lightly and season with lemon juice, pepper and salt, to taste.

Cozze in Blanco

- Prep Time: 35 Minutes
- Cook Time: 25 Minutes
- Serves: 6

Ingredients
- 2 tablespoons of yellow onions
- 4 cups of mussels
- 2 tablespoons of licorice liqueur
- 2 tablespoons of chopped garlic
- 1 tablespoon of chopped fresh basil
- 2 tablespoons of extra virgin olive oil
- Juice of half a lemon

Lemon Butter Sauce

- 2 tablespoons of minced garlic
- ¼ cup of real butter
- 2 tablespoons of cold butter
- w̄ cup of fresh lemon juice
- 2 tablespoons of yellow onions (minced)
- White pepper to taste
- Kosher salt to taste
- 2 tablespoons of dry white wine

Steps

1. To clean the mussels, leave them to soak in a bowl of cold water for 8-10 minutes, then scrub with a stiff brush until clean. Then scrape off the beard with a sharp knife and rinse a couple of times in cold water or until the rinsing water appears clear.
2. Put a large pan over medium heat, add oil and allow to heat for a few minutes, then put in the mussels and cook covered for 3-5 minutes or until the mussels begin to open.
3. Add garlic and onion, stir and cook covered 1-2 minutes or until fragrant, then set aside.
4. To make the butter sauce, put the real butter in a pan over medium heat until fully melted, remove from heat and let rest until the milk particles settle at the bottom.
5. Skim the oil from the top and throw away the sediment, then sauté the garlic and onion in two tablespoons of the clear butter.
6. Stir in the white wine and lemon juice, then season with pepper and salt to taste and allow to simmer for 3 minutes or until it loses at least half its moisture.
7. Remove from heat and combine with cold butter until fully melted and creamy.
8. Put the mussels back on medium heat, add lemon juice, liqueur, lemon butter sauce and basil. Cook for 1-2 minutes or until heated through, then serve into bowls.

Pasta

Linguine Pescatore

- Prep Time: 10 Minutes
- Cook Time: 15 Minutes
- Serves: 2

Ingredients
- 8 mussels (thoroughly washed)
- 3 shrimp
- 12 ounces of cooked linguine
- 1 ¼ cup of marinara sauce

- 3 scallops

Steps

1. Put all the listed ingredients (except the linguine) in a medium pan and sauté for 7-10 minutes or until the mussels are cooked and opened.
2. Toss with cooked linguine and allow to cook for 2-3 minutes or until the linguine is properly heated.
3. Serve garnished with fresh cilantro.

Pasta Sostanza

- Prep Time: 5 Minutes
- Cook Time: 10 Minutes
- Serves: 6

Ingredients

- 8 mushrooms (diced)
- 1 onion (diced)
- 8 tablespoons of Panko bread crumbs
- 1 can of artichoke hearts (drained)
- 1 tablespoon of olive oil
- Salt and pepper to taste
- 2 ½ tablespoons of minced garlic
- 10 large spinach leaves (chopped)

- 2 cans of diced tomatoes with juice
- ¾ cup fresh mushrooms (chopped)
- ½ teaspoon of oregano
- 8 ounces of fettuccine
- ½ teaspoon of rosemary

Steps

1. Cook the onions in a medium saucepan over medium heat for 10 minutes, stirring frequently until they just start to caramelize.
2. Add chopped mushrooms and minced garlic and cook for 1-2 minutes.
3. Add the diced tomatoes, oregano and rosemary, stir and allow to simmer for 2-3 minutes.
4. Season with pepper and salt, then cook until the sauce begins to thicken and lose moisture.
5. Cook the fettuccine in a large pot of boiling water until al dente, then drain.
6. Remove the saucepan from heat, add basil and artichoke hearts, stir and cover until the basil wilts.
7. Pour the fettucine into the sauce and toss to combine, sprinkle with Panko crumbs and serve.

Beef, Chicken and Seafood

Rib Agrodolce

- Prep Time: 40 Minutes
- Cook Time: 1 Hour 50 Minutes
- Serves: 4

Ingredients
- 1 bay leaf
- 5 pounds of baby back ribs (cut in four)
- 1 ½ teaspoon of basil
- ½ teaspoon of marjoram
- 1 carrot (chopped)
- 2 cloves of garlic (minced)

- 4 teaspoons of grill seasoning
- ½ teaspoon of thyme
- ½ teaspoon of lemon zest
- 2 tablespoons of unsalted butter
- 2 cups of low-sodium chicken broth
- 1 cup of diced tomatoes in juice
- 1 onion (chopped)
- 2 cups of red wine
- ½ teaspoon of rosemary
- 2 tablespoons of finely chopped fresh parsley
- 1 rib of celery (chopped)

Sauce

- ¼ cup of sugar
- w̄ cup + 1 tablespoon of balsamic vinegar
- 1 scallion (thinly sliced)
- Freshly ground black pepper to taste
- Salt to taste

Steps

1. Set your boiler rack on the middle tier of your oven, turn to broil, then set the temperature on high and allow it to preheat for 5-10 minutes.
2. While the broiler preheats, season the ribs with the grill seasoning and allow to stand at room temperature.
3. Lightly grease a broiler pan, then place the ribs on it and sear on both sides for 4-5 minutes.
4. Set the oven to bake and put the temperature to 300°F.
5. Put the butter in a large pan and melt over medium heat. Add onion, carrot, lemon zest, garlic and celery. Stir and cook for 4-5 minutes, stirring occasionally until the veggies are soft
6. Add canned tomatoes with juice, wine and broth, then stir to combine. Put in the spices, then allow to boil over high heat for 2-3 minutes.

7. Transfer the ribs to a roasting pan, top with sauce, cover with aluminum foil and bake for 60-75 minutes or until the ribs are tender.
8. Remove the ribs from the pan and set aside to cool.
9. To make the sauce, remove the bay leaf, then put the vegetables and liquid from the pan into a blender and process until smooth and thick (do so in batches if necessary).
10. Pour the mixture back into the pan, add sugar and vinegar, stir and bring to a boil over medium heat.
11. Allow the sauce to cook for 15-20 minutes or until the mixture reduces by half.
12. Put the rib backs on a broiler pan, drizzle some sauce over them and broil on high until browned.
13. Remove and serve garnished with scallions.

Tilapia Nocciola

- Prep Time: 15 Minutes
- Cook Time: 15 Minutes
- Serves: 6

Ingredients

Tilapia
- 2 tablespoons of canola oil
- 6 tilapia fillets
- Pepper and salt to taste
- Grape tomatoes (to garnish)
- 1 cup of hazelnuts (coarsely ground)
- 2 large eggs

- ¾ cup of Panko crumbs

Lemon Butter Sauce
- 2 tablespoons of sherry
- 2 cloves of garlic (minced)
- ¼ cup of chopped basil
- 4 tablespoons of butter
- Salt and pepper to taste
- ½ cup of heavy whipping cream
- ¼ cup of lemon juice
- 1 teaspoon of lemon zest
- 1 tablespoon of chicken stock

Steps

To Make Tilapia
1. Heat the oil in a large pan over medium-high heat and allow it to heat for 1-2 minutes.
2. While the oil heats, put the crumbs and hazelnuts in a shallow bowl and the eggs in another. Season both with a pinch of pepper and kosher salt, stir until well combined, then set aside.
3. Dip the fillets in the egg mixture, then dredge in the crumb mixture until properly coated.
4. Cook the fillets in two batches for 3-4 minutes on each side until cooked through and the breading is golden and crispy.
5. Remove from heat, then put in a bowl and cover with plastic wrap to keep warm.

To Make Lemon Butter Sauce
1. Melt the butter in a medium saucepan over medium-low heat. Add garlic and cook until fragrant and soft.
2. Add chicken stock, sherry and lemon juice, stir and allow to cook until the mixture loses half its moisture, about 5 minutes.
3. Put in the lemon zest and whipping cream and stir until sauce starts to thicken, then allow to cook for 2-3 minutes.

4. Remove from heat and add chopped basil, stir to combine.
5. Put the tilapia fillets on a serving platter and drizzle a generous amount of lemon butter sauce over it.
6. Serve garnished with grape tomatoes and enjoy!

Spiedino Di Mare

- Prep Time: 10 Minutes
- Cook Time: 5 Minutes
- Serves: 2

Ingredients
- ⅛ teaspoon of white pepper
- 4 scallops
- 4 tablespoons of lemon butter
- Fresh chopped parsley (to garnish)
- 2 tablespoons of extra-virgin olive oil
- 4 shrimp
- ⅛ teaspoon of kosher salt
- ¼ cup of Panko crumbs

Steps

1. Soak up 2 bamboo skewers in water for 30 minutes.
2. Season the shrimp and scallops with pepper and salt, then drizzle with olive oil before coating with bread crumbs.
3. Skewer the scallops and shrimp separately, then grill 3-5 minutes on each side or until cooked through.
4. Serve garnished with chopped parsley and melted lemon butter on the side.

Chicken Bryan

- Prep Time: 10 Minutes
- Cook Time: 40 Minutes
- Serves: 4

Ingredients
- ¾ cup dry white wine
- 4 boneless, skinless chicken breasts
- 8 tablespoons of butter
- 2 tablespoons of chopped basil
- 8 ounces of goat cheese
- ½ teaspoon of salt
- 2 tablespoons of sun-dried tomatoes
- 2 tablespoons of lemon juice

- ¼ teaspoon of freshly ground black pepper
- 2 tablespoons of olive oil
- 2 teaspoons of chopped garlic
- ¼ cup of chopped white onions

Steps

To Make Chicken

1. Place the chicken between two pieces of plastic wrap and pound until half an inch thick, then remove, rinse and pat dry with a paper towel.
2. Season the chicken with pepper and salt, then brush with olive oil until properly coated.
3. Grill chicken for 3-4 minutes on each side or until golden brown, then remove and plate before covering with plastic wrap to keep warm.
4. Slice the goat cheese into four for each piece of chicken and set aside until ready to use.

To Make Sauce

1. Sauté the garlic and onions in two tablespoons of butter over medium heat until fragrant, about 3-4 minutes.
2. Add lemon juice and wine, then allow to simmer until the mixture loses half its moisture, then add three tablespoons of butter and stir until fully melted and well incorporated.
3. Turn off the heat and add the rest of the butter and stir until melted and sauce is thick.
4. Strain the sauce to remove garlic and onion, then pour back into the pan and add the tomatoes and basil.
5. Put the chicken on a serving platter, place the mozzarella slices on each piece of chicken then drizzle a generous amount of sauce over it.
6. Serve and enjoy!

Pizzas

Chicken Alfredo Pizza

- Prep Time: 15 Minutes
- Cook Time: 25 Minutes
- Serves: 4

Ingredients

- ¼ cup of flour
- 1 (12-inch size) store-bought pizza dough
- ¼ cup sliced green onions
- ¼ teaspoon of pepper

- 2 tablespoons of grated Parmesan cheese
- 2 teaspoons of olive oil
- ¼ cup of shredded Asiago cheese
- 2 boneless, skinless chicken breasts (sliced)
- ¾ cup of Alfredo sauce
- ½ teaspoon of salt
- ½ cup of shredded mozzarella cheese
- 3 cloves of garlic (minced)

Steps

1. Preheat your oven to 425°F.
2. Grease a 12-inch pizza pan and spread the dough out until it is barely touching the edges of the pan.
3. Put into the oven and allow to bake for 5-7 minutes or until the crust is golden.
4. Put the flour, salt and pepper into a zip-lock bag, seal and shake to combine, then add the chicken and toss to coat.
5. Remove the chicken and pat off the excess flour before placing on a piece of waxed paper.
6. Put the oil into a large skillet and cook the chicken over medium heat until the crust is brown and crispy.
7. Remove from the heat and put in a colander to drain.
8. Spread the Alfredo sauce on the pizza crust until it is just a few inches shy of touching the edge.
9. Top with the fried chicken, then sprinkle with Asiago, Parmesan, mozzarella and green onions.
10. Put the pizza back into the oven and bake for 10 more minutes or until the cheese is melted at the top.

Margherita Pizza

- Prep Time: 35 Minutes
- Cook Time: 10 Minutes
- Serves: 3

Ingredients

- Semolina to handle
- 8 fresh basil leaves (chopped)
- 2 ripe Roma tomatoes (sliced)
- Extra virgin olive oil (for brushing)
- Freshly ground black pepper (to taste)
- 1 ball of pizza dough
- 5 ounces of mozzarella (thinly sliced)

Steps

1. Place a pizza stone in the middle rack of an oven and preheat at 550°F for 30 minutes.
2. Spread the dough out until it is at least 12-inchs wide, then sprinkle a clean, dry surface with semolina and place the dough in it to make it easier to handle.
3. Brush the dough with olive oil, then top with tomatoes and mozzarella slices.
4. Pick up the dough with a pizza peel and place on the pizza stone.
5. Bake for 8-10 minutes, then remove from the oven and top with basil before cutting into slices using a pizza wheel.
6. Sprinkle it with pepper and salt to taste, then serve hot.

Chapter 6
The Old Spaghetti Factory™

The Old Spaghetti Factory has been in business since 1969 and currently has 40 restaurants in the United States. They have managed to keep their customers satisfied with fresh, tasty meals that I am sure you can't wait to make at home. Well, now you have many recipes to pick from. Which shall it be?

Appetizers

Olive Tapenade

- Prep Time: 10 Minutes
- Cook Time: 5 Minutes
- Serves: 7

Ingredients
- ½ teaspoon of thyme
- 1 ½ cups of pitted green olives
- 1 loaf of Italian bread
- ¼ cup of capers

- 1 cup of extra virgin olive oil
- 2 ½ cups of pitted black olives
- ½ teaspoon of salt
- ½ teaspoon of dried crushed oregano
- 1 tablespoon of minced garlic
- ½ teaspoon of freshly ground black pepper
- 2 tablespoons of fresh lemon juice

Steps

1. Put the capers, black olives, olive oil, garlic, green olives, pepper, oregano, salt, thyme and lemon juice into a food processor and pulse until smooth.
2. Transfer the mixture to a container, cover and refrigerate until ready to use.
3. Combine 1 teaspoon of minced garlic and 4 tablespoons of extra-virgin olive oil in a small bowl, then slice the bread into four.
4. Brush the bread slices with olive oil mixture on both sides of the Italian bread.
5. Grill both sides of the bread until golden brown. Remove from heat, then cut each piece in half.
6. Put the olive tapenade in a small bowl and serve with grilled Italian bread on the side.

Sicilian Cheese Bread

- Prep Time: 10 Minutes
- Cook Time: 10 Minutes
- Serves: 4

Ingredients

- ½ cup of Mizithra cheese
- A pinch of paprika and pepper
- 1 loaf of Italian bread
- ⅛ teaspoon of Worcestershire sauce
- ¼ cup of softened butter
- ¼ teaspoon of garlic powder
- ½ cup of shredded mozzarella cheese
- 1 tablespoon of grated Parmesan cheese

Steps

1. Cut the bread crosswise, then half the cut pieces lengthways (keep the rest of the bread for later).
2. Combine the rest of the ingredients in a small bowl, then spread an even layer on the cut side of the bread.
3. Arrange the pieces of bread on a baking sheet, cut side up.
4. Bake for 10 minutes at 400°F or until the cheese is fully melted.

Pasta

Mizithra Pasta

- Prep Time: 5 Minutes
- Cook Time: 9 Minutes
- Serves: 8

Ingredients
- 1 cup of butter
- 16 ounces of cooked spaghetti (hot)
- Fresh basil (chopped)
- 1 cup of finely grated Mizithra cheese

Ingredients

1. Melt the butter in a small saucepan over medium heat until golden brown, stirring frequently.
2. Remove from heat and pour into a tempered clear bowl, then allow to settle so that the sediment settles at the bottom.
3. Pour the butter into another large bowl again, separating the clear butter from the sediment.
4. Add the pasta and toss until well combined.
5. Add half of the cheese and mix properly, then serve topped with the other half of the cheese.
6. Garnish with fresh basil and enjoy!

OSF's Manager's Special

- Prep Time: 10 Minutes
- Cook Time: 10 Minutes
- Serves: 4

Ingredients

- 1 cup of shredded Mizithra cheese
- 1 tablespoon of olive oil
- 24 ounces of spaghetti noodles
- 1 ½ cups of marinara sauce
- 1 pound of ground beef
- 1 cup of butter
- 1 clove of garlic (minced)

Steps

1. Cook the pasta in a large pot of boiling salted water until al dente, then drain and set aside.
2. Melt the butter in a small pot over medium heat, stirring frequently until the butter becomes golden brown.
3. Once browned, remove from heat and put in a bowl for serving.
4. Cook the meat and garlic in a large frying pan over medium heat until brown and cooked through.
5. Pour in the sauce, stir and cook for 2-3 minutes, stirring occasionally.
6. Put some spaghetti on a serving platter, top with some meat sauce and browned butter and shredded Mizithra cheese.
7. Serve and enjoy!

Sauces and Salads

White Clam Sauce

- Prep Time: 15 Minutes
- Cook Time: 15 Minutes
- Serves: 6

Ingredients
- 4 cups of half and half
- 6 tablespoons of butter
- 2 cans of clams (chopped)
- 1 teaspoon of salt

- 2 cloves of garlic (minced)
- 1 teaspoon of ground thyme
- ½ onion (finely chopped)
- 3 tablespoons of flour
- 3 stalks of celery

Steps

1. Put the onion, butter, celery and garlic into a medium saucepan and cook over medium-low heat until the butter is fully melted and the onion is soft but not brown.
2. Put in the flour, stir until well combined to make a roux.
3. Drain the can of clams and save the juice for later.
4. Pour the clam juice into a separate saucepan, add half and half, salt and thyme, then allow to simmer for 5-10 minutes over medium heat.
5. Add the roux to the clam juice mixture and cook until the sauce begins to thicken, then put in the clams and cook for 3-5 minutes.
6. Remove from heat and serve over your favorite pasta.

Chicken Caesar Salad

- Prep Time: 10 Minutes
- Cook Time: 20 Minutes
- Serves: 4

Ingredients

For The Dressing
- 1 tablespoon of white wine vinegar
- 1 clove of garlic (minced)
- ½ cup of grated Parmesan cheese
- 2 anchovies (mashed)
- 5 tablespoons of mayonnaise

For The Salad
- 2 boneless, skinless chicken breasts
- 1 medium ciabatta loaf
- 1 large head of Romaine lettuce (leaves separated)
- 3 tablespoons of olive oil

Steps

1. Preheat your oven at 350°F.
2. Cut the bread into large pieces using a bread knife, spread over a greased baking sheet, then brush with two tablespoons of olive oil.
3. Sprinkle a dash of salt over the bread and bake for 8-10 minutes, flipping occasionally until evenly browned.
4. Rub the chicken breasts with the remaining of the olive oil, then place the oiled chicken in a heated pan over medium heat until sizzling. Sear for 3-4 minutes on each side or until cooked through, then remove and shred into bite-sized pieces once cool enough to handle.
5. Combine the mashed anchovies with minced garlic in a small bowl, then add white wine and grated Parmesan. Stir until thick, then season with pepper and salt to taste.
6. Rinse the Romaine lettuce leaves, then pat dry with a piece of parchment paper.
7. Cut the leaves into large pieces, then put into a large salad bowl. Add shredded chicken and browned bread.
8. Drizzle the dressing over the salad and toss until well combined.
9. Sprinkle with some grated Parmesan, toss and serve immediately.

Specials

Spaghetti Vesuvius

- Prep Time: 15 Minutes
- Cook Time: 25 Minutes
- Serves: 4

Ingredients
- Salt and pepper to taste
- 1 pack of smoked bacon
- 125 grams of fresh mozzarella cheese (cut into large cubes)
- 1 onion (chopped)

- 1 teaspoon of balsamic vinegar
- Sugar to taste
- 2 cans of chopped tomatoes
- 3 cloves of garlic (minced)
- 2 tablespoons of olive oil
- 16 ounces of cooked pasta

Steps

1. Fry the bacon with olive oil in a medium skillet over medium-high heat for 2-3 minutes or until lightly browned.
2. Add garlic and onion, stir and allow to cook until soft and fragrant, about 2 minutes.
3. Add chopped tomatoes and vinegar, stir, then season with sugar, pepper and salt to taste. Allow to simmer over medium heat for 15-20 minutes
4. Serve over cooked pasta and top with mozzarella.

Shrimp Fettuccine

- Prep Time: 10 Minutes
- Cook Time: 20 Minutes
- Serves: 4

Ingredients

Fettuccine Alfredo
- 1 cup of half and half
- 4 tablespoons of unsalted butter
- 1 pound of fettuccine
- 1 cup of grated Parmesan cheese
- 1 egg yolk (lightly beaten)

Garlic Butter Shrimp

- ¾ teaspoon of red pepper flakes
- 2 pounds of shrimp
- 1 teaspoon of grated Parmesan cheese
- 1 teaspoon of garlic salt
- 3 tablespoons of softened butter

Steps

For The Garlic Butter Shrimp

1. Combine all the ingredients (except shrimp) in a bowl, then transfer to a pan and allow the butter to melt over medium heat.
2. Add the shrimp and cook for 2-3 minutes on each side until cooked through, then remove from heat and keep warm until ready to use.

For The Fettuccine Alfredo

1. Cook the fettuccine in a large pot of salted boiling water until al dente, then drain.
2. Melt the butter over medium heat in a small saucepan, add grated Parmesan and half and half, stir until well combined, then allow to cook until the cheese is fully melted.
3. Add the egg yolk and allow to cook until the sauce starts to thicken, stirring frequently, about 3-5 minutes.
4. Remove from heat and serve over cooked fettuccine, topped with garlic butter shrimp.

Desserts

New York Cheesecake

- Prep Time: 30 Minutes
- Cook Time: 1 Hour 55 Minutes
- Serves: 10

Ingredients

Crust
- 2 tablespoons of sugar
- 1 ½ cups of graham cracker crumbs

- 5 tablespoons of melted butter
- ⅛ teaspoon of salt

Filling
- 6 large eggs (lightly beaten)
- 4 cups of cream cheese (at room temperature)
- ½ cup of sour cream
- 1 teaspoon of lemon zest
- 4 teaspoons of vanilla extract
- ¼ teaspoon of salt
- 3 tablespoons of all-purpose flour
- 2 cups of sugar
- 2 teaspoons of freshly squeezed lemon juice

Steps
Crust

1. Preheat your oven to 375°F and set an oven rack in the middle tier of your oven.
2. Wrap a ten-inch spring-form pan with a large piece of aluminum foil, covering the bottom and the sides completely so that the seams of the foil are tucked inside the pan. Repeat this process with another piece of foil, then grease the inside of the pan with some butter or coat with a thin layer of cooking spray.
3. Combine the melted butter, salt, cracker crumbs and sugar in a medium bowl, then press into the bottom of the greased pan.
4. Smoothen the top with the broad side of a wooden spoon, then bake for 10 minutes at 400°F.
5. Remove the crust and reduce the temperature to 325°F, allowing the oven to heat until ready to use.
6. Bring a medium pot of water to boil.
7. Put the cream cheese, flour and sugar into the bowl of an electric mixer and mix on medium speed using the paddle attachment for 1 minute or until smooth, scraping down the sides frequently.
8. Add lemon juice, vanilla, salt and lemon zest, then mix on low.
9. Add the eggs slowly, mixing on low until well incorporated.

10. Add the cream and mix until well incorporated (do not over-mix).
11. Pour the batter over the baked crust, then place the pan in a large roasting pan.
12. Pour the hot water into the roasting pan, being careful not to pour it into the cake pan. Once the water is at least an inch high around the cake pan, put it in the oven and bake for 90 minutes or until the cake sets.
13. Remove the roasting pan from the oven and set aside to cool with the cake pan in it, about 50 minutes.
14. Once cool, remove the cake pan and peel off the foil wrapped around it.
15. Seal the pan with plastic wrap and refrigerate overnight.
16. When ready to serve, carefully remove the sides of the spring-form pan, leaving the cake on the base of the pan.
17. Cut into slices and serve drizzled with berry sauce.

Chocolate Mousse Cake

- Prep Time: 45 Minutes
- Cook Time: 15 Minutes
- Serves: 10

Ingredients

Cake

- 1 teaspoon of white vinegar
- ½ cup of all-purpose flour
- 2 tablespoons of canola oil
- ¼ teaspoon of baking soda
- ¼ cup of sugar
- w̄ cup of water

- 2 tablespoons of fine cocoa powder

Chocolate Mousse
- w̄ cup of 35% heavy cream
- 200 grams of dark chocolate
- ½ cup of sugar
- 1 teaspoon of gelatin
- 2 tablespoons of water

Steps

To Make Cake
1. Move the rack to the middle tier and preheat your oven to 350°F.
2. Grease an eight-inch spring-form pan with some butter and line the bottom with a piece of parchment paper.
3. Put all the dry ingredients into a large bowl, add oil, water and vinegar and whisk until well combined and smooth, then pour into the pan.
4. Bake for 10-12 minutes, then remove the pan from the oven and place on a wire rack to cool.

To Make The Mousse
1. Put the chocolate into a microwave-friendly bowl and microwave for 2 minutes on high, removing to stir frequently.
2. Once the chocolate is melted, remove from the microwave and set aside to cool for a few minutes.
3. Put the water into a small bowl, sprinkle the gelatin and let sit until it blooms, about 4-5 minutes.
4. Heat four tablespoons of the heavy cream in a saucepan over medium heat, add sugar and allow to cook until the sugar dissolves, stirring frequently.
5. Remove from heat and slowly stir in gelatin until it dissolves completely.
6. Pour the cream into the bowl of melted chocolate and stir until well combined.

7. Whip the remaining cream in another bowl with an electric mixer on high speed, until stiff peaks start to form.
8. Slowly fold the cream into the chocolate mixture until well combined, then spread onto the cake, using a spatula to level the top until smooth.
9. Refrigerate for 4-6 hours or overnight, then remove the sides of the spring-form pan. Cut into slices and serve.

Chapter 7
Romano's Macaroni Grill™

Romano's Macaroni Grill was founded in 1989 and has remained on top of their game by using fresh ingredients from small, locally-owned Italian farms. This is something many customers appreciate because everyone wants to be sure of what they are eating. These fresh ingredients also give their meals strong and unique flavors as fresh ingredients are an important part of Italian cuisine. So, if you have green thumbs, wouldn't you think it a good idea to grow some vegetables in your garden to add some freshness to your meals?

Antipasti

Calamari Fritti

- Prep Time: 20 Minutes
- Cook Time: 3 Minutes
- Serves: 6

Ingredients

- 1 egg (lightly beaten)
- 450 grams of whole squid (cleaned)
- Lemon wedges (to serve)
- 2 cups of all-purpose flour

- 1 cup of milk
- Sea salt to taste
- 5 fresh basil leaves (chopped)
- 2 teaspoons of paprika
- Vegetable oil (for frying)
- Freshly ground pepper to taste

Tomato Basil Sauce

- 1 can of crushed tomatoes
- 3 tablespoons of extra-virgin olive oil
- 4 fresh basil leaves (shredded)
- A pinch of sugar
- 2 cloves of garlic (minced)
- Freshly ground pepper to taste
- Kosher salt to taste

Smoked Jalapeño Aioli

- ½ tablespoon of freshly squeezed lemon juice
- 1 cup of mayonnaise
- 1 tablespoon of chopped Italian parsley
- Salt to taste
- 1 clove of garlic (minced)
- 2 cans of chipotle peppers in adobo sauce

Steps

1. Clean the squid under cool running water, then pat them dry with a paper towel.
2. Slice the squid into half-inch rings, then cut off the tips of the tentacles.
3. Combine the egg and milk in a bowl and beat with a fork until well combined.
4. Add the basil leaves and mix well.
5. Put the sliced squid in the milk mixture and toss to combine, then refrigerate for 15-20 minutes.

6. Heat one cup of vegetable oil in a medium pan over medium-high heat.
7. Combine the paprika and flour in another bowl, then season with pepper and salt to taste.
8. Remove the calamari from the fridge and dredge in the flour until properly coated.
9. Fry for 2-3 minutes or until the coating is golden brown and crispy, then remove from heat and set to drain on a piece of parchment paper.

Smoked Jalapeño Aioli

1. Put all the ingredients for the sauce in a food processor, pulse until smooth, then pour into a bowl and allow to sit until ready to serve (can be done before calamari).

Tomato Basil Sauce

2. Heat the oil in a small pan over medium heat for a minute. Once hot, put in the basil and garlic, then cook until soft and fragrant, about 2 minutes.
3. Stir in the sugar and crushed tomatoes, season with kosher salt and pepper to taste, then allow to simmer for 8-10 minutes, stirring frequently.
4. When the sauce is ready, put in a small bowl and serve on the side with fried calamari and jalapeño aioli.

Stuffed Mushrooms

- Prep Time: 20 Minutes
- Cook Time: 30 Minutes
- Serves: 6

Ingredients

- ¼ teaspoon of salt
- 6 tablespoons of butter
- 2 tablespoons of shredded Parmesan cheese (optional)
- 1 pound of mushrooms
- ⅛ teaspoon of pepper
- 3 tablespoons of minced red bell pepper
- ¼ teaspoon of Italian seasoning blend
- 2 green onions (minced)

- 1 cup of Panko crumbs
- ½ cup of crab meat

Steps

1. Cut the stems off the mushrooms, trim off the ends and wash both parts separately. Drain and set aside until ready to use.
2. Heat two tablespoons of butter in a small pan over medium-low heat until melted, then allow to cool for a few minutes before brushing over mushrooms.
3. Grease a shallow baking dish with some butter, then set aside.
4. Heat the remaining butter in a skillet over medium heat, add minced red pepper, green onions and minced mushroom stems, stir and cook for 2-3 minutes.
5. Add crab meat, bread crumbs and Italian seasoning, stir again and allow to cook for 5 minutes.
6. Turn the cap of the mushrooms up and stuff each of them with spoonfuls of the crab meat mixture, then top equally with shredded Parmesan cheese (optional).
7. Bake for 15-20 minutes at 350°F until the mushroom caps are soft.
8. Remove from heat and serve immediately.

Beef, Chicken and Seafood

Chicken Scaloppine

- Prep Time: 20 Minutes
- Cook Time: 25 Minutes
- Serves: 4

Ingredients

Lemon Butter Sauce
- 2 cups of soft butter
- ¼ cup of white wine
- ½ cup of lemon juice

- ½ cup of heavy cream

Pasta and Chicken
- 6 ounces of cooked pancetta
- 1 tablespoon of capers
- Chopped fresh parsley (to garnish)
- 1 tablespoons of vegetable oil
- 1 pound of cooked capellini pasta
- 2 tablespoon of butter
- 1 ½ cup of chopped artichokes
- ½ cup of sliced mushrooms
- 2 cups of flour
- 6 chicken breasts

Steps

For The Sauce
1. Heat the white wine and lemon juice in a small saucepan over medium heat. Allow to boil until the liquid is reduced by a third.
2. Add the cream and allow to simmer for 3-4 minutes or until the mixture starts to thicken.
3. Stir in the butter and allow to cook until melted and well incorporated, then season with pepper and salt to taste.
4. Turn off heat and keep warm until ready to use.

5. For The Pasta And Chicken
6. Cook the pasta according to the instructions on the pack, then drain and set aside.
7. Heat the butter and oil in a large skillet over medium heat.
8. Coat the chicken with a light dusting of flour until well coated, then fry in oil until brown and well cooked, about 3-4 minutes on each side.
9. Remove the chicken from the oil, then add mushrooms and cook until soft.

10. Put the chicken back and cook for 1-2 minutes, then pour in half of the lemon butter sauce and toss until the chicken is well coated.
11. Put the pasta n a serving platter and top with chicken mixture and a bit more sauce over it.
12. Serve garnished with chopped parsley and enjoy!

Parmesan Crusted Sole

- Prep Time: 20 Minutes
- Cook Time: 15 Minutes
- Serves: 3

Ingredients
- ½ teaspoon of garlic powder
- 6 sole fillets
- 3 medium eggs
- 1 ½ cups of Panko crumbs
- 4 tablespoons of olive oil
- 1 cup of milk
- ½ cup of shredded Parmesan cheese
- 4 tablespoons of butter

- ½ cup of flour
- ½ teaspoon of pepper
- ¼ teaspoon of salt
- 4 tablespoons of minced fresh parsley

Lemon Beurre Blanc
- ⅛ teaspoon of white pepper
- ⅛ teaspoon of kosher salt
- 1 cup of white wine
- 4 tablespoons of heavy whipping cream
- 1 stick of butter (cut into cubes)
- 1 tablespoon of minced shallots
- 1 tablespoon of white wine vinegar

Steps

For Lemon Beurre Blanc
1. Combine the vinegar, wine and shallots in a small saucepan and allow to cook over medium heat for 2-3 minutes until the liquid is mostly reduced and a little thick.
2. Add the heavy whipping cream and cook until the mixture is reduced by half. Reduce the heat and add the butter, stirring frequently until fully melted and well incorporated.
3. Season with pepper and salt and allow to cool until sauce is creamy and thick, about 2-3 minutes.

For The Crusted Sole
1. Put the Parmesan, Panko crumbs and parsley into a food processor and pulse until smooth, then transfer to a bowl.
2. Beat the eggs in another bowl, add milk and stir until well combined, then put the flour in a shallow bowl.
3. Season the fillets with garlic powder, pepper and salt. Roll them in the flour until coated, dip in egg mixture, then dredge in the Panko crumbs mixture until well coated.

4. Heat butter and oil in a large non-stick pan for 1-2 minutes. Gently put in the fillets and allow to cook for 2-3 minutes on each side or until golden and cooked through.
5. Remove from heat and serve topped with lemon beurre blanc.

Chianti Pork Chop

- Prep Time: 15 Minutes
- Cook Time: 20 Minutes
- Serves: 2

Ingredients

- 1 teaspoon of rosemary
- 1 cup of red wine
- 2 tablespoons of olive oil
- ½ cup of olive oil
- ½ cup of chicken broth
- 2 cloves of garlic (minced)
- 1 pork chop (1 pound)
- 3 large mushrooms

Steps

1. Rub the pork chop with salt and pepper and allow to sit for 3-5 minutes.
2. Wash the mushroom and trim off the ends, then set aside.
3. Heat the oil in a skillet over medium heat, sear the pork for 2 minutes on each side or until browned.
4. Once browned, add garlic and mushrooms and sauté for 2-3 minutes until soft.
5. Drain the excess oil and add wine and chicken broth, then cover and cook for 2-5 minutes (depends on how tender you want your pork to be).
6. Flip the pork, add rosemary, stir and allow to cook for 2 minutes.
7. Remove pork from heat and allow sauce to cook until it thickens.
8. Serve the pork chop with the sauce drizzled over it and enjoy!

Pasta

Lobster Ravioli

- Prep Time: 45 Minutes
- Cook Time: 15 Minutes
- Serves: 2

Ingredients

- 2 cups of light cream
- 1 pound of cooked lobster meat (minced)
- 2 teaspoons of light sherry
- ¼ pound of fresh mushrooms (washed and diced)
- 1 teaspoon of diced shallots
- 2 ½ teaspoons of flour

- 2 ½ teaspoons of butter
- 2 ravioli pasta sheets

Sauce

- Pepper and salt to taste
- 2 teaspoons of flour
- 2 cups of light cream
- ¼ teaspoon of paprika
- 1 tablespoon of brandy
- 2 teaspoons of butter

Steps

1. To make the lobster ravioli, melt the butter in a pan over medium heat. Put in the shallots and cook until soft, stirring frequently.
2. Add the mushrooms and minced lobster, stir and cook until mushrooms start to soften, about 2 minutes.
3. Sprinkle the flour over the mixture, stirring continuously so that it doesn't stick to the pan.
4. Stir in the sherry and light cream and allow to cook over low heat for 2-3 minutes or until sauce starts to thicken, then remove from heat and set aside to cool.
5. Line a sheet pan with wax paper, then dust with corn flour and set aside.
6. Roll out the ravioli sheets, then cut them into 2-inch squares.
7. Scoop 1 teaspoon of the mixture onto one of the squares, cover with another and carefully seal with a ravioli tool. Repeat this process for the rest of the ravioli, then place on the pre-lined sheet pan.
8. Bring a large pot of salted water to a boil over medium heat, add a dash of oil, then slowly add the raviolis, one at a time (make sure to keep them separate).
9. Cook for 3-5 minutes or until al dente, then gently remove with a skimmer.

To Make Sauce

1. Melt the butter in a small pan over medium heat, add brandy, flour, paprika and light cream, stir and allow to cook for 2-3 minutes or until sauce starts to thicken.
2. Season with pepper and salt. Then remove from heat and keep warm until ready to use.
3. To serve, put some of the sauce in a flat soup bowl, add raviolis, top with more sauce, then garnish with parsley before serving.

Pasta Milano

- Prep Time: 10 Minutes
- Cook Time: 15 Minutes
- Serves: 6

Ingredients

- 4 ½ cups of cooked bow-tie pasta
- 12 ounces of sliced mushroom
- 1 ½ stick of butter
- 6 tablespoons of grated Parmesan cheese
- 4 ½ cups of roasted garlic cream sauce
- 18 ounces of sliced grilled chicken (restaurant bought or home-made)
- 2 tablespoons of sliced Italian parsley

- 12 ounces of sun-dried tomatoes

Steps

1. Cook the pasta in a large pot of salted boiling water until al dente, then drain and keep warm.
2. Melt the butter in a large pan over medium heat, add shredded Parmesan cheese and roasted garlic cream sauce, stir and cook for 2-3 minutes.
3. Add chicken and cook for 1-2 minutes or until heated through.
4. Add the pasta into the sauce and stir until well combined.
5. Serve garnished with chopped Italian parsley.

Desserts

Sea Salt Caramel Gelato

- Prep Time: 5 Minutes
- Cook Time: 15 Minutes
- Serves: 5

Ingredients
- ½ cup of caramel
- 4 cups of heavy cream
- ½ cup of sugar
- 10 egg yolks

- 1 teaspoon of sea salt

Steps

1. Heat the cream and salt in a small saucepan over low heat.
2. Slowly combine a small amount of the egg yolks and hot cream in a separate bowl, then pour mixture into the rest of the egg yolks and stir until well combined before adding the rest of the hot cream (this is to prevent it from curdling).
3. Pour the mixture back into the saucepan and allow to simmer over low heat for 3-5 minutes, stirring frequently.
4. Remove from heat and pour into a bowl and refrigerate until cool, then add caramel and stir until well combined.
5. Freeze for 5-10 minutes or until it reaches the right consistency.

Romano's Cannoli

- Prep Time: 30 Minutes
- Cook Time: 15 Minutes
- Serves: 8

Ingredients

Cannoli
- ½ cup of white wine
- 1 tablespoon of sugar
- 1 ½ tablespoon of butter
- ¼ teaspoon of salt
- 2 cups of all-purpose flour
- 1 egg yolk
- Canola oil for frying

Filling

- ¼ teaspoon of cinnamon
- 3 pounds of ricotta cheese
- 1 cup of mini chocolate chips
- 2 cups of confectioners' sugar
- 1 ½ tablespoons of lemon juice
- 2 cups of heavy cream

Steps

1. Heat two cups of canola oil in a large pot over medium heat for 2 minutes.
2. Combine the sugar, flour and salt in a medium bowl, add butter and mix by hand until the mixture is sandy and coarse.
3. Add the white wine and egg yolks and mix until you get a smooth dough.
4. Put the dough in a zip-lock bag and refrigerate for 15-20 minutes.
5. Roll out the dough, then use a cookie cutter to stamp out rounds. If you do not have a cookie cutter, place a round topped cup over the dough and press down. Repeat this process until you have cut out all the dough, then reroll the scraps and repeat until the dough finishes.
6. Put a metal cannoli tube in the middle of the cut out dough, roll, then seal the edges with a few drops of water.
7. Pick the cannoli with a pair of tongs, then place in the pot of hot oil and fry, flipping frequently so that it cooks evenly.
8. Once browned, remove from oil and gently pull out the tube, then set aside and allow to cool completely before filling.
9. For the filling, mix all the ingredients (except chocolate chips) using an electric or hand mixer until smooth.
10. Pour the mixture into a piping bag and pipe into the shells.
11. Dip both ends of the stuffed cannolis in chocolate chips until lightly coated, then serve.

Chapter 8
Maggiano's Little Italy™

Maggiano's Little Italy was founded in 1991 in Chicago. As the name implies, their restaurants will satisfy your craving for Italian food. They serve the best of Italian soups, pasta and salad, which we will be exploring together.

Appetizers

Steamed Mussels

- Prep Time: 20 Minutes
- Cook Time: 10 Minutes
- Serves: 2

Ingredients
- 1 tablespoon of freshly squeezed lemon juice
- 20 mussels (thoroughly cleaned and scraped smooth)
- ½ teaspoon of chopped basil

- 2 tablespoons of cannellini beans
- ¾ cup of chicken stock
- ½ tablespoon of minced garlic
- ½ cup of white wine
- 2 tablespoons of sun-dried tomatoes
- 2 tablespoons of butter
- ½ tablespoon of chopped parsley
- Salt and pepper to taste

Steps

1. Combine the garlic and wine in a pan over medium heat.
2. Once hot, add the mussels and cook covered on high until the mussels open, about 5 minutes.
3. Put in the remaining ingredients, stir and allow to simmer over medium heat for 2-3 minutes, then season with pepper and salt to taste.
4. Serve the mussels in a bowl, drizzle with sauce, then serve with 2-3 slices of garlic toast.

Spinach and Artichoke Al Forno

- Prep Time: 20 Minutes
- Cook Time:20 Minutes
- Serves: 15

Ingredients

- ½ cup of sliced scallions
- 2 cups of canned artichokes (drained and rinsed)
- 1 cup of heavy cream
- 2 cups of shredded Asiago cheese
- 3 tablespoons of olive oil
- 2 cups of sautéed spinach (drained and sliced)
- Pepper and salt to taste
- 1 tablespoon of grated parmesan cheese

- ¼ cup of chopped sun-dried tomatoes

Steps

1. Preheat your oven to 350°F.
2. Put the scallions, heavy cream, spinach, Asiago cheese, olive oil, tomatoes and artichokes in a large bowl, stir until well combined, then season with pepper and salt to taste.
3. Transfer the mixture into a greased oven friendly bowl, then top the mixture with the shredded parmesan cheese.
4. Place the bowl in the middle tier of the oven and bake for 20 minutes at 350°F.
5. Remove from the oven and serve with slices of Italian bread.

Soups and Salads

Tuscan Sausage and Orzo Soup

- Prep Time: 20 Minutes
- Cook Time: 50 Minutes
- Serves: 8

Ingredients
- 1 tablespoon of Italian seasoning
- 1 pound of Italian sausage (casing removed)
- 2 teaspoons of fennel seeds (crushed)
- 2 celery sticks (finely sliced)

- 2 bay leaves
- 4 cups of chicken broth
- 1 tablespoon of olive oil
- 1 teaspoon of red pepper flakes
- 1 can of cannellini beans
- 2 carrots (chopped)
- 1 ½ cups of orzo
- 1 can of stewed tomatoes with juice
- 3 cloves of garlic (minced)
- 1 onion (thinly sliced)
- 2 tablespoons of ketchup
- Romano cheese for topping (optional)

Steps

1. Cook the sausage in a large pot over high heat until well browned, stirring frequently.
2. Add the celery, onions, garlic, crushed fennel seeds, carrots, Italian seasoning and pepper flakes.
3. Season salt and freshly ground black pepper to taste, then sauté until all the vegetables start to soften.
4. Add the broth, tomatoes, beans, ketchup and bay leaves, stir and bring to a boil, then set the heat to low and allow to simmer for 25-30 minutes.
5. Cook the orzo separately. Once done, drain and toss with olive oil to prevent it from sticking.
6. Add the orzo to the soup and cook for 1 minute.
7. Scoop the soup into bowls and serve topped with grated Romano cheese.

Maggiano's Salad

- Prep Time: 20 Minutes
- Cook Time: 0 Minutes
- Serves: 10

Ingredients

Salad

- Corn oil (for frying)
- 5 cups of chopped Romaine lettuce (cut into bite-sized pieces)
- ½ cup of thinly sliced prosciutto
- 1 red onion (thinly sliced)
- 5 cups of chopped iceberg lettuce (cut into bite-sized pieces)
- ½ cup of crumbled blue cheese

Dressing

- ⅛ teaspoon of dried oregano
- 1 tablespoon of Dijon mustard
- 2 cups of vegetable oil
- 2 teaspoons of granulated sugar
- Freshly ground pepper to taste
- ¾ cup of water
- w̄ cup of red wine vinegar
- Salt to taste
- 2 teaspoons of minced garlic

Steps

1. Heat half a cup of corn oil in a large skillet over medium heat, add prosciutto and cook until it browns, about 2-3 minutes.
2. Once browned, remove from heat and place on pieces of parchment paper to drain excess oil. Allow to cool, then crumble and set aside.
3. To make the dressing, combine the sugar, mustard, water, vinegar and garlic in a medium mixing bowl, then season with salt to taste.
4. Slowly stir in the oil, then whisk until well combined and the sugar is completely dissolved.
5. Add the oregano and pepper and whisk again until well combined.
6. Toss the cheese, lettuce, prosciutto and onion in a large salad bowl, drizzle some dressing over the salad and toss to coat, then serve immediately and refrigerate any leftover dressing for later.

Steaks, Chops and Veal

New York Steak Al Forno

- Prep Time: 20 Minutes
- Cook Time: 15 Minutes
- Serves: 3

Ingredients
- Salt and pepper to taste
- 1 New York steak (large)
- ¼ cup of sliced gorgonzola cheese
- ½ cup of sliced red onion

- 1 tablespoon of chopped parsley and basil
- 1 tablespoon of softened butter
- 1 tablespoon of garlic butter
- ¼ cup of balsamic sauce
- 3 ounces of roasted portabella mushrooms

Herb Marinade
- ¼ cup of chopped fresh thyme leaves
- ½ cup of olive oil
- ¼ cup of minced garlic
- 1 tablespoon of freshly ground whole black peppercorns
- ¼ cup of chopped fresh rosemary leaves
- ¼ cup of chopped fresh sage leaves

Steps

1. To make the herb marinade, put all the ingredients into a blender and pulse until smooth (add 2 tablespoons of water if difficult).
2. Rub the pepper and salt into the meat, add two tablespoons of the herb marinade and rub until the meat is coated with the mixture.
3. Put the meat in a broiler and cook for 3-4 minutes on one side over medium heat or until a brown crust forms, then flip and cook for the same amount of time or until the other side is well browned too.
4. Spread the garlic butter sauce on the steak halfway through the cooking time and let coat.
5. Sauté the mushrooms and onion in a pan over medium heat until they are both soft, add the balsamic glaze, stir and allow to cook for a minute or two.
6. Add the butter and chopped parsley/basil, stir and cook until butter is fully melted and well incorporated.
7. Put the sautéed mushrooms and onion mixture at the bottom of a large round plate, top with browned steak, then top with crumbled cheese.
8. Serve hot.

Beef Medallion

- Prep Time: 15 Minutes
- Cook Time: 30 Minutes
- Serves: 4

Ingredients
- ¾ cup of dry wine
- 2 cups of beef broth
- ¼ teaspoon of freshly ground black pepper
- ¾ cup of whipping cream
- 2 tablespoons of mixed dried wild mushrooms
- 1 teaspoon of roasted garlic
- 2 teaspoons of canola oil
- Salt to taste

- ¼ cup of diced shallots
- 8 beef medallions
- 1 tablespoon of softened butter

Steps

1. Preheat your oven to 350°F.
2. Soak the mushrooms in a bowl of warm water for 20 minutes or until soft. Strain and reserve the liquid to be used later.
3. Heat one teaspoon of oil and the butter in a pan over medium heat, add shallots, mushrooms and roasted garlic, then cook until shallots start to brown, about 4 minutes, stirring frequently.
4. Pour in the wine to deglaze the pan for 2-3 minutes, then add the broth and allow to simmer until the mixture loses half its moisture, about 8 minutes.
5. Rub the pepper and salt into the beef, heat the remaining oil into a large skillet over medium heat, then sear the meat for 2-3 minutes on each side.
6. Put into the oven and cook for 10-20 minutes until tender.
7. Remove from the oven and serve topped with a generous amount of sauce.

Veal Marsala

- Prep Time: 10 Minutes
- Cook Time: 20 Minutes
- Serves: 4

Ingredients

- ¾ cup of low sodium chicken broth
- 8 veal cutlets
- 2 ounces of mixed mushrooms (sliced)
- Salt and pepper to taste
- ½ cup of sweet marsala
- 1 shallot (sliced)
- 3 tablespoons of unsalted butter
- 1 tablespoon of chopped fresh rosemary leaves

- 3 cloves of garlic (crushed)
- 3 tablespoons of olive oil

Steps

1. Rub some salt and pepper all over the veal cutlets.
2. Heat two tablespoons of oil and butter in a large skillet over medium heat, add veal cutlets and cook for 2-3 minutes on each side or until browned, then remove and keep warm until ready to use.
3. Heat the remaining oil in the skillet, add garlic and sauté until soft and fragrant, then add mushrooms and cook for 2-3 minutes or until the moisture from the mushroom dries.
4. Season with pepper and salt to taste, then add the marsala and cook for 2-3 minutes.
5. Add the rosemary leaves and broth, stir and cook for 4 minutes, then add the cutlets and cook for 1-2 minutes, pouring the sauce over the veal while stirring.
6. Stir in the last tablespoon of butter and cook for a minute or until the butter has completely melted.
7. Put the cutlets on plates and scoop the sauce over them, then serve and enjoy!

Chicken and Seafood

Whole Roasted Chicken

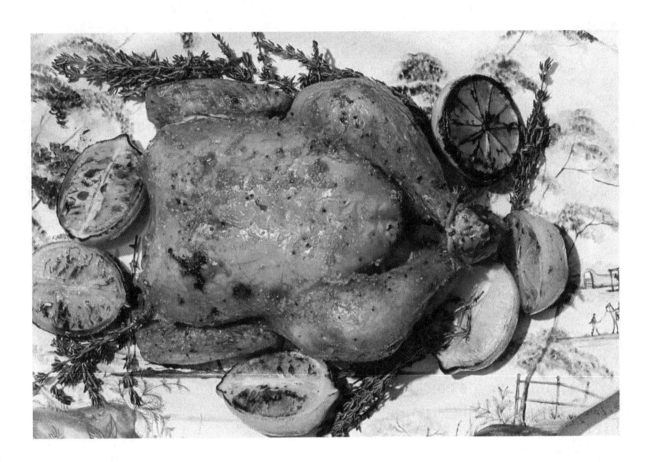

- Prep Time: 25 Minutes
- Cook Time: 1 Hour
- Serves: 6

Ingredients

- Salt and pepper to taste
- 1 whole chicken (washed and dried with a paper towel)
- 2 tablespoons of lemon zest
- ½ cup of softened butter

- 2 tablespoons of olive oil
- 4 lemon wedges
- ¼ cup of sliced onions
- ¼ cup of chopped fresh rosemary leaves
- 2 ½ tablespoons of freshly squeezed lemon juice
- 3 cloves of garlic (minced)

Steps

1. Preheat your oven to 425°F.
2. Put the olive oil, butter, lemon zest, garlic, and rosemary into a medium bowl, stir until well combined, then set aside.
3. Rub some salt and pepper all over the chicken and inside the cavity.
4. Brush a generous amount of the butter mixture into the chicken, making sure it is properly coated.
5. Drizzle the lemon juice all over the chicken and stuff with chopped rosemary, two lemon wedges and sliced onions.
6. Put the chicken on a roasting pan and put into the oven. Bake for 40-45 minutes, remove from the oven and baste with more of the butter mixture.
7. Put back into the oven and bake for 10-15 minutes or until golden brown.
8. Remove the chicken from the oven and let it cool for 10-20 minutes before serving.

Garlic Shrimp and Shells

- Prep Time: 15 Minutes
- Cook Time: 20 Minutes
- Serves: 2

Ingredients
- ¼ cup of white wine
- ¼ pound of shrimp (peeled and deveined)
- ½ pound of cooked shell pasta
- ¼ cup of extra-virgin olive oil
- 1 tablespoons of garlic butter
- ½ cup of clam juice
- ¼ teaspoon of freshly ground black pepper
- Pepper and salt to taste

- 1 cup of fresh tomatoes (remove seeds, peel skin and slice)
- 4 fresh basil leaves (torn apart)
- ¼ cup of marinara sauce
- 1 tablespoon of minced garlic

Steps

1. Marinate the shrimp with ground black pepper, salt to taste and half of the olive oil.
2. To prepare the tomatoes, dip in a bowl of hot water for less than a minute. Once the skin has softened, peel it off, then squeeze the tomatoes to remove the seeds before slicing into bits.
3. Heat the rest of the olive oil in a large skillet over high heat, add the shrimp and sauté until they start to pinken, about 3 minutes.
4. Add the minced garlic and sauté until fragrant, about 1 minute, then put in the tomatoes, clam juice and white wine, stir and bring to a boil.
5. Reduce the heat to medium, add garlic butter, marinara sauce and basil, stir and allow to cook for 1-2 minutes.
6. Put in the pasta shells and simmer until al dente, then season with pepper and salt to taste.
7. Serve hot.

Baked Shrimp Oreganata

- Prep Time: 15 Minutes
- Cook Time: 25 Minutes
- Serves: 8

Ingredients

- 3 tablespoons of grated Parmesan cheese
- 16 medium shrimp with tail on (peeled and deveined)
- 1 cup of low-sodium broth
- ¼ teaspoon of freshly ground black pepper
- ¾ cup of Panko crumbs
- 5 tablespoons of olive oil
- 1 medium lemon (quartered)
- 1 tablespoon of lemon juice

- 2 cups of chopped tomatoes
- ¼ teaspoon of paprika
- 3 tablespoons of finely minced garlic
- 2 tablespoons of chopped parsley
- 2 ¼ cups of softened butter
- 1 cup of white wine
- 5 tablespoons of chopped fresh basil

Steps

1. Preheat your oven to 400°F.
2. Season the shrimp with a tablespoon of minced garlic and ground black pepper, then set aside.
3. Whip the butter with a whisk until thick and smooth, add shredded Parmesan, lemon juice, chopped parsley and half of the chopped basil, stir until well combined, then add the Panko crumbs and mix properly.
4. Refrigerate for 2 hours.
5. Fold the shrimp with the tail tucked inward so that they seem curled in a fetal position. Place on a greased or foil-lined sheet pan.
6. Scoop the butter mixture over the shrimp, molding them into small balls.
7. Sprinkle the shrimp with paprika, then put into the oven and bake for 10-12 minutes or until the gratin butter is golden brown.
8. While the shrimp cooks, heat the olive oil in a sauté pan, add the rest of the garlic and sauté until the garlic starts to brown.
9. Put in the tomatoes and cook for 2-3 minutes, stirring frequently.
10. Pour in the white wine, stir and cook until the liquid is almost dry.
11. Add the low-sodium stock and chopped basil and cook for 3-5 minutes.
12. Remove from heat and scoop onto a large platter. Put the shrimp oreganata in and garnish with quartered lemon.
13. Squeeze some lemon juice over it, then serve

Specialties

Lasagna

- Prep Time: 40 Minutes
- Cook Time: 2 Hours 45 Minutes
- Serves: 10

Ingredients

Filling
- 3 pounds of ricotta cheese
- ½ teaspoon of black pepper
- 4 whole eggs

- ½ cup of all-purpose flour
- 1 cup of Parmesan cheese
- 1 ½ teaspoon of minced garlic
- 1 ½ teaspoon of salt

Assembly
- 1 pound of Italian sausage
- 1 cup of Parmesan cheese
- 6 fresh pasta sheets
- 1 jar marinara sauce
- 1 ¼ cup of grated provolone cheese
- 1 pound of ground beef
- 14 cups of lasagna filling
- 1 teaspoon of Italian seasoning

Steps
1. Combine Parmesan cheese, eggs, garlic and ricotta cheese in a small bowl and mix properly.
2. Add salt, pepper and flour, mix properly, then set aside.
3. Put the ground beef and Italian sausage in a large sauté pan over medium heat, add Italian seasoning and cook until browned, drain off excess oil and set aside until ready to use.
4. Spread half of the marinara sauce at the bottom of a medium baking pan.
5. Put a sheet over the sauce, then top with three cups of the lasagna filling over the pasta sheet. Spread ¾ cups of the meat over the lasagna filling, top with a quarter cup of marinara and shredded Parmesan, then place another pasta sheet over it. Repeat this process until you have a total of five fillings and six layers of pasta.
6. Put the pan in the oven and bake for 2 hours and 30 minutes at 350°F or the internal temperature of the lasagna is 155°F.
7. Remove from the oven and top with grated provolone and allow to melt before cutting into portions.
8. Serve with grated Parmesan and extra marinara sauce.

Homemade Gnocchi

- Prep Time: 20 Minutes
- Cook Time: 30 Minutes
- Serves: 4

Ingredients
- 1 tablespoon of minced garlic
- ½ teaspoon of salt
- Grated Parmesan cheese (to serve)
- 2 tablespoons of olive oil
- w̄ cup of vodka
- 1 pound of gnocchi
- 5 tablespoons of chopped fresh parsley
- 1 can of whole tomatoes (with juice)

- 3 tablespoons of chopped fresh basil
- ¼ teaspoons of red pepper flakes
- ¼ cup of water (reserved from cooking pasta)
- ½ cup of heavy cream
- ¾ pound of sliced Italian sausage (casing removed)
- ¼ cup of minced onion
- 1 tablespoon of garlic butter

Steps

1. Cook the gnocchi in a large pot of water until they start to float to the top, then drain and reserve a quarter cup of the pasta water.
2. Put half of the tomatoes (with juice) into a blender and puree until smooth, then chop the rest.
3. Put the oil in a saucepan and allow to simmer for a minute, then add pureed tomato and onion, cook for 2-3 minutes or until the onions soften, stirring occasionally.
4. Add red pepper flakes and garlic, stir and cook for a minute.
5. Add chopped tomatoes and season with half a teaspoon of salt.
6. Remove from heat and pour in the vodka, stir until well combined, then simmer over medium heat for 10 minutes or until the alcohol has dried completely.
7. Gently stir in the heavy cream until well incorporated, then cook for 2 minutes.
8. Add parsley, basil, garlic butter sauce and sliced sausage and simmer on low until the sausage is cooked through.
9. Put in the cooked gnocchi and toss until well coated, then add the reserved pasta water if the sauce is too thick (skip if not needed).
10. Serve the gnocchi topped with shredded Asiago and chopped parsley.

Mushroom Ravioli Al Forno

- Prep Time: 40 Minutes
- Cook Time: 15 Minutes
- Serves: 12

Ingredients

Fresh Egg Pasta Dough
- 1 teaspoon of olive oil
- 3 cups of all-purpose flour
- 5 egg yolks
- ½ cup of cake flour
- 5 whole eggs
- A pinch of salt

Cream Sauce

- A pinch of dry thyme
- 4 cups of heavy cream
- 2 tablespoons of olive oil
- ¼ cup of diced Spanish onion
- ½ cup of white wine
- 4 cloves of garlic (mashed)
- 1 bay leaf
- Pepper and salt to taste

Mushroom Filling

- Pepper and salt to taste
- 4 pounds of mushroom
- 1 cup of heavy cream
- 1 ½ cups of aged Asiago cheese (grated)
- ½ teaspoon of freshly thyme
- 1 ¼ cup of white wine
- 1 tablespoon of minced garlic
- 8 tablespoons of butter
- 1 pound of Spanish onion (diced)

Steps

1. To begin, put the eggs, flour and olive oil into a food processor and pulse until a smooth, loose dough is formed, about 2 minutes.
2. Knead the dough on a clean, floured surface, then cut the dough into 6 equal pieces and allow to rest for 30 minutes.
3. Put the dough into a pasta machine and allow to run, folding it into thirds every time it is run through. Repeat 8 times until the dough is silky smooth or less if you want it thicker.
4. To make the filling, melt the butter in a heavy-bottomed skillet over medium heat. Add garlic and thyme and sauté until brown and fragrant, about 1 minute.
5. Put in the cream, wine, mushrooms, stir and season with pepper and salt to taste, then allow to cook until almost dry, about 2-3

minutes.

6. Remove from heat and add Asiago cheese, then mix well.
7. Pour the mixture into a food processor and pulse until smooth, then set aside and allow to cool before using.
8. Scoop two tablespoons of the cooled mushroom filling onto each pasta sheet, fold and cut into two-inch squares before sealing the raviolis.
9. Heat the oil in a heavy-bottomed pot over medium heat and allow to simmer for a minute.
10. Add garlic, onions, bay leaf and thyme and sauté until garlic and onions are soft and fragrant, about 30 seconds.
11. Add wine, then season with pepper and salt to taste. Stir and cook on high until the wine starts to dry, about 2-3 minutes.
12. Add the heavy cream and allow to simmer over medium heat until sauce starts to thicken, then strain the sauce through a mesh sieve.
13. Gently put in the mushroom-filled raviolis (about 35-40, depending on the thickness) in a large pot of salted boiling water, cook for 2-3 minutes, then drain.
14. Pour the cream sauce into a large sauté pan, heat for 1-2 minutes.
15. Remove the pan from heat and add the raviolis. Toss gently in sauce until well coated.
16. Serve topped with grated Parmesan and garnished with chopped parsley.

Desserts

Vera's Lemon Cookies

- Prep Time: 10 Minutes
- Cook Time: 20 Minutes
- Serves: 8

Ingredients

- 1 cup of confectioners' sugar
- ¾ cup of softened unsalted butter
- 1 teaspoon of lemon zest (grate lemon zest before juicing)
- 2 egg yolks

- 2 tablespoons of freshly squeezed lemon juice
- ½ teaspoon of vanilla extract
- 2 cups of all-purpose flour
- ¼ teaspoon of kosher salt
- ¾ cup of granulated sugar

Steps

1. Combine the sugar and butter in a bowl and mix until fluffy using an electric mixer.
2. Add vanilla, egg yolks and salt, mix again until well combined.
3. Add the flour, small amounts at a time until well incorporated.
4. Cut the dough in half, then roll each piece into one-inch logs.
5. Wrap the logs in wax paper and refrigerate for 25-30 minutes or until firm.
6. Preheat your oven to 350°F.
7. Cut the logs into slightly thick, round pieces and place them on a parchment lined baking sheet, keeping them at least an inch apart.
8. Bake for 15-20 minutes or until golden.
9. Remove from the oven and let cool on the baking sheet for 5-10 minutes, then move the cookies to a cooling rack.
10. Combine the lemon juice, confectioners' sugar and lemon zest in a small bowl and whisk until thick, then dip each cookie in the glaze and let sit for 15 minutes or until the glaze sets completely.

Chocolate Zuccotto Cake

- Prep Time: 30 Minutes
- Cook Time: 0 Minutes
- Serves: 6

Ingredients
- 1 round chocolate cake
- 3 ¼ cups of chocolate frosting

Filling
- ¾ cup of Samballa Sambuca
- 1 bittersweet chocolate
- 2 cups of heavy cream

Steps

1. Break the chocolate in chunks into a large microwave-friendly bowl. Put into the microwave and heat on high for 1 minute, stirring occasionally.
2. Remove from the microwave and let it cool for 2-3 minutes.
3. Combine the Samballa Sambuca and the cream in a large mixer and whip for 2-3 minutes at medium speed, until creamy and smooth.
4. Add the chocolate and whip until well incorporated, scraping down the sides and bottom at regular intervals.
5. Line a medium steel bowl with plastic wrap, then cut the top off the cake, keeping the scraps for later.
6. Cut the cake into four equal layers using a turntable, then carefully place one of the layers at the bottom of the plastic-lined steel bowl, pressing down gently until it sits firm.
7. Scoop some of the filling onto the cake and top with another layer. Repeat this process until you have three layers of filling.
8. Top with chocolate frosting and level with a palette knife, then refrigerate until firm.
9. Cut into slices and serve.

CPSIA information can be obtained
at www.ICGtesting.com
Printed in the USA
BVHW011441220621
610211BV00008B/2093